William Minto, William Bell Scott

**Autobiographical Notes of the Life of William Bell Scott**

William Minto, William Bell Scott

**Autobiographical Notes of the Life of William Bell Scott**

ISBN/EAN: 9783337006921

Printed in Europe, USA, Canada, Australia, Japan

Cover: Foto ©Andreas Hilbeck / pixelio.de

More available books at **www.hansebooks.com**

# Autobiographical Notes

## OF THE LIFE OF

## WILLIAM BELL SCOTT
### H.R.S.A., LL.D.

And Notices of his Artistic and Poetic
Circle of Friends
1830 to 1882

EDITED BY W. MINTO

*Illustrated by Etchings by Himself
and Reproductions of Sketches by Himself and Friends*

VOL. II

NEW YORK
HARPER & BROTHERS, FRANKLIN SQUARE
1892

# CONTENTS OF VOL. II

## CHAPTER I

PAGE

DR. SAMUEL BROWN—SIR WALTER AND LADY TREVELYAN
AND MY PICTURES AT WALLINGTON—JOHN RUSKIN     1

## CHAPTER II

FIRST APPEARANCE OF A. C. SWINBURNE—AN AMUSING
EXPERIENCE WITH THOMAS CARLYLE—DEATH OF
DR. SAMUEL BROWN     14

## CHAPTER III

RÉSUMÉ OF LETTERS FROM FRIENDS IN LONDON, 1856-58
—ADDITIONS TO THE CIRCLE THERE     28

## CHAPTER IV

RÉSUMÉ OF LETTERS FROM FRIENDS, 1859-60-61—THE
ROSSETTIS, HOLMAN HUNT, WOOLNER, MUNRO,
ETC.—LADY TREVELYAN—MISS BOYD .     46

## CHAPTER V

DEATH OF MRS. ROSSETTI—ANECDOTES OF WALLINGTON—MY SERIES OF PICTURES OF BORDER HISTORY BEING FINISHED, I LEAVE NEWCASTLE—RETURN TO LONDON      64

## CHAPTER VI

PENKILL CASTLE AND MISS BOYD—DEATH OF SPENCER BOYD—MY PAINTING OF THE STAIRCASE—MACLISE      73

## CHAPTER VII

LETTERS FROM HOLMAN HUNT, JERUSALEM, 1870-71 .      88

## CHAPTER VIII

1868 TO 1870—MY "KING'S QUAIR" PICTURES AT PENKILL FINISHED—D. G. R. SPENDS AUTUMNS 1868-69 THERE WITH US—RECOMMENCES HIS POETIC STUDIES—THE FRANCO-GERMAN WAR—MY REMOVAL TO 92 CHEYNE WALK, SEPTEMBER 1870      107

## CHAPTER IX

LETTERS FROM D. G. ROSSETTI, AUTUMN 1871, AT KELMSCOTT—ON HIS OWN POETRY THEN IN PROGRESS—ALSO ON MINE      127

## CHAPTER X

1872—Rossetti's Illness—Stobhall     168

## CHAPTER XI

1873—My last visit to Italy—Dr. Franz Hueffer—F. M. Brown     182

## CHAPTER XII

The Rising Generation in Poetry, 1875 .     192

## CHAPTER XIII

My Poems published 1875—Alma Tadema—My "Dedicatio Postica"     202

## CHAPTER XIV

Holman Hunt's Picture "The Flight into Egypt," now called "The Triumph of the Innocents"     221

## CHAPTER XV

Spiritualism     235

## CHAPTER XVI

Death of G. H. Lewes and George Eliot—Of R. N. Wornum—Of Sir Walter Trevelyan and Lady Pauline .     244

## CHAPTER XVII

MORE DEATHS—THOMAS DIXON OF SUNDERLAND—
    RICHARD BURCHETT—SOLOMON HART .    264

## CHAPTER XVIII

ARTISTIC INQUIRIES, 1879-80    278

## CHAPTER XIX

PENKILL—A. (MISS BOYD), 1880 .    291

## CHAPTER XX AND LAST

MY "POET'S HARVEST HOME"—DEATH OF ROSSETTI    303

## CHAPTER XXI

CONCLUDING CHAPTER BY EDITOR .    321

# LIST OF ILLUSTRATIONS

## VOL. II

### ETCHINGS AND PHOTOGRAVURES

| | |
|---|---|
| Portrait of Author. Profile. *Etching by himself* | Frontispiece |
| A. C. Swinburne. *Etching by W. B. S.* | To face page 18 |
| Miss Boyd. *Drawn by D. G. R. Etched by W. B. S.* | 56 |
| Penkill Castle. *Photogravure* | 74 |
| Staircase of Penkill. *From a painting by A. Hughes* | 82 |
| Design for Door, South Kensington. *By W. B. S.* | ,, 170 |
| Fireplace, etc., at Stobhall. *By W. B. S.* | 172 |
| Exterior of Hall, Penkill. *Photogravure* | 324 |
| Interior of Hall. *From a painting by A. Hughes* | 326 |
| Bedroom in Penkill Castle. *Photogravure* | 328 |

### FACSIMILES OF SKETCHES

| | |
|---|---|
| "Mr. Porcupine." *Sketch by Lady Pauline Trevelyan* | page 52 |
| Roll Moulding, Penkill Castle | ,, 74 |
| D. G. R. in Bennan's Cave. *Sketch by W. B. S.* | ,, 115 |
| Human-headed Vases. *Sketch by W. B. S.* | ,, 289 |
| In the Glen at Penkill. *Sketch by H. A. Bowler* | ,, 296 |
| Monograms of Scotch Lawyers in 16th Century | ,, 301 |

# CHAPTER I

DR. SAMUEL BROWN—SIR WALTER AND LADY TRE-
VELYAN AND MY PICTURES AT WALLINGTON—JOHN
RUSKIN.

NOTWITHSTANDING my reluctance to re-enter Edinburgh, I had many occasions to go there, and to find myself among friends. One of these most pleasant to meet was Samuel Brown, who had established his laboratory in suburban Portobello. His physical science repudiated my poem *The Year of the World*, or rather, I should say, discredited the perfectibility of the human creature, although it carried him in his own theories any length in ameliorating the conditions of the body! As years passed on his health prevented his working and deprived him of the mental exuberance so exciting and amusing in earlier life, and he, like so many others, returned to his native lair to die. His and my brother's latest literary circle gradually broke up; he saw nothing of Professor Nichol, De Quincey, and even of Gilfillan, and other younger men; and his most assiduous friend Mrs. Crowe, whose cares for him were almost as great as those of his devoted wife, disappeared from Edinburgh through a deeper species of malady than even his own. The *Night Side of Nature* and the *Seeress of Prevorst* had taken too strong a hold of her mind, quick and active as it was; her faith in new and unknown conditions of life suspended that in the ordinary laws of nature. Still she was constant to Samuel Brown, her bodily strength being unimpaired, till one Sunday morning, leaving her bed, she quietly escaped the observation of her attendants, and armed only with a card in her hand inscribed with three mystical marks which she believed rendered her invisible, sallied out to visit him. Fortunately it was a Scotch Sabbath-day, not a soul was within sight. She had gone but a few steps in George Street, not far from her own door, when she was met by an astonished medical friend known to both, who threw over her his top-coat and took her back to her house. This was the painful gossip of the time, and in effect this lady, so much respected by the Edinburgh literary coteries, vanished from among them. In fact, except Samuel's cousin, Dr. John Brown, the author of *Rab and his Friends* and much else; and some early friends—Ballantine, Steell, now Sir John, the sculptor, Sir William Harvey, the painter of Covenanter celebrity—I knew so few that I could walk the streets a whole day without being recognised.

De Quincey was the last left of the illustrious literati of the previous generation, and he had become more and more erratic in his habits. I have always found original genius of a concentrated and peculiar kind the most dangerous endowment; it is only the Shakespeare or the Goethe who can carry out unalloyed the specific energy, and retain manhood and rational common sense in all the affairs of life; poets like Byron or Shelley could not do so.

However, this chapter is intended to deal with other matters, and I introduced Dr. Samuel Brown, not to describe his circle, but because he was the means of bringing me into communication with the Trevelyans, my dear and helpful friends of so many years. Sir Walter and Lady Trevelyan were among the admirers of Samuel Brown, and at his desire she wrote the review that appeared in the *Scotsman* newspaper of my *Memoir* of my brother David. When my little book of poems (*Poems by a Painter*) was published in 1854, I sent it to Sir Walter, at Wallington Hall, a large modern mansion near Morpeth which they preferred to Nettlecombe Court, their lovely Elizabethan house in Somerset. I received in reply a pressing invitation to visit them.

It was a long drive at that time after alighting from the railway at Morpeth. About midday, as I approached the house, the door was opened, and there stepped out a little woman as light as a feather and as quick as a kitten, habited for gardening in a broad straw hat and gauntlet gloves, with a basket on her arm, visibly the mistress of the place. The face was one that would be charming to some and distasteful to others, and might in the same way be called rather plain or rather handsome, as the observer was sympathetic or otherwise. In a very few minutes the verdict would be understood and confirmed by the lady, whose penetration made her a little feared. This habit of looking well at a stranger and concluding correctly about him has always been fascinating to me, even when seasoned with the mild satire generally associated with penetration. Why not enliven life by that play, innocent on the tongue of the amiable, mild in the hands of a lady who knew reply was out of court, and beneficial too from so trenchant an observer as the possessor of the hazel eyes that saw through one and made him careful to avoid affectation of any complexion, such care being his only safety in the interview?

Lady Trevelyan said she was going to look at her own garden, and asked whether I would accompany her, or enter and make myself known to the familiar of the family, Mr. Wooster, the only inmate at that moment, Sir Walter having been called from home at an hour's notice. I went with her and in half an hour we were old friends; she had asked many questions, and received the directest and truest answers. In each case she showed that she liked my plain speech and recognised it to be genuine and unconventional, and in her own way felt grateful and pleased. Walking on from one spot to another, she made me acquainted with various picturesque features and little nooks she had sketched, with the bulrushes and water-lilies. I rowed her across one of the artificial ponds before we returned and entered the house.

It was fortunate that I had Lady Trevelyan these few days all to myself, Sir Walter being so difficult to become acquainted with. Not that he drew a line round himself as many do whose only recommendation in the world lies in their belongings, but he was a man of few words, and many unacknowledged peculiarities. Inheritor too of the bluest blood, his name, spelt the same as now, being in the Doomsday-book for the same Devonshire property the family still possess, though a Whig by descent and a philosophical leveller in some respects by inclination, the inherited habits of thirty generations were not to be cast aside.

With all Lady Trevelyan's discrimination in art matters and acquaintance with the works of old masters and with living modern artists, she had not risen above the Turner mania; and the exponent of Turner, Mr. Ruskin, I soon found, held an overpowering influence over her. Many incidents had conduced to this. She had taken his part before, and was now prepared indignantly to stand by him again. At Oxford she had been especially amused by some of the dons confessing to her they had hoped better things of him than his present course indicated, spending his time writing about pictures!

Wallington House had been a quadrangle, but the interior court, open to the sky, had been long found productive of only damp and cold, and Dobson, the architect of so many able works in the North of England, turned this blind space into a saloon by opening the walls into arcades and covering the whole by a coffered roof. Paved and surrounded by hot-water pipes, the whole house was made comfortable and a place provided for pictures and decoration, which I was to supply. When this was determined on in the beginning of 1856 I drew out a scheme, and Lady Trevelyan prevailed on me to consult Mr. Ruskin, which I did with strong misgiving. I sent him a sketch of a compartment, telling him at whose instance I had done so, wishing him to think over the scheme and give us such suggestions as might occur to him. His reply was not very useful, but such as it was I may enter it here. My design was that the lower pilasters between the pictures should be filled by tall plants— as foxglove, bulrush, corn of different kinds, and so forth—painted on the stone, and the spandrels with spreading foliage of native trees—oak, lime, elm, and others,—the upper tier of pilasters to be only panelled, and the spandrels decorated sparingly with grotesques as they approached the ceiling, which was rich in stuccoed Roman mouldings and pateras. In a few days Lady Trevelyan, then [May 1856] living at Tynemouth, enclosed his answer, saying, "The enclosed came yesterday. Mr. Ruskin was at Amiens when he wrote, on his way to Geneva.

He was quite knocked up, and is obliged to be absolutely idle for some time. He says in his letter to me that even if he were well he does not think he could help us. He likes the plan very much."

DEAR MR. SCOTT—I am quite *vowed* to idleness for a couple of months at least, and cannot think over the plan you send. I am as much in a fix as you are about interior decoration, but incline to the *All Nature* in the present case, if but for an experiment. The worst of nature is that when she is chipped or dirty she looks so very uncomfortable, which Arabesque don't. Mind you must make her uncommonly *stiff*. I shall most likely come down and have a look when I come back in October.

So get on that I may have plenty to find fault with, for that, I believe, is all I can do. Help you I can't.—But am always, truly yours, J. RUSKIN.

I did get on, beginning the series of pictures with the "Building of the Wall of Hadrian";[1] and in the autumn, visiting London, I willingly agreed to go to him if he would let me, expecting much pleasure, if not also advantage, from listening to the

[1] [This seems to be a slip of memory. At least the first of the series to be completed and exhibited was "St. Cuthbert on Farne Island," which was exhibited in the rooms of the Literary Society at Newcastle in November 1856. "The Building of the Roman Wall was exhibited in July 1857, and the remaining six appeared at regular intervals in the following order, "The Death of Bede," "Danes descending on the Coast at Tynemouth," "The Spur in the Dish," "Bernard Gilpin," "Grace Darling," "Iron and Coal." The whole series of eight pictures was exhibited at the French Gallery in Pall Mall at the end of June 1861. References to the various pictures, as in the course of composition, occur in the subsequent notes and letters.—ED.]

most eloquent writer and most enthusiastic hero-worshipper of this or perhaps of any age. On reaching town I found an invitation to dine at Camberwell, the note saying that he "understood I wished to gain some information about the teaching pursued at the Working Man's College," which we could visit afterwards. He knew I was attached to the Department of Art; indeed the note was addressed there. The Working Man's College repudiated every point of the curriculum of the Government system, and there was an impertinent jealousy in the mind of every one of the teachers, all volunteers as they were, carrying on the art classes at that unendowed seminary. I felt it necessary to answer that this was a mistake, at least in any particular way; that Lady Trevelyan wished me to make his acquaintance; but if he liked in a friendly manner to receive me on that ground, I should be very pleased to accept his invitation, and to accompany him afterwards to Red Lion Square, the evening in question being his evening there. I mentioned this to Rossetti, who volunteered to go with me self-invited.

These particulars and the others following are of little value, but are necessary to make my future relation to Mr. Ruskin understood; he may never, however, be mentioned in future pages. There are natures sympathetic to each other, and there are others antipathetic. I endeavoured to be very modest, and tried to be agreeable, but it was of no use. I had sent him my little volume of poems at the lady's desire, and D. G. R. asked him what he thought of the book; he pretended to be surprised it was mine. His late visit to Edinburgh led us to talk of Scottish artists, when he mentioned David Scott, some of whose works had been pointed out to him. He thought they possessed some quality in colour, but nothing else, though he believed the artist had valued himself on quite other qualities! "Scott's brother, you mean," suggested D. G. R., whereat he again simulated surprise. This was still followed by some other supercilious pretence, and I could bear him no longer, thought I would have a good-humoured reprisal, and the conversation turning soon, of course, on Turner, I said the evidence of the personality and talk of a man was in the most of cases conclusive as to the character of his works, and I told Thomson of Duddingston's anecdote of his "introdoocing a bit of sentiment" into the view of the place where Harold Harefoot fell [see vol. i. p. 84]. At this Gabriel laughed, and asked him if Turner really talked in that way, and how he got over that sort of thing. The poisonous expression of his face was a study. His hero-worship of Turner was not an affectation at all; but his overpowering passion in talk as in writing was a determination to find out qualities no one else could see, and to contradict or ignore those evident to every one else.

We drove in to Red Lion Square, and here I found drawing from copies as preliminary practice, drawing from beautiful ornamental objects or human figures—everything indeed to be seen in academic or Government schools of art practice—ignored. I remembered F. M. Brown's class in Camden Town, where all the pupils were drawing from *wood-shavings*. Instead of these, here every one was trying to put on small pieces of paper imitations by pen and ink of pieces of rough stick crusted with dry lichens! He drew my attention to the beauty of these as giving the pupils a love of "nature"! but I suppressed my expression of dissent in the presence of the young men. What astonished me was Rossetti's abetting of such frightful waste of time, especially as I found Woolner, who had a modelling class, teaching the human figure.

I came away feeling that such pretence of education was in a high degree criminal; it was intellectual murder: not one of the young men who attended at the Working Man's College ever acquired any power of drawing. The only one who could ever be quoted was employed by Ruskin to copy Turner's drawings, which he could do before he entered the class; he copied them by elaborate stippling, covering an inch or so in a day! I found Miss Siddal was then in the South of France for her health, Ruskin having persuaded her to go. His wealth and entire carelessness about it enabled him to do very kind things, and this was the cause of his influence as much as his rhetorical genius. In a letter a short time before, D. G. R. had told me about his volunteering at the Working Man's College. "You think I have turned humanitarian perhaps,

but you should see my class for the model! None
of your *Freehand Drawing-Books* used. The British
mind is brought to bear on the British *mug* at once,
and with results that would astonish you." This
was what any one would have expected from him,
the British *mug* being interpreted living model!
and walking home I reminded him of this letter,
but I did not find him communicative or even explanatory. I concluded he planted himself into the
party that evening just to see and hear what passed
when I was face to face with Ruskin and the class
drawing from bits of stick. He was my dearest
and, I may say, most attached friend, my admiration
in poetry and, to some degree, in art too; but I
wished he could or would act and speak in a more
manly and ingenuous manner. Why could he not
have acknowledged Ruskin's liberality to Lizzie
Siddal, and yet objected to etching with a pen from
lichenous sticks!

Let me finish here with Mr. Ruskin. In 1861 I
think it was, after the last of my eight pictures was
placed, and instead of arabesques on spandrels of
the upper circle of arches in the hall, Sir Walter
had agreed to my painting eighteen scenes from
the ballad of *Chevy Chase*, Ruskin, who had not
been there since his eventful visit with his wife and
Millais, at last accomplished his visit to paint one of
the pilasters. Lady Trevelyan had kept for him
the great white lily, commonly called the Annunciation Lily, but the modesty of the professor would
not allow him to take that sacred flower. No; he

would take the humblest—the nettle! Ultimately wheat, barley, and other corn, with the cockle and other wild things of the harvest-field, were selected, and he began, surrounded by admiring ladies, Miss Stewart Mackenzie, then on the eve of her marriage with Lord Ashburton, and others being guests at the time. At dinner we heard a good deal about the proficiency of the pupils at the Working Man's College, and next morning he appeared with his hands full of pen-and-ink minute etchings of single ivy leaves the size of nature, one of which he entrusted to each lady as if they had been the most precious things in the world. He took no notice of me, the representative of the Government schools. I could stand by no longer. He had been giving lessons on drawing, had set Miss Mackenzie to draw a table, prohibiting her to make a preliminary general sketch, but directing her to begin at one corner and finish as she went on; this being next to impossible, she had applied to me, but I had declined to interfere. Now I could not remain silent, so I gave them a little lecture on the orthodox method of teaching and the proper objects to be used as models, and in a very cool, confident way showed the sensible women, as they all were, that spending so much time niggling over a small flat object with a pen was teaching nothing, but ruining the student for any application of art except that of retouching and spoiling photograph card portraits. I asserted that long practical knowledge made me certain of what I said, and I appealed to him to tell us if he had ever found any young man apply what he had thus learned to any purpose whatever? The revulsion in the minds of my audience was visible at once; he grinned in contemptuous silence. The subject was dropped.

# CHAPTER II

FIRST APPEARANCE OF A. C. SWINBURNE—AN AMUSING EXPERIENCE WITH THOMAS CARLYLE—DEATH OF DR. SAMUEL BROWN.

By midsummer of the year after I received my commission to paint the eight pictures at Wallington,[1] I had got the two ladies, Lady Trevelyan and Miss Capel Lofft, fully interested and occupied on the decorative portions of the saloon work, and my first picture was in its place. They worked under my direction, so that I was very frequently in that quarter, and very soon I began to recognise a little fellow who used to pass my post-chaise on the road descending from Cambo to Wallington. He was always riding a little long-tailed pony at a good pace towards the village. He had the appearance of a boy, but for a certain mature expression on his handsome high-bred face, which had bright, coarse yellow hair flowing on his shoulders, and flashing out round his head. On his saddle was strapped a bundle of books like those of a schoolboy. He

[1] [*i.e.* in 1857.—ED.]

recognised me as quickly as I did him, and the conscious look he gave in passing raised my curiosity, which was soon gratified by finding him one day kissing his hand to Lady Trevelyan at the door of the Hall, and by my learning that he was the grandson of a neighbouring baronet, Sir John Swinburne, and was now spending his school recess at Capheaton, his grandfather's house, whence he rode over to read with the incumbent at Cambo.

Cambo was a very little village on the top of an ascent of a mile from Wallington, with an inn exhibiting a swinging signboard which gave it the name of the Queens, as it showed on the south side the head of Queen Elizabeth painted by Lady Trevelyan, and on the other towards the north that of Mary of Scots by Miss Capel Lofft. Many a pedestrian and disciple of Isaac Walton knew this sign, and remembered it as a deception and a snare; as no beverage but tea, coffee, and ginger-beer—the best of things, but not to their liking—was to be had within this temperance hostelry. This quietest of villages had the smallest of churches, where Sir Walter read the lessons from his own pew, and the amiable clergyman, Algernon's tutor, went through all the forms the same as if he had had an audience of five hundred; suffering, too, from a nervous agitation when he mounted the pulpit that made him catch his breath and hem between the sentences. He used to dine every now and then at the great house, where Lady Trevelyan, who took a motherly care of Algernon, used to ask him how his pupil went on, receiving always the same answer, that he was too clever and never would study.

Swinburne must have been at this time about eighteen, but from his small figure and from his boyish style of manners, though he had been at a public school for several years and was now about to enter Balliol, he gave the impression, as said before, of greater youth. This caused him to be so treated, which treatment, again, made him affect to be younger than he was. At this time, and long after it, he could, so to speak, believe what he liked, or rather, what the people he liked chose to expect to be true. He had got a prize for French, which made him childishly proud, and, indeed, made him all his life delighted with that tongue—the most unfortunate for poetry—a fact it was impossible for him to admit. This was, I think, the only success he made at school or college, which none of his intimate friends could fathom, as he was able to acquire without trouble, and had a memory enabling him to recite long poems by once reading. When he began to write poetry, which he was always fond of reciting, he never needed to carry his manuscript about with him!

A few days after my first meeting him he appeared with the prize-book, entering the saloon where we were all at work hopping on one foot, his favourite expression of extreme delight. It was a large edition of *Notre Dame de Paris* gorgeously bound, with illustrations by Tony Johannot; but the exuberance of his delight was so comical that even

Lady Trevelyan could not resist a smile, and Miss Capel Lofft, a very nervous person, begged him to sit down quietly and show her the prints. For my part, not yet recognising in this unique youth the greatest rhythmical genius of English poetry, I looked on with wonder as at a spoilt child. The whole forenoon that book was never out of his sight. If it lay on the table his eyes were always wandering to it. The fascination of first love was nothing to this fascination; and when we all adjourned for an interval to the garden, there it was tightly held under his arm, while he ran on before backwards and ran back to us again, and the sharpest of eyes were fixed on him with their amused but maternal expression.

Can it have been that this school prize-book, the *Notre Dame de Paris*, made Victor Hugo his hero for life? I do not mean to suggest that egotism was the key to his feelings. Far from that; he was altogether free from that unamiable selfishness. And much as he loved and admired his own advantages, internal or external, it was in the frankest spirit of admiring what was good; his friends' excellent qualities were equally loved and admired. He had the greatest power of loving his friends, and bearing with them. His enthusiasm was measureless.

From small beginnings great results arise. From one step to another, his own natural temperament impelling him, and these trifling incidents determining its direction, the Gallo-mania that has been the *motif* in so much of his writing became a proclivity infecting all the young verse-writers and critics of the day. The sound of Swinburne's verse, which is in danger of becoming tedious by his unbounded facility of repeating the same rhythm exactly, and the Gallo-mania associated with it, have been the two characteristics of this decade or longer. At this moment [1877] I know half a dozen ambitious and innocent young men who talk of the literature of our neighbours as if it were altogether delightful, and as if they, each one of them, had discovered the fact, and that Victor Hugo, too, was the greatest of possible poets and mortals. Was it all because Algernon Swinburne when a boy had *Notre Dame de Paris* presented to him at school?

In 1860, when his first drama was published, I painted a small portrait of him in oil. He used to come in and live with us in Newcastle, and when I was out or engaged he was to be seen lying before the fire with a mass of books surrounding him like the ruins of a fortification, all of which he had read, and could quote or criticise correctly and acutely many years after. This portrait used to arrest him long afterwards, when he visited me, as if it was new to him. He was delighted to find it had some resemblance to what he called his portrait in the National Gallery. This was the head of Galeazzo Malatesta in the picture of the Battle of Sant' Egidio by Uccello, which certainly was not merely the same type, but was at this time exceedingly like him.

I soon began to look for him every time he had written ballad or scene that pleased himself, and his

advent had the charm of sunshine or champagne on one with many burdens conscientiously borne, and an extreme love of an idleness I could never indulge. He was a creature above all the ills of life or difficulties of art, emancipated from ordinary annoyances. He was not like Rossetti, self-tormented by the ambition to paint, which he could not do to his own satisfaction till late in life; nor distracted by responsibilities like myself. His pockets were always crammed with papers; still he recited quires of manuscripts without consulting them. But his nervous excitable nature could not stand strain: pain was nothing to him, yet he would not bear the slightest inconvenience a moment. One morning he had a toothache, and at once determined to have the tooth out. He would not stand it another minute; off he would go to the dentist, and I should accompany him. It was a mighty grinder, and the operator exerting his whole muscular force, lifted him from the seat without extracting the tooth. I held his head, the grinder broke; Swinburne swore, not against the dentist, but against the tooth, and had it out piecemeal without complaining!

In future years, amidst the wear and tear of poetical composition, when living in London—when Oxford had been left behind, with its quiet habits —we used to wonder how his amazing physical powers stood the hard usage he gave himself. But the stock he came from was a good one, and I recollected how his grandfather, at the time of my

Wallington work, astonished the doctor. This doctor, who used to ride past Wallington, to and from Capheaton, told us one morning that Sir John, then more than ninety years of age, had ruptured the tendon-Achilles, and could not put his foot to the ground. Of course, the conclusion formed by the surgeon was that the old gentleman would never walk again, the restoration of the tendon at his age not being thought possible. He would not, however, keep his bed; in a few weeks he was well again!

I may here enter a very droll passage with the gruffest and most ungenial of all mortals, though one of the intellectual potentates of the age and of all time, Thomas Carlyle. In the attempt to refresh my memory about Swinburne, I find I have nearly missed out my third adventure with that redoubtable friend and fellow-Scotchman. Bound to him for ever, as I have said, by his prompt notice of the lying report circulated by the bookseller's canvasser, I sent him my book of *Poems by a Painter*, as the volume has been often called, from its having an etched frontispiece with these words under it. Critics are tired out by repetition of the same kind of work, and, with a load of new books waiting for their manipulation, they hurry over what does not at the first instant arrest them; my respected friend Carlyle, though not a professional critic, was a hard-worked and slowly industrious littérateur, and could not find leisure to look at anything in my little book, except the frontispiece, which, however, he had not studied to good purpose. Like the Irish editor who would not prejudice his mind by perusing the book, he wrote me the following note, that startled me not a little:

CHELSEA, 26th October 1854.

DEAR SIR—I have, with many thanks for your goodness to me, received your pretty little volume. Everywhere in it I find proof of your assiduity, your ingenuity, —in short, of your talent for doing something much more useful in the world than writing rhymes never so well. If you will take any advice of mine in this matter (which I hardly expect you will) then know that according to my notion a man's *speech* is next to nothing in comparison to the man's *deed*; what he can *do* and practically perform, not at all what he can *speak* or *sing*, is the first question we ask of every man; to which I only add that if the man *has* anything to say, he had better say it than sing it, at this time of day.

Silence, with pious thought and strenuous practical exertion superadded, will do much more for a man of worth and parts than any speech can or could. You may depend upon it I have nothing but goodwill towards you, though I say these unwelcome things.—I am, yours very truly, T. CARLYLE.

This note, its manner as well as its meaning, puzzled me more the longer I thought of it. I had only been in his house once or perhaps twice, it is true, but my circle was his circle, and in every way I was favourably known to him. Besides, I had some vague recollection of having seen or heard the very same kind of sententious elocution before. It seemed an echo of something written by him I had seen in a newspaper. My first feeling soon gave way to one of mirth at the absurdity of a man whose *doings* had been very feeble indeed, only as a parish schoolmaster at Kirkcaldy, and who had subsided into endless objurgatory prose speech, but for which neither I nor any other man above the village blacksmith in that *lang town* would ever have heard of him. I tried to be still on the friendliest terms with him, and in a fortnight wrote him as follows, endeavouring, in fact, for an explanation:

NEWCASTLE, 11*th November*, 1854.

MY DEAR SIR—I am in receipt of your note on my little book of Poems. I acknowledge a very considerable influence possessed by your feelings and opinions written or printed ; and therefore cannot help writing a word or two in reply to your note of the other day.

Of all men in the world, I appear to myself precisely the last whom it is necessary to remind that what a man *does* is more important than what he says or sings. Ever since boyhood I have had burdens fall to my share that left me no possibility of doubting the superior efficacy as well as the imperious necessity of ceaseless activity and tangible work. The habit of *doing* has thus become so natural to me that the smallest interval of time is filled up by work—if not for others, then for myself ;—thus I endeavoured to establish my brother's claims by publishing his *Memoir*, and thus, too, I sent you this little volume of Poems illustrated by myself. *My* habit of doing brings upon me *your* warning against writing, *i.e.* idle talking and singing !

The oddest thing is that yours is the warning voice, since maxims the most opposite are so frequently to be found in your writings. You may (must?) have forgotten the circumstance long ago, but I once had the temerity to write you regretting the absence of a Hero of Work, an Art-Hero, from your book of hero-worship. Curious it is, and a little funny, to find myself replying to your late note as I do now.

But, after all, the thing I most want to say is, that my book of Poems *is something done*, not merely said or sung, but for the most part experienced, and in some part felt to the marrow of my life. If it were merely good singing, it would meet approval from a greater number than it is likely to do as it is.

My dear Mr. Carlyle, with much respect, yours,

W. B. S.

In a few days the mystery was solved : I received the following :

CHELSEA, 16*th November* 1854.

MY DEAR SIR—It is too certain I have committed an absurd mistake, which indeed I discerned two weeks ago with an emotion compounded of astonishment, remorse, and the tendency to laugh and cry both at once ! The truth is I am pestered with incipient volumes of verses from young lads that feel something stirring in them ; on the frontispiece of your little volume, I read Printer (not Painter, as I should have done), nor did your written note, in the hurry I was in, recall to me your identity ; fancying, therefore, it was an ingenious printer lad in your coaly town, who was rashly devoting his extra gifts, evidently rather valuable ones, to the trade of verse-making, I wrote and admonished (hastily reading five or six stanzas here and there), in the singular manner you experienced ! Never was a more distracted *qui pro quo.* On discovering that Printer was Painter, and hearing that *you* had published a volume of Poems, I at once found my " Idle Apprentice " converted into a grave, earnest man, of mature mastership, with a beard almost as gray as my own, whose surprise at my reception of him it was at once ludicrous and horrible to picture to myself ! This is the naked truth ; and I hope you will find in it an explanation of everyhing.

For the rest, I must say, you take the affair, even in its unexplained shape, in a spirit which I must call chivalrous, and in every way humane and noble, for which accept praises and thanks from me, very cordial indeed. I need not add that verses of your writing, were they only the sport of well-earned leisure, come under a very different rubrick from verses by my supposed young gentleman playing truant; and are likely to be much more deliberately read and judged of in this place; and that my doctrine about work and speech was, and continues to be, so far as I can perceive, precisely your own.

On the whole, I will ask you to come and see me again, if you can spare half an hour (3 to 4 P.M.), while in London; to consider me reading your new Poems (as my purpose was) the first spare evening I have; and always, as remembering with pleasure and respect the friendly man, recognisable as an earnest fellow-labourer in the vineyard, whom I once saw here.—You may believe me, yours very sincerely, T. CARLYLE.

I had signed myself "with much respect" his, as the right thing to do, writing as I did, but, after all, I did not feel my respect quite so great now that the explanation had come. He had a stereotyped form of discouragement for the young, even although the idle apprentice could do what he now professed to respect, finding it the work of a middle-aged friend! I did go to see him again, and in the course of conversation he told us over again the same story he had told me before, and in the exact same words! The story was of his visit to the field of the Battle of Dunbar, in an autumn afternoon, and seeing Irish reapers resting all along the road after their long, weary journey. Like the tenor of my letter, this story was evidently prepared as a show-piece of descriptive elocution! Alas! yet it had become so perhaps only after the publication of the *Cromwell.* Whether or not, I cannot open any of his greater works without thinking of him as one of the greatest men of the time.

Let me take up here and enter, for the last time, perhaps, in these desultory pages, the name of a dear friend who remains in my mind associated with Carlyle, and still more with my brother, and others belonging to a cycle now closed and shut away by the door of death—

> The door of gold
> That mortal eyes can not behold.

Samuel Brown ought certainly to have left an honourable name in various walks. He perceived the underlying truth in scientific things by the supreme intuition of the discoverer, while the way to show it to others he had still to find. His instincts were sure, while his experimentalism did not always answer. I remember his venturing on the now very generally accepted idea that colour would be found to be one, not three components, blue and yellow being light and darkness, leaving red as the inherent appearance of physical things. This as far as I understood him at the time, but then came the difficulties of experiment, which was necessary—"Triumphant Analysis," of which he was so fond of talking, having reached its limit. But the social influence he possessed, by means of his specific learning and wonderful power of ready speech, has left a deeper impression and a more charming recollection of his personality than his chemical discovery, or supposed discovery, relating to the atomic theory, his essays, admirable as they were, or his drama, *Galileo Galilei*, which is about as good as Carl von Gebler's later celebration of the same hero. He might have made any reasonable success as a physician, I venture to think; but he, like my brother, would have no medium success; their triumphs were to be in the highest walk, and both failed—not for want of genius, but for want of talent.

His cousin, John Brown, who has left a more lasting name, but whom I had only met in an accidental way, wrote me that Samuel was going down very fast. My last sight of him was at his native place, Haddington, still brimful of speculation on his favourite topics, though furnace and crucible had quitted his hand. I have none of his letters to embellish my narrative withal, as they were gathered in by his wife, with a view to publication, after he was gone; but I may preserve one from the author of *Rab and his Friends*, written a few days after his death:

MY DEAR SCOTT—Let me thank you most cordially for your note. I knew it would go to your heart, for few men loved him as you did, and as he knew you did. I could not write anything. I tried and broke down. I send the *Scotsman*, which is by his unfailing nurse, J. C. B. The *News* is, I think, by Professor Nichol. It is all so sad, so pathetic; such a mournful eclipse of so much brightness and power; the sun going down while it is yet day, the tree withering in its spring leaves; and without one word of complaint from him. He appeared before the time was ripe, and has paid the forfeit. Do you remember old Grotius's epitaph on the Schoolmaster? The idea is from the tenses of the verb—

*Præsens*
Imperfectum
Perfectum
Plus quam perfectum
FUTURUM.

Always glad to hear from you for your own sake, as well as for your brother's and Samuel's.—Yours,

J. BROWN.

*September* 1856.

# CHAPTER III

### RÉSUMÉ OF LETTERS FROM FRIENDS IN LONDON, 1856-58—ADDITIONS TO THE CIRCLE THERE

I MUST now return to my London circle of friends, as I may properly call the new school of painters, and other men with whom they were associated. For some time after attaching myself to the "School of Design," on visiting London I kept up some association with my former friends by visiting them, especially Frith, O'Neil, and Egg. But I found the game was not worth the candle; all these had found entrance into the Academy, and that made a difference to them—similar, in a way, to the change which takes place on the ordinary young woman when she gets married, has a house of her own, and has little more to expect in life. I wholly dissented from Frith's treatment of Pope in his picture of Lady Wortley Montague laughing at him in contemptuous fashion, however well painted it might be. I could not tell him I thought it represented the characters of the poet and the lady from the point of view of the cad, but I thought so. Egg was a valuable man in a way, but without power of any kind whatever.

Other old friends were gone out of town, or dead, as Poole, Meadows, or Patric Park, sculptor.

To explain the mutual relation and activities of my newer friends I must recur to their letters, as far as they have been preserved. Taken year by year they may be amusing.

From Woolner in May 1855. He says there is very little artistic news: growlings, of course, at the Academy Committee. They hung Millais—even Millais their crack student—in a bad place, he being too attractive now; but that celebrity made such an uproar the old fellows were glad to give in and place him better. Millais' amusement when Woolner wrote was to go about and rehearse the scene that took place at the Academy between him and the ancient magnates, especially the horse-painter, Abraham Cooper. Hunt had not yet returned from Jerusalem, nor did Woolner know when he would return.

Tennyson is publishing some new poems, most lovely things: I think them the best he has done. I hope you have heard of the new illustrated edition of his works, to appear with all our set in it, if Rossetti can be got to work. There is to be an engraving of my medallion of the royal Alfred for frontispiece. I have made a new one of him, much better than the last; also a new Carlyle, better than the old one. Carlyle is extremely pleased with it, and says it is the best likeness of him that has ever been done. That brute beast, the public, begins to think there is a glimmering of sense in the much-ridiculed *Latter-Day Pamphlets*. The stone which the builders rejected, etc.; but every one must bide his time. Concerning Wentworth's statue, which brought me home, it has turned out a failure. Wentworth has resolved on founding a fellowship at the Sydney University with the money instead.

This is at least fifteen hundred out of my pocket, coming back to England when I did.

"It was the only chance I ever had of making any money," Woolner says in the despairing way of young fellows, and ends with the reflection: "Throwing up a certainty for promises which prove false does not sweeten one's temper."

From Alexander Munro, a little while later [October 1855].

I have delayed writing till after my return from Paris, where I have been to see the Great Exhibition with D. G. R. I got home on Tuesday, but Rossetti only returned to-day. We enjoyed Paris immensely, in different ways of course, for Rossetti was every day with his sweetheart [E. S.], of whom he is more foolishly fond than I ever saw lover. Great affection is ever so to the mere looker-on, I suppose. Well! well! Hamon's pictures are indeed lovely, but Decamps is the great fellow; Ingres is often stupid, and Delacroix's drawing often bad. The grand sight was the Emperor and his court blazing in gold and colour at the distribution of medals; the Empress looking more lovely than ever, her head and neck very gracefully bending like a bell-flower. Old Horace Verney was there, resplendent in decorations from every country but ours. I spent one delightful evening with the Brownings, who are living in Paris; the Trevelyans I did not meet, although they were there.

William Rossetti writes [June 1855] in a long letter difficult to epitomise. I had asked him about Woolner in my last, so he also gives me the account of the Wentworth statue having gone among the "were to be."

Poor old sturdy Woolner is done again; he thinks of returning to Australia, where he was going on swimmingly, staying a year or two, then finally back to England. Allingham's little volume, such as it is, is about ready, illustrated by Hughes with woodcuts, also by Millais and Gabriel. Hunt, when he wrote last, was to leave Jerusalem shortly, and to be at Constantinople before now. I have a long-pending engagement to meet him at some point on the Continent on his way home. He has not had any picture ready to send over from the East for the Exhibition, but a life-size crayon of his father, admirably finished, has been rejected; they wanted to do the same for Millais, but did not dare. Are you aware he [Millais] is now at Perth, whither he started last Monday, to be married (to-morrow I think). Such is the scene at present on the stage of that curious and mournful tragi-comedy. Ruskin himself, for whom almost exclusively Gabriel is now engaged painting, has been very unwell of late, poor fellow, and is staying at Tunbridge, but he will be back to town on Thursday. I have met him repeatedly, and know few men I like better.

This is very pretty of William. He was the most amiable and generous of friends and brothers. Here is something from Gabriel on the same matters, and to the same effect. I wish I could transcribe it all, ending as it does with a sonnet.

I see your book in Mudie's last list [he says], together with *The Angel in the House*, whose gifted author's face must afford a fine rainbow study, since that vile stuff in the *Athenæum*. [This was an amusing review in verse, exactly like that of the poem reviewed, but printed as prose.] However, his book, it seems, is selling at a hundred a month. I remember you asked me how I liked it. Oh, it's done to a nicety, really well and extra well. But I know I need not read it again, although the author is asking his friends all round to do so, and marginise on it suggestions for the new edition. But the book is a first-rate one in its way. Allingham is shortly to be out with a new or a demi-semi-new volume, for which I have not yet ceased to be astounded at having drawn an illustration on wood in a moment of enthusiasm, but if it is not well cut it shall be cut out. I have been asked by Moxon to do some for the *Tennyson*, and said I would, but don't know whether I shall, as all the most practicable subjects have been given away already—my own fault, however, as I had been asked to choose long ago. Millais—but perhaps you have heard variously about him! In painting he is hard at work apotheosising the fire-brigade [painting his picture of the children saved from a house on fire]. Hannay—did you see his *Satire and Satirists*? a real book, the best he has done—is going to publish *Nettle-Flowers, a Collection of Epigrams*, etc., and means to contract for a few cudgellings in a mild way, as advertisement. Here is a rough recollection of one:

PRIAPUS HIGG *loquitur*.

With fraud the church, the law, the camp are rife,
Nothing but wickedness! O weary life!
I must console me with my neighbour's wife.

W. M. R. again, dated December 1856. He sends "many thanks for the *Leaves of Grass*, which I have not yet received from Woolner, but shall be eager to read as soon as I get it. Woolner and others denounce the book in the savagest of terms; but I suspect I shall find a great deal to like, a great deal to be surprised and amused at, and not a little to approve,—all mingled of course with a lot of worse than worthless eccentricity." Soon after he adds, "The *Leaves of Grass* has come to hand,

My best expectations are more than confirmed by what little I have read as yet; and Gabriel, who has had nothing but abuse for it hitherto, tends even towards enthusiasm. You could not have given me anything I should better like to receive." This was the introduction of Walt Whitman's work to the English literary world. A travelling bookseller, who had been in America, and been all through the war with Whitman, had brought over a number of copies of the first edition, an eccentric man of republican principles and very hard-up. In America the book being ignored by all booksellers, who declined at first even to lay it on their counters, he had got a quantity of copies and was now trying to sell them at Sunderland by Dutch auction. Thomas Dixon, my constant friend, a perceptive man and a public-spirited, though then only a working cork-cutter, sent the book to me as a curiosity. Instantly I perceived the advent of a new poet, a new Americanism, and a new teacher, and I invested in several copies. The one I sent to W. M. R. was the cause of his editing the English edition, which raised Whitman into a celebrity.

At that moment I had induced Woolner to visit Sir Walter Trevelyan with me, which was a fortunate circumstance in his professional career, as he carried away a commission for a marble group to occupy the centre of the hall, and this was the beginning of his great success. W. M. R. goes on to speak of this group, which was to carry out, express, or typify in some manner, the result of all the history I was then painting round the walls.

What is Woolner's "centre sculpture for the Hall" at Wallington to be, do you know? I asked him about it just after receiving your note, and he did not seem to have any distinct idea of either the subject or the extent of the commission. I hope it will be a good one, and that he will make a good thing of it, for really it is beginning to be high time he should take up his proper position. Of Lady Trevelyan I saw but little when I met her at Mrs. Loudon's, but she seems particularly frank, unaffected, and good-humouredly willing to be pleased. I had more conversation with Sir Walter—a fine-minded man, of both natural and acquired dignity. He would do well for Don Quixote—not the Don of the caricaturist, however. Both spoke most lovingly of you [which gave me great pleasure]. *Aurora Leigh* [just published] was sent to Gabriel, and also to Woolner, by Mrs. Browning herself, and both are unboundedly enthusiastic about it. I have read as yet something less than two books of it, stuffed and loaded with poetic beauty and passionate sympathy and insight. It is certainly better than only a succession of fine things, though, even to take the book from that point of view, it would be quite a wonderful thing of the kind. I confess, however, I stand somewhat taken aback at the prospect of the 14,000 lines of blank verse, introspection, and humanitarian romance, and I would not venture to name any early day for coming to the end of it. I have alluded to Thomas Seddon's death [Hunt's friend who died in the East]. You have probably met him among our set in London, though I am not certain. He was doing good service in the application of the Pre-Raphaelite principle to landscape of historic interest, such as Jerusalem, Egypt, etc., and in a year or more would have made a very decided position. His sudden death from dysentery at Cairo at the age of thirty-five is very melancholy, both for his own family and for the wife he had married only a year and a half ago. Hunt, like the fine fellow he is, was the first to suggest that some public recognition and substantial fruit of his exertions might be attained by exhibiting the works he has left. I am just setting off to a meeting at Brown's where four or five of us are to talk the matter over. [The result was a subscription which purchased and presented to the National Gallery the picture of Jerusalem.]

Now for a rapid dash at our news. Hunt is painting at his "Christ and the Doctors in the Temple," having established himself for the present in the Crystal Palace for some use that he can turn the Alhambra Court to for the background. Gabriel has done four of his Tennyson designs, and is preparing with some seriousness to paint an altar-piece for Llandaff Cathedral—subject, the *Nativity*. Millais is still at Perth. Woolner, well on with his Tennyson bust in marble. Arthur Hughes, with sufficiency of commissions and also a baby. Hannay is writing for the *Quarterly*. The Brownings are back to Florence; their presence in London was most delightful to all of our set who know them. Brown, who has not yet begun his picture of "Work," has done a small oil portrait of me, capital in painting and likeness, which he has presented to my mother.

Gabriel follows a month later or so (February 1857) from 14 Chatham Place, where he remained so long:

I have been meaning to write you ever since Brown showed me the photograph from your noble picture of "St. Cuthbert." I had not, in the state of sleepy worry in which one lives here, woke up to the consciousness that such things were being done, and it came to me as a most delightful surprise. I shall hope some day to see the original. I suppose it is the only picture existing as yet of so definitely "historical" a class, in which the surroundings are all real studies from nature; a great thing to have done. The sky and sea are sky and sea, and the ancient boats are all real as if you had got such things to sit to you. The whole scene too, and the quiet way in which the incident is occurring, at once strike the spectator with the immense advantage of simple truth in historical art over the "monumental" style. The figures all seem very fine, although their lower limbs are out of focus in the photograph. The only one which at all fails to satisfy me is the priest in the centre; but perhaps you are right in curtailing him of much individuality. [This figure represents Bishop Theodore, an Oriental from Smyrna, whom I had consequently made very dusky in complexion. He accompanied the young King of Northumbria to the island of Cuthbert's hermitage, having celebrated mass before embarking. I represented him apparelled for the celebration to give contrast to the hermit's wrapper. This may be considered by some a sacrifice to pictorial convention; if so, it is the only one in the picture, or, as far as I know, in any of the series of pictures.] A succession of works such as this cannot fail to establish your reputation. I hear you are now at work on the " Building of the Roman Wall." One of the future subjects, " Barnard Gilpin taking down the Gauntlet," should inspire you; it will be a glorious opportunity for a stirring work. I have done a few water-colours in my small way lately, and designed five blocks for Tennyson, some of which are still cutting and maiming. It is a thankless task. After a fortnight's work my block goes to the engraver, like Agag, delicately, and is hewn to pieces before the—Lord Harry!

    ADDRESS TO THE D——L BROTHERS

      O woodman, spare that block,
      O gash not anyhow;
      It took ten days by clock,
      I'd fain protect it now.
        Chorus, wild laughter from Dalziel's workshop.

Your friend W. J. Linton did two for me. [I am delighted to quote his good opinion.] I am convinced he is a long way the best engraver living, now that old Thomson is nearly out of the field. But unluckily the two that went to Linton were just the least elaborate. All the most careful ones have gone to Dalziel, and have fared but miserably, though I am sure the greatest pains have been bestowed upon them. Yesterday I made Linton's acquaintance, as he came to town on business; he seems a most agreeable fellow.

Two young men, projectors of the *Oxford and Cambridge Magazine*, have recently come to town also from Oxford, and are now very intimate friends of mine. Their names are Morris and Jones. They have turned artists instead of taking up any other career to which the University generally leads, and both are men of real genius. Jones's designs are marvels of finish and imaginative detail, unequalled by anything unless perhaps Albert Dürer's finest works; and Morris, though without practice as yet, has no less power, I fancy. [Such is D. G. R.'s first impression of the two close friends and men of original genius. Besides, he goes on to say]: He [Morris] has written some really wonderful poetry too, and as I happen to have a song of his in my pocket I enclose it to you. [This song has been lost, or possibly returned; I cannot find it, or remember what it was.]

Gabriel writes again in March 1857, sending me three numbers of the *Oxford and Cambridge Magazine* containing three poems of his. Regarding one of these he wants to protest that it appears in the same number with a praise of one of his pictures, quite innocently on his part:

The praise was written by my most kind friend Vernon Lushington [whose name I now heard for the first time] before I knew of his intention, and I never saw it till ready for press. The poem had been some time in the editor's hands, and got put in unluckily just then. *Non mea culpa.*

He says again :

I hope some day to see your pictures ; but also think there ought to be some steps taken, if possible, to show them in London when several are completed.[1] Could not they be fixed only temporarily in the Hall at present? I shall not forget to keep photographs of my blocks for Tennyson for you. Besides these three I have done two more, which W. J. Linton has cut well, and of which, therefore, I need not regret having no photograph. I have forwarded your "Seddon" subscription to William. About the new art paper, it is to be feared it will not come to anything : Ruskin bites not. You asked about the capitals (botanical) for the Oxford Museum. I have not undertaken any, but promised some time ago to design the sculpture in the arched doorway to the street —how call you it?—but have not, however, heard from Woodward [the architect of the museum] very lately. He is, as you surmise, well worth knowing, but is the stillest creature out of an oyster-shell.

Woodward had appeared as a guest at Wallington, and also Dr. Acland, and I had designed the first of the capitals of pillars which were to form a series all round the museum supporting the gallery, and were expected, by combining four or six plants on each cap in a Gothic manner, to represent all the botanical classes. That year, on visiting Oxford, I found some of these cut by the O'Sheas, very good indeed ; but those expert stone-carvers disliked copying drawings—could only, in fact, improvise with a vague resemblance to the copy.

Again in June 1857 Rossetti writes me, mainly on my new picture of the "Building of Hadrian's

---

[1] [The pictures were ultimately exhibited, when the series of eight was completed, at the French Gallery in June 1861.—ED.]

Wall" and about a small semi-private exhibition opened by the set or coterie—we may as well call a spade a spade—in Fitzroy Place, accessible by free tickets, which exhibition was a forerunner of the Hogarth Club, constituted a year after. I will not, however, indulge myself again in transcribing his praises. Here are his tidings about the two friends from Oxford :

> Morris has as yet done nothing in art, but is now busily painting his first picture, " Sir Tristram after his Illness in the Garden of King Mark's Palace, recognised by the Dog he had given to Iseult," from the *Morte d'Arthur*. It is being done all from nature of course, and I believe will turn out capitally. His chum Jones, who is by far the most advanced of the two, is getting commissions fast, and has done some wonderful cartoons in colour for stained glass, which would delight the soul of you. He has an order for an oil picture from Mr. Plint of Leeds, and has done me the honour of choosing for subject my "Blessed Damozel," which he is to illustrate in two compartments. I have no doubt it will be in *our* next year's exhibition. I hope you will send us one of your pictures, but I have as yet no idea of their size. [This picture was never done, Mr. Plint having died.]

Thus my circle of friends was being gradually enriched by those I met. Swinburne and others, under the friendly wing of Lady Trevelyan ; and these notices in London letters were the first intimations of the advent of two youths who were both destined to fill an important place in the intellectual history of our time. They were undergraduates together at Oxford at the time D. G. R.'s poetry brought them to him in connection with the *Magazine*, in which they were both actively concerned—Burne-Jones feebly, however, and William Morris enthusiastically, as he contributed many wonderful tales and some poems.  They were then fast friends, and they have remained so ever since.  The powers of the two men were, however, very distinct, although at this their starting-point they were both equally bent on becoming artists.  Morris's first step in this direction was to article himself to George Edmund Street, then located in the University town as architect to the diocese.  He paid his premium, and soon tiring of the regular office work, left it off, and they both, as we have seen, appeared in London.  Morris was entirely his own master, but E. B. J.'s course of action was not so free, as he had a father living, and it was only by the mediation and warm assurance of Rossetti as to his son's extraordinary talent that the paternal bias to the Church for his son's career gave way; D. G. R. told me.  Perhaps the best of Morris's tales in the *Oxford and Cambridge Magazine* were "Gertha's Lovers" and the "Hollow Land," but all of his contributions were unmistakable in imaginative beauty, and will some day be republished.

At this time the Union debating club-house and library was just finished building.  Those interested in it, Dr. Acland, Mr. Woodward, the architect, and others, accepted the offer on the part of Rossetti—I think it must have been mainly in his hand, as he asked me to join in the work—to surround the gallery of the great room with life-size subjects from the romance of the Round Table. Both of these youths went into the scheme ; Arthur Hughes also, and a youth whose name has not yet adorned these pages, Valentine Prinsep. The work was voluntary ; the remuneration was to be the honour ; the expenses of living there while the work was going on and the bills for colours being defrayed by the Union. I did not avail myself of the invitation to join the party, as I had fortunately other occupation. But will it be believed, not one of the band from first to last knew anything whatever of wall-painting and its requirements! It was simply the most unmitigated *fiasco* that ever was made by a parcel of men of genius. The " great work " Gabriel as we see holds out hopes of Morris accomplishing, that begun by Rossetti himself, and the one next it by Valentine Prinsep all went rapidly on, but only apparently, as they were painted in water-colours on the irregular brick wall merely whitewashed! The wall being a common brick wall meant to be primed with plaster, one might have expected even the architect Woodward would have expostulated. He did not : the edges of all the bricks caught the dust ; and as no adhesive medium, so far as I could discover, was used, the powder colours rubbed off the flat surfaces. When I saw them only a few months after they were executed,[1] they were beginning to be

[1] [In an old pocket-book containing entries about this visit to Oxford, which seems to have been in June 1858, I find a note of Mr. Scott's impressions of the Union paintings, which is worth transcribing.—ED.]

"The paintings by the new-school artists in the Union are very unintelligible. By this time they must have largely disappeared. Still the remains are curiously interesting, and ought to be preserved.

What gave Morris his proper position was the publication in the following year (1858) of the *Defence of Guenevere*. This book was and is the most notable first volume of any poet; many of the poems represent the mediæval spirit in a new way, not by a sentimental nineteenth-century-revival mediævalism, but they give a poetical sense of a barbaric age strongly and sharply real. Woolner wrote to me at the time of publication, "I believe they are exciting a good deal of attention among the intelligent on the outlook for something new." Nevertheless, like Swinburne's first volume, the book was still-born. The considerable body of perfectly-informed but unsympathetic professional critics are, strange to say, so useless as directors of public taste that they have never yet lifted the right man into

interesting. They are poems more than pictures—being large illuminations and treated in a mediæval manner, not studied from nature nor endeavouring to represent nature indeed—at least not restricting the means of suggestion by the limitation of correct imitation. The drawing is such as men who have scarcely practised at all can do without the model before them, and the colour is all positive, like mediæval work, the execution stippling like a miniature. The conception of the whole artistically, the method of working, and the character of colour and design are undoubtedly all due to Rossetti; indeed the work is properly his work, Morris also showing in the roof the originality one might expect from his character as a poet. This is shown in Rossetti's picture being so much more perfect than the rest. In it the stippling is admirably expressive of the detail, but in all the others it means nothing. However, this stippling with a little brush is simply the result of his habit of painting nothing but little water-colours. The invention in his picture and in some of the others is most lyrical and delightful."

his right place at once.  After repeated volumes had attracted public favour, both of these little volumes were reprinted ; the original impression having been returned to the paper-mill, this destination being the successor to "the trunkmaker" of old times.

I have quoted one of Rossetti's letters expressing great praise of one of my Wallington pictures.  I might have quoted many more.  The admiration for the scenic treatment and the accessories in the "St. Cuthbert" picture, for the sea and the sky, the birds, and other matters, which he repeats with still increasing emphasis of other following pictures, suggests a few remarks.  I have always believed the best unofficial education for an artist is daily sketching, keeping a pocket sketch-book as Thomas Sibson, a friend too soon lost, as already noticed, was in the habit of doing.  If he in this way records every characteristic action, every beautiful feature or form he observes, not only in the accidents of society or active human life, but also in vegetation or among the lower animals, he will be real and natural in expressing whatever he invents.  "All painted from nature" is very excellent, as Rossetti says Morris is doing at the Union ; this, however, meant merely that he got sunflowers into the gallery, but as he could not get Tristram along with them the sunflowers were so obtrusive he only showed Tristram's head over them!  The best professional education for a *painter* is perhaps scene-painting, but for designing, thinking pictorially, the vital habit necessary is observing and recording, however slightly and transiently, the multitudinous aspects of life.

The absence of this habit made Holman Hunt, the most conscientious of men and the most realistic of painters, a slave to the circumstances under which he worked; and D. G. R., poet and imaginative inventor, who never made a memorandum of any thing in the world except from the female face between sixteen and twenty-six, was torn to pieces by the waste of energy and excruciating difficulty entailed by the getting of his picture backgrounds reasonably right. I shall not say true to life or nature—*that* he never considered; but he would unwittingly make the wall of a house only two inches thick, or its perspective entirely wrong. In the water-colour picture I got Lady Trevelyan to commission, "The Virgin in the House of St. John," he had to introduce a distaff; after spending weeks in looking for one he drew one "out of his head," and made the lint drawn from the top of the mass looking somewhat like a smoking chimney in the painting. True Italian as he was, he never went home even as tourist, where he could have seen the old women about Rome still using the distaff; he cared for nothing, in short, but what he invented. Had he gone he would never have sketched the old women with distaffs. He would have come back as ignorant as he went pictorially, but wiser in every other respect. I prevailed on him to alter the fallacy, but even after explanation he could not make it right. In the little vignette for his sister's

*Prince's Progress* he made an open window looking on a garden in which was a labyrinth; this he actually represented as the *plan*, not the picture, of a labyrinth! I knew at once he had taken it from the plan of the labyrinth at Hampton Court given in the sixpenny guide to that locality. He would rather buy the book, and not trouble to go into the maze itself!

He has all his life been occupied and absorbed in his own conceptions of art or of poetry. But we cannot live by bread alone; life is multiform, and art for art's sake is a narrow field. Without the faculty of observation the ideal becomes simply the unreal. Jones is a painter by nature; the aspect is everything to him, the reality little. Rossetti is a poet, and feels the core of the matter to be all-important; but his powers of observation of the actual world are nearly nil. I mention these defects in the accessories of his pictures as an argument for the value of sketching from nature; they were infinitely insignificant compared with the richness of invention, purity of feeling, and loveliness of the figures represented in the works of each of these men.

# CHAPTER IV

RÉSUMÉ OF LETTERS FROM FRIENDS, 1859-60-61—THE ROSSETTIS, HOLMAN HUNT, WOOLNER, MUNRO, ETC.—LADY TREVELYAN—MISS BOYD.

I HAVE now arrived at a period when painting occupied all my days and nights too, though I still conducted the School of Art. I shall therefore have little to say about myself, and shall again fall back upon letters, such as were annually saved from the waste-basket of the year at Christmas. Not any of these letters were other than friendly and accidental, but as they relate mainly to passing events, their want of elaboration is no defect, and no confidences are violated by what I shall extract.

Sometimes a sketch or a verse, even satirical or caricature in a good-humoured way, recalls more vividly still the impression of the passing moment. Louis Napoleon, or, as Swinburne called him, "the Beauharnais," was now in his glory; Victor Hugo, and others dear to all of us, were refugees. Swinburne, always possessed by some pet subject of hatred or admiration, was carried away by ungovernable fury at the success of the wretched adventurer, or weak-minded innocent, now settled in the Tuileries, and practised his ingenuity in inventing tirades against him, sometimes full of humour and splendour, at other times grossly absurd. Lady Trevelyan, always ready to enter into his mood, used to assist him; but learning he was going to accompany his family to France, she predicted that he would be caught by the police, and sketched the fate that awaited him. The figure of A. C. S. addressing the people was wonderfully good.

1. The first letter I find is from my best friend and letter-writer of that day (1st March 1858), W. M. R., relating to the formation of the Hogarth Club, of which I have spoken before. All the names on the list of the proposed Portfolio Club and many more were enrolled, the only important one not among them being that of Millais, who could not join a body including Ruskin. The only non-artistic members I remember meeting were Vernon Lushington and his brother Godfrey, sincere and intelligent lovers of art and its professors; and in many ways Vernon was and is one of the most admirable of men—I knew little of Godfrey. This club *ought* to have been still in existence, and under able management it should have by this time taken a place only second to the Royal Academy in professional importance, but its existence was short. Ruskin was the first dissentient: the committee invested in a billiard table, which he took as an insult, as he could play at no games, so he left; then the arrange-

ment of an Exhibition open to the public on payment, instead of a changeable show of pictures open only to the members' friends, brought up conflicting opinions. Strangely enough, F. M. Brown was the opponent of the scheme; the club broke up under the pressure of the struggle.

The most important picture shown on these semi-private club occasions was Martineau's "Last Day in the Old Home." The two most popular of all the thousands of works afterwards shown in the International Exhibition of 1862 were it and Brown's "Last of England," in which he painted himself and his wife, with the infant Oliver (afterwards to be mentioned) in her lap. I may say of this picture parenthetically, that it represents what might have been a fact in F. M. Brown's career. When Woolner went to the gold-fields, and Holman Hunt was hesitating about giving up painting, Brown had similar plans floating in his mind, only, being of a reticent nature, and also slow to act, he neither talked of them nor put them in practice, except in the way of producing this record of them after he had found some small successes at home. These successes were in finding a "patron" or two, the principal being my friend James Leathart of Newcastle, who, with my advice, made an excellent collection of the works of the new men—Holman Hunt and Millais to begin with, then Rossetti and Arthur Hughes, Martineau, and above all, F. M. Brown.

II. Here is a long note from Holman Hunt,

much of it, however, about his affairs, which it is needless to quote. The rest is mainly about a new medium in painting and other matters of his studio, highly worthy of record to the initiated. It is dated, Tor Villa, Campden Hill, Kensington, 11th February 1860, while he was finishing—a long process extending over years—his "Christ in the Temple." He says he had put away my "good-natured letter" to answer at leisure, and now he finds it a month and a half old, and is

> overpowered by the feeling that no protestations of mine will convince you of the pleasure I had in receiving it. You know, however, that we are not always able to do what we like best, and so will believe that I would have sat down to have a chat with you about varnishes and about my present plans and engagements long ago, if I had been able. . . . Well then: I seldom mix my copal and turpentine together, not because there would be any danger to the permanency of the work by such proceeding, but only because the character of the surface obtained thereby is not so pleasant to my taste as the fat full firmness got by paint in its pure state as mixed with oil, or when compounded only with copal. To avoid the excess of this quality when it becomes difficult to work, I often begin by modelling all out with a turpentine dilution of the copalled pigment. When I repaint over old work, I often, too, soften the surface of the dry ground, and modify the colour of it with washes of turpentine colour, a dodge which has many advantages, not the least being that it enables the two coats of paint to combine together, as if painted at once, and thus obviates the danger of one tearing up the other. You will, I daresay, have found out the same plan, and by this time may have got over all your difficulties with copal. . . .

I had written him about a small water-colour, a

commission from a friend long in hand, but he was unable even yet to say much, his great picture being not yet quite finished, and in its last tedious state of finish he was afraid to think of the smallest subject of another kind, lest he should be seduced from the little scrapings and stipplings-up of odd corners, which was his present labour. When he had finished this Temple picture, he said he would have to do the same service for two other Eastern pictures brought home, and several sketches, which would exhaust his present Oriental mania, so that he would be glad to clean his brushes and palette for open-air practice somewhere in a green field with daisies and country lasses sprinkled about. This would only be a temporary aberration, however, for he cannot believe that art should let such beautiful things pass away, as are now passing in the East, without any exertion to chronicle them for the future.

So I promise to return in spirit to the land of the good Haroun Al Raschid, if I can't get there in the body before the year is out. The little subject Mr. Crawhal wants [this was the water-colour picture a friend in New-castle wanted from one of Hunt's illustrations to Tennyson's poems] will scarcely require me to fight the fates in the East, so I think I may promise to have it done and forwarded to him, or kept here for his refusal, without the danger of its being touched up by the hand of a quarantine officer at some Syrian seaport, with the sharp punch which promotes ventilation at all risks in articles passing through his hands. The important picture for Mr. Leathart is a more serious affair, because I don't see how I can paint it out of the rotation of commissions which are of some depth—and with my slow brushes will require some time. As I never or rarely undertake special commissions for settled subjects, but merely let the friends, one after another, whose names are down, have the refusal of each as finished, it is possible that I may have something earlier than would seem likely. I always try to paint every new picture as unlike the one last painted as possible, so people are frequently taken by surprise when I show them my work, and thus pictures not my worst at all, pass six or seven applicants before they are taken up. . . . [He hopes I won't dread incommoding him if Mrs. Scott and I should be coming to town, and will be his guests.] I live so regularly that a lady would not be in my way at all; but I will not interfere with your earlier plans. If you come alone, however, you could not be more conveniently posted, or with more pleasure to your host, than here.

This note, with its conscientious particularity and exactness of detail, and kind, candid, and friendly spirit, is very characteristic, and the press of commissions shows the mighty revolution in his fortunes after the popularity of the "Light of the World" had confirmed his position.

III. The process of finishing here described is in curious contrast to that indicated by Rossetti in a letter received about the same time, 13th November 1859, both having been leaders in the same movement. He says:

I have painted a half figure in oil, in doing which I have made an effort to avoid what I know to be a besetting sin of mine, and indeed rather common to P.R. painting—that of stippling on the flesh. I have succeeded in quite keeping the niggling process at a distance this time, and am very desirous of painting, whenever I can find leisure and opportunity, various figures of this kind, chiefly as studies of rapid flesh painting. I am sure that among the many botherations of a picture where design, drawing, expression, and colour have to be thought of all at once (and this, perhaps, in the focus of the four winds out of doors, or at any rate among somnolent models, ticklish draperies, and toppling lay figures), one can never do justice even to what faculty of mere painting may be in one. Even among the old good painters, their portraits and simpler pictures are almost always their masterpieces for colour and execution, and I fancy if one kept this in view one must have a better chance of learning to paint at last. One of the things I have finished last you have seen—the "Sir Galahad." But far more than that anything done I have been struggling in a labyrinth of things which it seems impossible to get on with, and things which it seems impossible to begin.

This letter is of infinite importance in the history of Rossetti's painting. It marks the first success in life-size oil-painting, and the practice of his whole later art-life has shown increasing mastery over half-length female figures of a similar type. Millais also before this time had protested that life was too short to continue painting in detail as he had done with such amazing rapidity and success. He was now married, full of commissions, and unable to take up half the success that lay to his hand. As to the remark about the old masters, Rossetti had not seen any of their chef-d'œuvres, never having been in Italy!

IV. Let me enter here some extracts from Lady Trevelyan's friendly notes. In her more familiar letters she used often to address me as Mr. Porcupine, the defensive creature being drawn neatly instead of the word, and sometimes indulge in very rare humour. We must be contented with only such extracts as will add to our narrative.

WALLINGTON, *May* 1860.

I have finished my panel and am prepared for any amount of abuse you may be pleased to bestow upon it. . . . I have not heard lately from Algernon, but what I hear of him is good. He has passed for his degree, and he has written a poem (for the Oxford competition on *The Loss of Sir John Franklin*) which his father and people like very much. I am glad the Academy have ill-used the Preraffs, it will perhaps lop off some rotten branches in the shape of weak brethren, who paint boneless imitations of the school and bring discredit on it. If these are convinced it is unpopular and does not pay they will give it up, which will be an unmixed good. I believe Mr. Ruskin is only going to Switzerland for the summer. He will never go away for a very long period while his father and mother are living. He has always said that but for them he would go and live in some favourite place in Switzerland. I shall be very thankful if he doesn't write the *Notes* this year, for he is quite tired with his last volume, which he is just finishing ; and if he does *Notes* at all, he should do them with all his strength instead of half in joke, and at the end of six months' hard work, while longing for a holiday. Is Hunt's bargain really concluded? We expect to go south on Monday, when I will write you again.

V. Next from London, June 1860:

I am glad to hear a good account of you from Sir Walter, and that he had the pleasure of entertaining the School of Art, students, inspector, and all, at a picnic. I can only wish you had had a finer day for it.

How was the light for seeing the Hall? Holman Hunt spent an evening here very well and jolly. He is finishing up odds and ends that have been put aside for the great picture, and is very diligent at rifle-drill. My brother Roland is also up and off to Walham Green every morning at seven, for ball practice, spending bushels of cartridges. Yesterday I sent you a paper about Captain Snow's Arctic search: he is to lecture at Newcastle on the 19th and collect subscriptions. Now I conjure you by all you believe in, misty philosophy, gooseberry pie, and anything else equally sacred to you, go to hear him and make others go. Do puff, do ventilate the subject and make others take an interest in it. If they don't care for the records and Journal, there is always a chance of finding some of the crew alive; if they don't care for those, they may be moved by our old flag going first round the world by the Arctic route and not leaving that triumph to the stars and stripes, which will be before us as sure as fate, if we don't mind. I have set my whole heart on this search; read the *Saturday Review* of this week about it. . . .

SEATON, AXMINSTER, *August* 1860.

VI. I have been very long without writing, but I have been awfully busy. I always am so here, where I am among my lace people. Sir Walter gave me your note about the spandrels. They have hung on hand shamefully, but as we have been away this summer, I suppose we shall stay at Wallington in winter, and then I'll paint the yew, and the fir, and anything one can get in winter, and be very industrious. Dreadful weather we have had, no painting out of doors, but I suppose it was all sunshine while you were with Miss Boyd—that was so of course. Holman Hunt wrote the other day to ask if the white lilies were to be had, and offered to go down and do them, but of course they are dead and gone weeks ago; so I told him if he will be in England next lily season, we would wait for that; but if not, he must come to us as soon as we get back and do dahlias, or sunflower, or

what we can get. He was just starting on a tour with
Alfred Tennyson to Brittany, and I have not got his
answer. This was a week ago. Things get on so
slowly here when we are away. Sir Walter has determined
not to leave till our school is finished and its work started.
Mr. Woodward is also designing some seaside houses
for us, but it is such a dear little place, I don't complain
of staying on. . . . We have been in the west of
Cornwall, where the red geranium grows up to the bedroom windows, and we found Mr. Nash painting at
Kyname Cove: he had been on the same picture for ten
weeks. . . . What are you doing now? smoking and
getting fat in your new studio? I expect to find you
fearfully fat and stupid when I come home. Is Grace
Darling finished? Is she fearfully and wonderfully ugly?
[I answered that Grace Darling was too far in storm to
be anything, but that the principal figure nearly the size
of life—the woman whose child had died in her bosom
unknown to her—was wonderfully noble, having been
painted from Miss Boyd.] Woolner can't get a block
of marble at present to do the Fairbairn children, so he
has been working on our group. Dr. Acland had a
gloomy voyage with the Prince to Canada. They were
in a dense fog as soon as they started, so wet a fog that
their clothes, beds, everything, were damp the whole time
till they were about 150 miles from Newfoundland, when
they suddenly sailed into bright clear air all ablaze with a
brilliant sunset, and they saw the fog behind them like a
thick white curtain from sea to sky.

\* \* \* \* \*

SEATON, *October* 1860.

VII. I think I had a letter from you since I wrote—
the one describing your "Grace Darling" picture, which we
have not yet seen, in which you go in as a great marine
painter, which, no doubt, you ought to be considering
your great love of the sea and your passion for voyaging
upon it, so that you are a sort of a fat peaceable sea-king.
Not like that "Cockney Turner," who used to go for a

voyage whenever he could, and had himself lashed to the mast to watch storms when they came.

\* \* \* \* \*

I am afraid we shall not see much of Algernon in the north now dear kind Sir John Swinburne is gone. What a loss he is! It seems ridiculous to feel as if a man of ninety-eight had died too soon, yet he certainly has, for he enjoyed life and added to the enjoyment of many other people. The shock of Sir Henry Ward's death was the exciting cause of his last illness.

I have been reading Mr. Woolner's poem. Some of it is very fine and there is a great deal of himself in it; but doubtless you will have seen or heard most of it. I was in some hopes that the Tennysons would have come to Wallington when we returned there, but that has had to be given up, and they have gone back to the Isle of Wight to receive some guests. Holman Hunt was left somewhere near Falmouth making sketches.

I have taken advantage of some fine days to try and make a little oil study of some plants out of doors, but of course I got into many troubles. Hang the oil-colours!! why do they look so bright and strong and jolly, and in two or three days go in and are all dim and dingy? The picture seems to want varnish. Must it wait for a year, till it is quite hard, before it is varnished? Now, I'll be civil if you'll help me—I hope Mrs. Scott is well, and that you've given up smoking.

Some allusions in these extracts require commentary. Above all others, there is the first mention of Miss Boyd, so dear to me from that time till the present moment of writing. On the 18th March 1859, though I have omitted to record the incident, while I was painting Bernard Gilpin addressing the borderers in the church of Rothbury after having taken down the gage of battle from

the wall, I had a visit from a lady some few years over thirty, ill and weary from watching by the death-bed of her mother. I had not heard her name before. She wanted to find a new interest in life, and thought to find it in art. She was somehow or other possessed, to me, of the most interesting face and voice I had ever heard or seen. I devoted myself to answer this desire of hers, and from day to day the interest on either side increased. At this moment I am sitting, on a fearfully wet day, in her old family castle, Penkill, in Ayrshire, where all these notes have been written. This ancient house has been my summer home and that of my wife, for many years, and all the friends, with few exceptions, mentioned in these pages have come to see us here; the winter half of the year Miss Boyd is our guest in London. As important in my life as Wallington, infinitely more so, indeed, the name will be or ought to be the principal one in my later pages.

VIII. From my dear W. M. R., 14th May 1860. He had kindly sent me a summary of about twenty pages of the history of Sordello—I ought to call it an explanatory essay on Browning's poem. Unhappily I thought this nearly as obscure as the poem itself. He says:

As to Sordello, I must give you up, hoping that the pains of heresy don't await you round the corner somewhere or other. The particulars of his life given—*not given*, you would say—by Browning are nearer the truth than most people suppose, or at least nearer some versions and hints of the truth, for his life is involved in great obscurity. I have read the notice of him in Nostradamus's *Lives of the Provençal Poets*, and there is an extended account of him in Tiraboschi's Italian literature which I shall look carefully into one day. [All of which he might very reasonably have saved himself the trouble of doing.] The sale of Hunt's picture is now settled; if the arrangement of which he told me yesterday week came to pass, as I cannot doubt it did, Gambart buys the picture with copyright for £5500, of which £3000 was to be paid last Wednesday, and the remainder in bills at eighteen months. This is a miraculous draught of fishes, though I have little doubt that Gambart, being a wide-awake man, will pay himself splendidly for the outlay by exhibition and engraving, and finally by the re-sale of the picture, which will have accumulated a huge reputation meanwhile. A little time ago the receipts at the door were £30 a day, and a very easy sum in arithmetic will show what this would come to throughout the year. I concur as to the poorness of what has been written about the picture. The one in *Fraser* ought to be above the average: it is by a son of Sir F. Palgrave. I have not seen it yet. The author has already published various things, especially an anonymous book called the *Passionate Pilgrim*, which evokes the enthusiasm of Patmore and some others. . . . I have always been curious to see what you make of "Grace Darling," and trust it will be in my power, as a conscientious and eminent critic, to pat your breakers on the head.

W. M. R. next asks me if I knew that Gabriel is about to marry or, perhaps, is now married to Miss Siddal, whom you have heard about and possibly seen? The family had been a little taken by surprise at receiving from him at Hastings, about a month before, the definite announcement of the forthcoming event, then to be enacted as soon as possible. Still later he had determined that it might possibly be on last Saturday, his thirty-second birthday. She is in the opinion of every one a beautiful creature with fine powers and sweet character. If only her health should become firmer after marriage, William thinks it will be a happy match. At all events he is glad that Gabriel is settled upon it. "He leaves Blackfriars, but I think has not yet managed to suit himself elsewhere." This sudden news was the first I heard of Gabriel's marriage; nor did either I or his own family hear directly from him for some little time after. Instead of leaving Blackfriars he at last appeared there with his wife, where he fitted up another room or two and continued to live till her death.

IX. Three months later (in the summer of 1860) I was for the first time visiting Miss Boyd and her brother at Penkill Castle in Ayrshire. My wife was in London, and writes me about the people she meets.

I am truly glad [she says] you are in such good company as Miss Boyd and her brother, and finding such delightful landscape subjects in the glen. . . . On Wednesday we drove to the top of Highgate Hill, where is S. Mary Magdalene Home. We spent a pleasant day with the sisters and penitents in the open air, the Bishop of London, etc. etc. . . . Christina is now an Associate, and wore the dress, which is very simple, elegant even; black with hanging sleeves, a muslin cap with lace edging quite becoming to her with the veil. Yesterday, at All Saints, whence Christina and I went to see Woolner and the marble group for Wallington, which is now going on. It is beautiful: and there, too, at last I have met Tennyson. In the evening we had a party of about twelve, among whom were Mr. E. Burne-Jones and his wife. She is pretty, a very little creature, indeed, and sang the ballad of "Green Sleeves" and others in loud wild tones quite novel and charming. E. B. J. I think extremely like a tall boy from school. William Morris and his wife also looked in, but only for a few minutes, having to go out of town by railway. You have not yet seen either of these ladies, and I now heard that Mrs. Gabriel Rossetti has not yet been seen in his mother's house, and has been invisible to every one. I can't think what countrywoman Mrs. Morris is like, not an Englishwoman certainly; but she did not untie her bonnet, their hour by the train being at hand. Mrs. D. G. R. has been ill—I suppose this preventing her coming out: she was really dangerously ill on their return from Paris, where she had been so well. Gabriel has been planning to take up his abode there. It seems Mrs. Madox Brown and her mother have been associated intimately somehow, so she is with her every day. All we little women looked quite diminutive beside Mrs. Morris.

These few words serve to show how nearly in point of time these matrimonial affairs came together; unless, indeed, the two now first mentioned above had not been late events, although the ladies were new to my wife. The Morris party going out of town indicates that the house he built after his marriage, the Red House, was already inhabited by them; and we must remember that the painting of the Union gallery at Oxford, if it had no artistic result, had an important one on the fate of William Morris. One evening, after the labours of the day, the volunteer artists of the Union regaled themselves by going to the theatre, and there they beheld in the front box above them what all declared to be the ideal personification of poetical womanhood. In this case the hair was not auburn, but black as night; unique in face and figure, she was a queen, a Proserpine, a Medusa, a Circe—but also, strangely enough, a Beatrice, a Pandora, a Virgin Mary. They made interest with her family, and she sat to them. Morris was at that time sworn to be a painter; she sat to him; he forthwith ventured to propose marriage, and here they were, starting for his new house at Upton. In this house I first saw her. It was designed by Morris in what he called the style of the thirteenth century. The only thing you saw from a distance was an immense red-tiled, steep, and high roof; and the only room I remember was the dining-room or hall, which seemed to occupy the whole area of the mansion. It had a fixed settle all round the walls, a curious music-gallery entered by a stair outside the room, breaking out high upon the gable, and no furniture but a long table of oak reaching nearly from end to end. This vast empty hall was painted coarsely in bands of wild foliage over both wall and ceiling, which was open-timber and lofty. The adornment had a novel, not to say startling, character, but if one had been told it was the South Sea Island style of thing one could have easily believed such to be the case, so bizarre was the execution. This eccentricity was very easily understood after a little consideration. Genius always rushes to extremes at first; on leaving the beaten track of every day no medium is to be preserved. The repudiation of whatever is modern in sentiment is immediate. There was the hatred of Louis XIV., and all possible relation to school advice and Birmingham taste. Morris did whatever seemed good to him unhesitatingly, and it has been very good: not "Songs of the Art-Catholic," certainly, but "Songs of mediæval life"; *The Earthly Paradise* has been the ultimate result. In ornament he succeeds not quite so well, but he has made an important position; by and by he will likely do better than anybody else.

X. Here under date of 5th October is something at last from D. G. R.; as usual, I make use of the letter only to carry forward my story—

Many thanks for your note with its inquiries regarding my wife, who I trust improves gradually. She is certainly stronger now than some months back, and the approach of winter does not seem to hurt her yet. We sent no cards, too much trouble you know, or certainly you would have got some. My wedding-trip was rather prolonged, and no place out of my studio must know me this autumn, in spite of various invitations, tempting to wife and self.

Soon after he writes again:

Lizzie is gone for a few days to stay with the Morrises at their Red House at Upton, and I am to join her there to-morrow, but shall probably return before her, as I am full of things to do, and could not go there at all, but that I have a panel to paint there. I shall soon be taking up Leathart's picture, almost immediately, but have been much interrupted lately by getting settled.

This was the picture he now called "Found," and this reference to it did not, I fear, really indicate any intention of taking it up. My friend Leathart had bought it at my recommendation, and paid for it, as the figures were nearly done, but strange to say, the background and the perspective baffled him. He never carried out the proposal to bring it down and paint it with me beside him at Hexham, but had tried to carry it out by himself over and over, and from the first had got the simple matter of perspective into a muddle. As years went on Leathart became impatient, the arrangement was annulled, with my intervention, to enable him to return the money: the picture never was finished.

I wish you could see how comfortable we have made ourselves. And, by the bye, we have always a spare bed-room, which please do not forget when you and Mrs. Scott come to town.

This friendly invitation was never available, indeed could only have been so for the next season: before a second summer D. G. R.'s married life was cut short by his wife's tragic death.

# CHAPTER V

DEATH OF MRS. ROSSETTI—ANECDOTES OF WALLINGTON—MY SERIES OF PICTURES OF BORDER HISTORY BEING FINISHED, I LEAVE NEWCASTLE—RETURN TO LONDON.

THE auguries of happiness from his marriage, entertained by some of Rossetti's friends, were frightfully dispelled. For myself, knowing Gabriel better than his brother did, though from the outside, I knew marriage was not a tie he had become able to bear. His former bachelor habit of working till 9 P.M., then rushing out to dine at a restaurant, was continued; Mrs. Siddal Rossetti, little accustomed to the cares and habits of domestic life, willingly conforming. She had become a genius in art, imitating her husband's inventions in water-colours in a way I clearly saw to be damaging to the peculiarities of his own works, though her uneducated performances were at once praised by him immoderately. After her death we heard nothing from Gabriel, or from any of the family, till he wanted me to be again his banker to enable him to leave Chatham Place, where he had not slept since the sad event. He then, after a temporary abode in Lincoln's Inn Fields, took the Chelsea house, 16 Cheyne Walk, where he remained, and began a professional success which increased through all the rest of his career.

To return for a moment to the great trial of his life. In ignorance of the main circumstances, and in obedience to a desire to comfort him, on receipt of his letter about leaving Blackfriars I ventured to tell him I never thought him fitted for a Benedict; but even to this he replied nothing, though long after his mental prostration had subsided, and his MS. book of poems was buried with her, I had to listen, alas, too much to the painful narrative. On the eventful night they had dined as usual at a café-restaurant; he had returned home with her, advised her to go to bed, and unheedingly taken himself out again. On his next and final home-coming he had to grope about for a light, and called to her without receiving a reply. What was said or done at the inquest I know not.

\*　　\*　　\*　　\*　　\*

\*　　\*　　\*　　\*　　\*

Time is the great physician, but for the next seven years, till his first autumn visit to Penkill in 1868, he wrote scarcely a line of poetry, except sonnets for pictures. Why he revenged himself thus on his distinguishing faculty I never could tell. When success in painting, properly speaking, first began on his acquiring a larger style on a large scale, he became for him proportionately gay and hospitable, carefully hiding the wound which, however, continued to bite like the Spartan's fox. He had a marquee erected in the garden in which he entertained in the evenings, and at same time constructed enclosures and cages for animals and birds. But, on the other hand, he began to call up the spirit of his wife by table-turning. Curious to be present at this serious divertisement, and not without hope of undeceiving him in this matter of spiritualism, I went one evening by appointment. I refused to make one at the table unless I saw the medium's feet all the time, as well as those of the table. This being indignantly objected to by him (not by her!) the *séance* was broken up. I never went back, objecting to see him believing so implicitly in a creature so abject.

This attempt of mine to be present was four years after his wife's death; it was in 1866, but long before that year a common friend had written to me: "One thing I must remember to tell you. Our old friend Gabriel has gone into spiritualism, and fancies he can call up bogies, and make them knock on a table. I am exceedingly sorry. There is only one consolation, it does not follow as a necessity that a man's friends will be obliged to confine him for such irrational doings. Many have done this for years, pursuing their ordinary avocations, insane only on one point." Other indications of unrest were soon apparent, resulting from a confusion between external realities and mental impressions, suggesting the question of what might further develop in future life.

To return to my own affairs. The suggestion that I should exhibit in London the eight large pictures, now drawing to a close, was carried out,[1] but Gambart pushed it over the season for other more promising ventures; the Exhibition did little good.

The decoration of Wallington, however, left room for other artistic labours besides my own, which deserve to be recorded. In one of Lady T.'s letters, already quoted, she speaks of Holman Hunt's going there to paint a pilaster, and Ruskin's visit to do so has been mentioned. Hunt never managed to do this, but Arthur Hughes and others did, especially Mrs. Mark Pattison, at that time lately married to the Master of Lincoln, and one of the most perfectly lovely women in the world. She is now distinguishing herself in literature, but then she gave proof of great ability in painting. The group in marble for the centre of the Hall suggests a little history. "Sturdy old Woolner," as W. M. R. calls him in a friendly colloquialism, was invited there through me. When I proposed the visit to him I found him in a disposition to revenge himself on the world at large for his want of success. At first he swore loudly that he would not go near any people with handles to their names; they were all "devastators of the day, maggots in the wounds of us poor devils who have to fight the battle of life; Carlyle thought so, and also Tennyson!" His phraseology was sometimes very strong, but his

[1] [In 1861, see vol. ii. p. 7.—ED.]

bark being worse than his bite, he did come, and was commissioned to prepare this sculpture. He was to summarise the result of all the surrounding history, a vague motive which at last suggested the beautiful work he produced, and which is now there.

The commission was a pleasant surprise to me, and was the beginning of immense success to him, but, unfortunately, it was the mistaken cause of the loss of my friend, Alexander Munro. Munro had been with me to Wallington more than once; the year before Woolner's visit he had there modelled both his host and hostess, afterwards executing one of them in marble ; and he jumped to the conclusion that but for me being interested in a brother poet, Woolner would never have stepped in. At the opening of the International Exhibition of 1862 the feud between the two sculptors—a feud of long growth previously—was the cause of a public scandal, through the Official Catalogue of the sculpture there collected giving vent to a murderous criticism against Munro's works. The sanction of the Royal Commissioners to the publication was withdrawn, but the evil was done. Munro never recovered his position, and, as the fates would have it, he was shortly after attacked by a mortal illness that sent him to Cannes to seek recovery, where he remained the rest of his life.

One more anecdote about ever-dear Wallington and its inmates. It was close upon Christmas of 1862, when we—that is, the Newcastle group, Miss

Boyd, Letitia, and myself—were preparing to change the scene by flitting to the wild sea-coast at Tynemouth for a holiday, when Woolner passed through on his way north to see Sir Walter. Two days later, early in the forenoon—when we were great-coated and packed for the railway, Swinburne suddenly appeared, having posted to Morpeth from Wallington early that morning. Why so early? he could not well explain; just thought he had been long enough there! he wanted letters at the post, but had not given his address! I could inquire no further; there appeared to be some mystery he did not wish to explain; we went by a later train, and he would accompany us. So we had him to walk with us by the much-resounding sea, when he declaimed the *Hymn to Proserpine* and *Laus Veneris*, two of the most lovely, perfect, and passionate among the triumphs of his best period of poetic performance, never to be forgotten when recited in his strange intonation, which truly represented the white heat of the enthusiasm that had produced them. The sea, too, was in sympathy, the breaking waves running the whole length of the long level sands towards Cullercoats, and sounding like far-off acclamations.

\*   \*   \*   \*   \*
\*   \*   \*   \*   \*

My series of pictures being finished, and a complete change effected in the organisation of Government Schools of Art, so that we early masters appointed by the Board of Trade had the option of retiring with a small pension; proximity to Edinburgh being besides unnecessary now my family was extinct; I returned to London in 1864.

When we prepared to leave Newcastle, we met with various demonstrations of kindness, in the way of public meetings, and I took with me a commission for a picture of the building of the "New Castle" by the son of William the Conqueror. Also for eighteen pictures for the upper spandrels of Wallington Hall, representing the history of Chevy Chase, from Earl Percy's going out to the bringing home of the dead.

If a man, artist, *littérateur*, or other, with a specific professional object, lives in the country, he may live a higher life than in town, but out of daily collision with other men, his fellows in literature or what not, he ceases to strive as they do for the objects they value. He sees better because he takes a bird's-eye view of the battle, and finds that many things struggled for are not worth having. The game is not worth the candle. Yet is it necessary for him to live in society— for even the poet. The acres of flatness in Wordsworth belong to the country life he led; his innovations and inspired work to his association with Coleridge and others.

We settled down in Elgin Road, Notting Hill. ... Being now again in London with an opportunity of entertaining my friends, I tried to bring some of them about me again, and I may here give some relics of the process. Meadows, I was one day told, was still to be seen about his favourite

Strand and Haymarket, so I sent him an invitation to meet some of the men of a newer generation. But he was in Jersey. Letter-writing was not in his line; but here is his reply, perhaps the only fragment of epistolary rhetoric the old boy ever indulged in.

> 1 TIVOLI VILLAS, ST. AUBEN'S ROAD,
> JERSEY, *September* 1867.
>
> MY DEAR SCOTT—Your kind recollection was like a glass of our toddy of old times in a cold night, or a sunbeam on a bleak world—a climax with the apex downwards—but you will observe by it that your invitation has driven me into fine writing. I should have seized with avidity the opportunity of meeting some of my old friends once more before I am made a cherub of, but you see it was not to be done. The wind is S.S.E. by north, and an antagonistic trifle of something like two hundred miles lies between us. Nevertheless the invitation was as agreeable as if it had been a chicken and a bottle of champagne. Being at this distance I know not if ever I shall see you again; the event must occur before we can be certain of it. I am living with Lucy and her husband, who think me an old fool not fit to be trusted alone, and perhaps they are right. But whether or no, I shall always remember W. B. Scott, and with him everything he can wish for himself.   KENNY MEADOWS.

G. H. Lewes I was sure of finding. He and *George* Eliot were shortly leaving town, but he invited me to dine with them and get acquainted with his new wife, whom I found the most bland and amiable of plain women, and most excellent in conversation, not finding it necessary to be always saying fine things. He, the plainest of men, was much improved with years, and yet as enthusiastic as ever. "I am often in that study of yours in Edward Street," he wrote, "where we passed the night 'talking of lovely things that conquer death.' We both hope to see you again." When they returned to town, I sent them both an invitation to dinner, which brought this reply :

THE PRIORY,<br>NORTH BANK, REGENT'S PARK.

MY DEAR SCOTT—Ever since we came to live in London, Mrs. Lewes has been forced to adopt the rigorous rule of not going out, nor returning calls, except to friends living out of town. On no other condition would life have been practicable (that is peaceful and workful) for us. This has also made me adopt the same rule, though less absolutely, and as I do sometimes make exceptions, I cannot refuse an old friend like you, so I shall gladly come to you on the 25th.—Yours, G. H. L.

# CHAPTER VI

PENKILL CASTLE AND MISS BOYD—DEATH OF SPENCER
BOYD—MY PAINTING OF THE STAIRCASE—MACLISE

WHEN we returned to London towards the end of 1864, Alice Boyd, whom I shall probably in future designate by her monogram Æ.B., also desiring to leave Newcastle, it was arranged that she should make her winter home with us. She was detained in the North by her brother's illness during our first winter in town, but every winter since she has been with us, and every year we have spent the late summer and autumn months at Penkill.

Penkill Castle, the ancient Ayrshire homestead of the younger branch of the Boyds, a family sufficiently historical in Scottish annals, had been suffered to fall into decay, the acres having been sadly diminished, and Spencer, the heir, living in England. When he came of age, he devoted himself to its restoration, re-roofing the early part and building a great new staircase instead of the narrow newel of former years.

This old building was so interesting to me with its recessed windows with stone seats and grooves half-way down the window-jambs, showing which portion had been glazed and which closed by shutters, that I puzzled out its history very completely. A large dormer window on the earliest part, ornamented with the nail-head, and a roll moulding  which terminated in a knot, George Edmund Street, certainly one of our best authorities for the history of our early architecture, thought could not be later than 1450; but in outlying places I see reason to think an ornament was retained later than it continued to be produced in more central places. Whatever date might be assigned to the first building, it was simply a square tower, a *peel* as it has been elsewhere called, consisting of four stories, the uppermost having two corner turrets, pierced with loopholes for defence. The lowest of these apartments, that level with the ground, was the stable, vaulted by means of thin stones embedded edgewise. Above this vault was the living-room, not large enough to be called a hall, paved with very thick red and yellow tiles. This room had probably been accessible only by a wooden stair outside, an arch in the rubble wall indicating where the door had been. Above this was the apartment called in ballads the "Ladies' Bower," divided no doubt by partitions, as here was a *garderobe* in the solid of the wall. A narrow stair in the end wall also reached this room

inhult castle

from the one below, and another similar ascended to an upper apartment, which may have had an outlet to a narrow promenade surrounding the roof. In 1628, on the marriage of the then laird, the narrow accommodation of this defensible house, typical of the later middle ages, was found insufficient, an outside stone staircase being built, and three large rooms added, still, however, with thick walls and small windows. Over the entrance to this narrow newel staircase was inserted a tablet bearing the heraldry of the two families, with their initials and the date 1628. Two rudely-carved oak chairs, with exactly the same heraldry, date, and initials, are still among the furnishings of the house, a large one with arms for the laird, and a little low one, a nursing-chair, for the lady. From the old times a high stone wall had enclosed the house, with a dove-cote at one corner and a gate defended by a movable grill or portcullis, which had latterly lain at the neighbouring smithy for a century till its final decay.

The last addition, that made by Spencer Boyd, had been done by renovating the whole building, and making ante-rooms and landings between the great new staircase and the rooms of both former buildings on each floor. These changes indicating the development of civilisation have a historical value: they bear an unmistakable evidence of our social national advancement, as the geological periods do of the development of the world at large.

The glen below the house was most interesting to me, and revived my ancient landscape proclivities.

Every summer for nearly ten years I painted there. The "friendship at first sight" was confirmed. Time could not strengthen it, but the impression or instinct of sympathy was changed by experience into satisfied conviction and confident repose. I speak of my own feeling of course. All my life I had tried for confiding affection both from men and women when I had a chance; had made many attempts to realise it without success. Not that I gave up the faith that two men who are not brothers by birth can be more than brothers by harmony of life. But while the fates had been against me with men, here at last was a perfect intercourse, made possible by the difference of the sexes. As we sat painting together by the rushing Penwhapple stream, in the deep glen, which D. G. R. afterwards commemorated, listening to the "*Stream's Secret*" before he put it into verse—and I too, by my three series of sonnets called *The Old Scottish Home, Outside the Temple*, and those entitled *Lost Love*, when there was a chance of Æ.'s health giving way; or in town during the long winter evenings reading a hundred books or enjoying whatever a London season cast in our path,—there had never occurred a misunderstood word or wish which might divide us. My wife had faith in us too, and Æ.'s brother as well.

But he was soon to part from her and his beloved old place. Their father having died when they were infants, and their mother having married again, they had been inseparable till the time when Æ. came to join us in London. This was in the spring of

1865. Her brother was to spend the following Christmas with us; we amused ourselves by decorating the dining-room with a large banderole inscribed *Welcome,* to receive him, and promised ourselves a pleasant time.

For a few days we made holiday. Spencer Boyd appeared quite well. His knowledge of architecture and love of it induced us to spend a day inspecting the clearing-out and refitting of St. Bartholomew's Church in Smithfield, where we chanced to witness an incident so curious as to be worth record, although it breaks in upon my narrative and delays the sad *dénouement.* The workmen were lowering the floor, which had become so silted up that the bases of the piers were covered. To do this they were removing the pavement, which was mainly of tombstones, and as we entered they were prising up a very heavy one, with an inscription still partially legible, having been protected by the floored seats placed over the entire nave at a later time. This was the tombstone of the hairdresser to His Majesty Charles II., one of the makers of the mighty wigs we see him painted in, but I forgot to transcribe his name; and packed in below was a large quantity—several wheelbarrows full—of white terra-cotta pins about half an inch thick by three and a half long, each end slightly enlarged. Neither the workmen nor their superintendent could guess what these were for, but we carried away some of them, and I found they were curling-pins for these great wigs of the period. The curling-pins were heated, and every long curl of the wig was wrapped round one of them. This is the latest instance known, I daresay, of the belongings of the deceased being buried with the owner.

The evening of that day Spencer died. We were sitting at tea; my dog and his were heard barking; he set down his cup, saying he would let them out; we heard him do so, but he did not return. By and by Alice, always careful about him, went out to ascertain what caused his delay, and in a little while I followed to hear her calling out his name at his bedroom door, which she had found locked on the inside. She had a presentiment that caused her to be dreadfully excited, so that I threw myself with all the force I possessed against the door, bursting it open, and we found him already dead. He had attempted to get into bed, but had been unable to do so. The first doctor who arrived undid his clothes, and I saw again the dark blue suffusion round the region of the heart I had seen on my brother Robert. He had died from the same disease of the heart.

I forbear to describe the grief on that endless night of the dearest of friends. We buried him in the wildest storm of snow I ever remember, in the family enclosure in the ancient ruin of Old Dailly Church. He was the last of the direct line of the Boyds of Penkill and Trochrague, who figure in Scottish biographical dictionaries under various headings: Mark Alexander, a soldier of fortune and writer of Latin and Greek poems, some printed at Antwerp 1592, others remaining in manuscript in the

Advocates' Library in Edinburgh ; Robert, Principal of Glasgow University, and his father ; and that very interesting and eccentric person Zachary, who wrote no end of curious poetry, very like Quarles in some points, but unique in the familiarity with which he treats his sacred heroes.

The summer after this sudden change to Æ.B., as we were driving in the neighbourhood of the little seaside town, Girvan, passing a place where had traditionally existed a tower, possibly the oldest house of the Boyds in these parts, we found a villa in course of building on the very spot. Robert M'Lean, the old coachman of the family, drew up and looking about him, pointed to the shattered stump of an ash-tree, and drew his mistress's attention to it. "That's it," was his emphatic announcement. I found on inquiry that this remainder of a tree was an after-growth from the *stool* of the last of a pair of great ashes once associated with the tower, long dear to the inhabitants of the little town, and that there was a rhyme current among them to this effect—

When the last leaf draps frae the auld aish tree,
The Penkill Boyds maun cease to be.

To defeat this prophecy, apparently approaching realisation, a piece of the old wood, bearing a young shoot still green and fresh, was cut off and carefully planted. "The popular prophecy is of course correct about us," said Æ.B., "but let us try if we can break the connection with the ash-trees"; so it was nursed carefully, perhaps too carefully, as an ash-tree is not quite at home in a heated greenhouse ; next summer it was still alive but its leaves were few, the second season it was gone.

Towards the end of the year, back in town again, I was preparing my winter's work in my studio, when the long banderole with the word "Welcome," turned up, a melancholy memento of Spencer Boyd's visit, and just then W. M. R. appeared, stepping out of a cab at the door. It was a holiday at the Inland Revenue office, he explained, and he had come to get me as a companion to visit Mrs. Marshall, the quondam washerwoman, now expert in calling up the bogies and making tables rap. I had tried various experiments in this matter of communicating with the dead, but without the smallest shade of success, but I would try again, and off we went, although I did not expect much, he having been present at his brother's on the evening I have mentioned.

The supposition of such communication is so irrational, environed on all sides with irrationalities, that I confess I only did try the experiment as an amusement, but William Rossetti had written down question and answer with all the circumstances of the interviews he had had with experts for years, and I was inclined to regard his judgment with respect on literary matters at least. Besides, the irrationalities in this species of spiritualism resemble those of some forms of religion that are sufficiently respectable. Invocation of saints is exactly the same ; saints are the bogies of good people long deceased, and they must be ubiquitous to answer every one's prayers, the same as those the *spiritualists* try to bring about us. Well, as we drove along in a rattling cab, thinking of the banderole I said to William I would ask for Spencer Boyd. There were two devotees besides ourselves with Mrs. Marshall and her son and daughter-in-law. The two men might have been confederates, but even then I think it was impossible that my writing could have been overseen. The room was upstairs, the largest room in the house of the moderately respectable domicile; and the two women, old and young, were as uncultivated and mentally unfurnished as the evil genius of D. G. R. already mentioned. We sat down at the table with the frowsy old mother, her smart daughter-in-law, and the two strangers. I wrote the name of my deceased friend on the interior of a half-unfolded letter, and then, as desired, I went along an alphabet, touching each letter, and the knocks came correctly, spelling *Boyd*. I began again and the knocks came correctly spelling *Spencer*, a rare name. I then asked if the spirit would tell me how long ago he died. "Ask it by months," said the girl, "saying one, two, and so on." The result was the knocks came at eight instead of ten months, not a great fallacy for a spirit who is reasonably supposed to keep no diary or pocket calendar. Where did he die? was my next question. "At *Eldon*," and with a little hesitation, "*Road.*" Elgin Road was my address, still this was nearly right, especially as there was a Lord Eldon as well as a Lord Elgin. But this very mistake, appearing to have a reason in it, as well as the young woman proposing I should ask by months for the period in my former question, indicated to a suspicious observer some previous knowledge. No other question was answered approximately right.

I went again to Mrs. Marshall with Mrs. Lynn Linton without good result; but this first interview, instead of giving me any addition to my faith in the table-rapping of spirits, had the opposite effect. I saw in the approximation to truth the clever guessing of the practised thought-reader by the expression of the countenance. Every card-sharper has this faculty, showing him how far he may go; and every successful schemer and man of law or business, with or without his consciousness of any impropriety, works by the same means. It was at best guessing nearly right while the first clue guided, and then farther and farther wrong. Reading the expression is the art, and I believe women who are not usually troubled by logic and habits of ratiocination are quicker than men in it. Miss Boyd and I have a game at bézique every evening, and I have found her a hundred times tell me what card I had drawn, simply by looking at me. "You have got a good card this time, I see! I believe it is the king—yes, the king, not the ace!" and so it has been.

The death of Spencer left his sister well disposed to carry out his pious work of re-edifying the old house, and she did so by proposing that I should paint with some pictorial history the great circular staircase which her brother had built. I selected as my subject a series of scenes from the lovely story of *The King's Quair*, the poem written by King James the First of Scotland at the end of his imprisonment at Windsor. This work, executed on the wall with oil pigments, the medium being wax dissolved in turpentine, encaustic in short, occupied me three or four months in each year, beginning in 1865 and ending 1868. The wall was three feet thick, and therefore taking very long to be free either of damp or of the corrosive quality of the lime. I had begun upon it rather too soon, occasioning some repainting, but I found this species of encaustic was almost perfect; most probably the pictures will now remain without further change.

Before determining on this method of wall-painting, the water-glass being then in successful use by Kaulbach in Germany, and as it appeared admirable in the hands of Maclise, in his great picture, finished two years before, "The Meeting of Wellington and Blucher," perhaps the noblest of all war-pictures ever done, though scarcely at all known to Englishmen, I consulted him. He was unknown to me. I availed myself of the introduction of Mr. F. G. Stephens, one of the original P.R.B. set of men, who had gradually dropped into his true field, that of daily and weekly critic of the art season. Slowness of imagination and want of artistic excitability prevent the mass of people and generality of critics from even accepting so mighty and dramatic a work as this in the Houses of Parliament, the meeting on the field of Waterloo of the two triumphant generals, simply because the painter has brought the elements of the historic scene into tragic proximity—closer together, in short, than they were on the wide area of the field of battle. Stephens was too cultivated to make any such prosaic detraction from the value of the picture in his writing about it in the *Athenæum*, and Maclise received his introductory note in a kindly spirit. I found him to be a large, phlegmatic, sad-voiced man, to whom success in life seemed to have brought no pleasure, nor had the possession of artistic genius adorned him with any social nimbus. He was then drawing to a close with "The Death of Nelson," on the opposite wall, and in it he had taken care to avoid the fault mentioned, fault in the eyes of the uninitiated, but no fault at all in an epic invention. He told me he had taken correct measurements of the deck of the *Victory* or of some other ship of equal dimensions, from gun to gun, had so planned every point included in the picture from careful observation and sketches, and had seen the corps of men (seven in number if I remember rightly) serve each gun as in action. No other mode of operation could have given so vivid an idea of the frightful daring of the old sea battles, when the great wooden hulls with a thousand men serving a hundred guns ran close together, yard-arm to yard-arm, and blew each other to pieces.

When I explained my object in seeing him, he gave me a slow sad look, and said his first advice was not to undertake such work at all. "But," he added after a moment, "if you do and adopt *water-glass* as your plan, you can have all my traps, which I am glad to be done with. I will make you a present of the whole remainder of materials. I hope to return to my studio and to the easel pictures which I wish I had never left!" Saying this he pointed to his whole array of pots of colour, palettes, and vessels, including the tin kettle sort of machine for steaming the work when done. His offer took me by surprise, especially as there was no opinion expressed as to the merits of this and other methods, or their comparative difficulties. I could not, of course, take advantage, or indeed reckon on such an offer, even if I had determined on the water-glass medium. This I expressed, adding my wonder at his state of regret, instead of triumph on the completion of such great works. "Well, yes, I daresay you are right. I know what they are, of course, but the people I have to please are such indifferent brutes and such ninnies. Nobody cares for the pictures after they are done, or wants them as far as I can see. Literally so, no one comes to see this now it is about done. I have asked the Ministers and others, and I see them passing in droves to inspect Herbert's 'Moses' there," pointing over his shoulder to the room where Herbert's picture was. "That convert to Romanism, the barrister, brings them in droves and Herbert is working the oracle, which I can't do, and shouldn't put myself into the necessity of doing, do you see. They look on him as a Michael Angelo —they even knock at the door of this my wooden chamber and inquire where the great picture is to be seen!" The outspoken candour of our one supreme English history-painter was almost painful; I could only assent to his disgust at oracle-working. "Well," he went on, "you think I need not care? Perhaps not, but as I am not going to do any more of this, but am about to return to what I like best in my studio at home, I have no more use for all these things."

This interview, showing me as in a glass, but not darkly, the true feelings of a true man, was not of much use to me in the matter in hand, but of infinite interest. A similar feeling, modified by the individual character of the speaker, I have encountered repeatedly in the best painters I have known. My brother for one completed his best works in a state of despair. When I went into D. G. R.'s studio to see his large "Dante's Dream," I found him in a similar state, hidden under a kind of ferocity; and I remember Holman Hunt, the success of whose "Christ in the Temple" was too great to allow of discontent, saying with a haggard expression of face, "It is well for once, but I'll be now found out. I can never do anything more!"

The cause of this, which has descended to us from the time of Michael Angelo himself, but is more peculiarly an insular disease nowadays, results mainly from the unpopularity of exceptional genius. The man as well as his work is shied by his professional associates as well as the public: he is not "one of us." There are exceptions where popular qualities are mixed with the unique merits that render a work peculiar and original, so ensuring the praise of the public and of the critics who cannot see, or will not risk recognition of the greater qualities. Popular qualities make work easy, and mitigate the mental strain. Among poets I have never seen any similar frame of mind follow publication, even when no recognition at all has followed. In this respect the fate of the painter is harder.

# CHAPTER VII

### LETTERS FROM HOLMAN HUNT, JERUSALEM, 1870-71

BEFORE returning to my own home circle I may give here some letters from Holman Hunt, then living in Jerusalem, struggling indefatigably, as he always did, with a new subject, this one being the "Shadow of Death." The tone of Hunt's mind and letters is in curious contrast to our idle experiments about spirit-rapping and such like stuff, but perhaps not so amusing. He has allowed me to give these letters verbatim.

JERUSALEM, *7th April* 1870.

MY DEAR SCOTT—I have a long time to stay here still, and I don't feel disposed to wait patiently until my return to England for the next communication with you. I send this scrap, then, as a threatener of future letters, and as a petitioner for some news and thoughts of yours.

You should see how grand I am in my desolate house here; it is about large enough for a family of ten or twelve, and I walk in dismal dignity about the unfriended rooms. Two servants attend upon me, and sometimes a country man or woman is staying here as a possible model. I assure you at first starting, even with my old experience, it required no ordinary perseverance and energy to get to work. The house was the first difficulty, and then the model-finding. The difficulties were all the greater to me because I had altogether forgotten my Arabic at first. Little by little now I am getting about as forward as I was when I left nearly fifteen years ago, and as I pay well, the procuring people to sit does not promise to be such a bother as formerly. One great trouble, indeed, is to know what to think of my own work. If I could show it to some one like yourself I might save much painful uncertainty.

You are one of the few men I know who would truly appreciate this country. When I say this, I remember very well some of your views about religious matters associated with Palestine, but you would be delighted with the number of realisations of ancient days and ways one feels as one goes about. We pass not merely from village to town, and from town to desert, or to an Arab encampment, lying down for the night's rest under the unscreened stars; but we pass from century to century, from Abraham to Cambyses, from Herodotus to Jesus Christ, then to Mohammed and so to the Crusaders. There are, too, such undreamed-of scenes as though they did not belong to this world, but rather to the moon. You know how above all my life-affections is my love of Christ, yet of late I had felt it to be time that I should take stock of thoughts which should never crystallise. Since leaving England I have been reading *Ecce Homo*, Renan's *Life of Christ*, etc., \* \* \* \*
\* \* \* also I have further re-read very attentively the whole Testament, marking down all its questionable points and comparing passages with determination towards unbiassed judgment, and the result is that I believe more defiantly than ever. You will think I am not consistent when I say further that I think the evangelists made many mistakes, that they did not themselves understand what had been said to them. But nevertheless, as the books stand, being written in absolute good faith, correctly reporting what

passed, this seems to furnish convincing arguments for the truth of their subject. As to Renan, with all the valuable and splendid observations in his book, I saw symptoms of bad faith in his search for truth, and I find his acumen very shallow, and his sentiment most tawdry, and this assisted in making me feel that Christianity, even in its highest pretensions, must be true. You will know I am not saying this in ignorance of critical and scientific theories. I wish I had you here to explain more thoroughly my way of accepting evidences. I should not hope to convert you, but think I should be able to show you ways of interpreting not at all generally propounded, and make you more prepared to see Christianity sending out fresh branches than you are now.

I ought to explain what I mean by "highest pretensions." I do not use the phrase in relation to the authority of the Church, I mean the direct supernatural origin and nature of Christ, that He really came down from heaven, from the dwelling-place of divinity, that He performed miracles, that He rose from the dead, and returned again into heaven,—there! I have almost written out the creed. My belief is that as man was a new development in animal life so was Christ to us. You may contend that this was by gradual evolution. My reply would be that nothing comes of nothing, and that a new perfection must be made by the Master Artist.

I am glad that you have been publishing the *Life of Dürer*, not that I know the book yet, but I rejoice, now that so many who know nothing about Art issue volumes in tens and hundreds about it, that an artist should once on a time say something derived from practical observation and experience. Professed critics—and I say it with all deference to our old friends who follow that line of business—are becoming a great impediment to true healthy art. They fabricate theories by brain machinery, every one has his law. To hear A. when at Rome propounding his dogmas was too edifying! I did not argue with him, because for the short time we were together we had much more entertaining talk. It is the same with B., somewhat the same with C., and also with D., who is of course a critic too. They talk as though they regarded artists as waiting for their orders. We, too, at times have our crotchets at nights, but the easel work of the following day modifies them: we determine, to wit, that on no occasion should the teeth be shown in a face, etc. etc., but some exceptional case is soon found when the ingenious idea will not do, another and another case for which it is not suitable arise, and then we give it up, perhaps even forget it, while as theorists we should have sworn by it to the end of our days. Art is now, it seems to me, becoming less hopeful in England, because two or three sets of influential artists are adopting "laws." To me their art is losing the vitality which gives worth of a lasting kind. Sculptors are most driven to become traditional, because there are so few subjects which they can take from passing life either for form or idea. Albert Dürer, to return to our particular subject, seems to me a greater man as a designer for engraving than in painting. All that I saw of him in Italy disappointed me. I had imagined much more perfect drawing and painting too than I found.

I am now reading an Italian translation of *Marc' Aurelio Antonino*. He strikes me as having been a sort of classical ———. His head never appeared to me that of a strong man, but until now I had never read enough of him to trust that impression. When I was a boy, a friend of mine who worshipped him used to talk much of him, and quote much; at that time his philosophy seemed to me more wonderful and comprehensive than it does now.

Have you lately given any attention to spiritualism? A painter who came here for a short time, who did not appear a fool though he was not a very wonderful artist, openly professed himself a thorough believer in it, and the evidence he advanced would have been convincing had he not been deceived. This I felt he must have been, when it came to light that a man he had trusted here, and who had acted as his interpreter, had robbed him in the most ridiculous manner from his very pocket, time after time. His great agent was Mrs. Marshall, and he declared that all the artists, naming several academicians, were taking it up. Here there seems to be something of the kind among the Moslems, but it is only practised in great secret. The reports of the proceedings are wonderfully like those of the spiritualists at home, although having *no tables* they are less ridiculous, and the manifestations are more material; they begin, however, by imploring the aid of Shaitan, or I would try to get them to operate here. I have no reason to believe in it, but I should have liked to examine it impartially. Mrs. Guppy came to Florence while I was there and startled some people, but on inquiry I found that the more sensible members of her *séances* had been convinced that she had recourse to imposture. Old Kirkup was still a believer; I should think by this time he must be a spirit himself.

How can you get on in London without Arabic? Tyib, mafish, inshallah, wakri, etc. etc., are surely words that no fellow can do without! Confess now, don't you often find yourself in difficulty for want of them? I select those because they have no gutturals. Have you heard of the drought we have had here? at last some supplies have reached us, not much, but enough to make painting in water-colour a possibility.—Yours ever,

W. HOLMAN HUNT.

This "scrap," as he calls the document, interested me much. The persistent dependence on the principles that recommend themselves to the common sense of the generality is notable, and the criterion by which he sets aside the trustworthiness of the advocate of Mrs. Marshall's miraculous powers is very characteristic. One of the most valuable features of Holman's intellect is his acute practicality in the ordinary affairs of life. Thus the man who let himself be robbed systematically was not to him a credible witness ; and he was perfectly correct. I wrote to him both about his views of the historical part of the New Testament and about other things. Happily it is not possible to enter *my* letter here, but this is his reply, dated Jerusalem, 10th August 1870:

MY DEAR SCOTT—I will take up the questions in your letter of the 26th May in the order in which they are presented. You are surprised, first, by my declaration that recent examination here in Syria of the history recorded in the Gospels has removed difficulties I was ready to admit. If I said that increased confidence had resulted from the opportunity of seeing the actual spots where the writers place the events, I was saying more than I intended. My objections were silenced rather by closer and more free-thinking examination of the records. Artistically I admire the country very much as suitable for such history, although I see it would not satisfy your requirements any more than it does those of the clergymen who come here, who confess, perhaps reluctantly, their disappointment with nearly one voice. This feeling of theirs forces me to recognise that they cannot bear the actual realisation of the subject. Their ideas are still mythical and vague, and thus it is difficult to regard them as happy and confident in their belief, since they cannot, like you, regard the history simply as a poetic dressing of half-forgotten facts. You start with the proposition that the history is supernatural, this in its most scientific sense ; my mind commences with the inquiry as to what is within and what without the pale of natural law.

You don't answer a question I put in my letter, whether you have had any *recent* experience in spiritualism? I have *never* had any, but I may take you as a witness to the fact that certain mysterious powers acting on others do exist in individuals, which science wholly rejected when they were first brought before the public. It will serve here to revert to the story of your visit to Mrs. Marshall, when she told you that within a twelvemonth a friend had died suddenly in your house, speaking with sufficient exactness to make you think she had had information of the death of Mr. Boyd. It may be said this information had been obtained by material agency, although the difficulties in the way of this solution were considered by you too great. Mesmerism in other forms remains beyond question, forms which were regarded as impossible when first announced ; what is or is not supernatural is not, you see, infallibly determined. My notions of this world and our life in it come from what I feel and see myself and hear from others. If no scientific explanation of what has occurred to myself can be given, I will not accept it for other and greater questions in history. Your difficulty in believing in the Godhead of Christ comes, as it seems to me, from your terribly distant idea of God. [He refers here to my holding by the "*Shorter Catechism of the Divines at Westminster*" definition of God : "*God is a Spirit, infinite, eternal, and unchangeable, in his power, wisdom, holiness, justice, goodness, and truth.*"] I come with no preconceived ideas of any kind to the subject ; I am ready to accept the most practical of the many presented to me, that which tallies best with the view of His purpose of increase in the goodness, justice, and love, which the world, as made by Him, exhibits. I have no fear of offending by not doing justice to His dignity, because I find that *men* who think of their dignity are poor creatures. And the discovery that man has invented an infinity of fables to incorporate his notions of deity, need only be kept in mind as a reason for scrutiny. . . . I see no difficulty in admitting the possibility of " supernatural " acts in connection with paganism. I believe entirely in the Dæmon of Socrates, and I credit, without hesitation, the possibility of a " revelation," in a dimmer way, to the Greeks, Egyptians, and Persians; but it was a lower grade than that of the Jews and Christians.

Perhaps, however, the strongest conviction I have on these subjects comes from the consideration of the effect of the two views (religion or no religion) on life. What is the reason of the dead-alive poetry and art of the day, if not in the totally material nature of the views cultivated in modern schools? Trying to limit speculation within the bounds of sense only must produce poor sculpture, feeble painting, dilettante poetry. What else could be produced when the mind revels only in the body's hopes? To measure and imitate the works of soul-inspired workers of previous ages is not producing the bread of life. It is foolish as it were to give a babe a lay figure for a wet nurse. I again wish you were here, not because I think the country would satisfy your poetic dreams, but because you would for the time be able to consider the question free from the influence of European artificial life.

With all the weakness of the men who conduct the business of religion, the noblest efforts of society are made by them. Who try to civilise the savage, to reclaim the convict? Who pick up the ragged boys from the gutter? who snatch the children from premature labour in pit or factory? who try to work out a plan of life without war? who try to raise women from infamy? "By their fruits ye shall know them" is an axiom simple and divine in wisdom. What, on the other hand, do your philosophers do? Surely nothing of an unselfish kind in comparison, although I thoroughly believe that much is left for them as counterpoise to the narrowness and rancour of bigots. In going over the Bible and Testament you will find lots of difficulties and objections if you are like me. I find man to be slow of conviction and still slower in change of habit, and the prophets have spoken oft and men have professed to be converted, and their actions have proved this to be delusion. I am sure that you would find wisdom by careful study which had not appeared before.

Everything shows me that this life itself is a trial and a question. I lately made out the parable of the unjust steward; what had seemed actually objectionable before, I saw in an instructive and interesting sense. But I must not go on to all eternity—though this convulsion of war may reach here any hour, and time close upon us before the closing of this sheet! Yet I must add a few words, for I had altogether neglected one of your arguments, viz. that of the physical absurdity of His body having been received up into the clouds (which are nothing, while astronomical distances are vacuums thousands of years away), and you find this part of the story to be explained by the cosmogony of the time that heaven was in the circumjacent sky. Now our artistic experience may give some illustration of the way in which God might work. In finding a desirable idea to illustrate we have a sense of its beauty not limited in any way. When we have to express this to others all manner of restrictions present themselves, from the nature of the language and the materials of our art, and from consideration of the intelligences we address. The object of the artist, as of the Creator, is to put the idea into material form, and I cannot think of any better way of suggesting that this One had escaped death than by making Him visibly ascend from this earth. What became eventually of the body it is scarcely in our province to determine; but since we are told that a condensation of gases in the atmosphere can make a solid body like a thunderbolt, it is competent for us to imagine that His body was resolved into its original elements, to be reorganised perhaps at a later time.

You ask about my subjects. As I am very anxious that you should see my pictures without any preconceived ideas in your mind, I would rather defer revealing them. I may perhaps in the spring get one of these finished, and I shall come with it to England, and then I shall ask you to tell me whether my work is good or bad. I am painting very hard indeed. I should like, meantime, to know what you are doing, for you are working among others and perhaps not keeping your subjects a secret.

But I must shut up now. Kind regards to your wife, and any friends you meet.—Yours ever,

W. HOLMAN HUNT.

I find among my papers of this next year, too, a continuation of the Holman Hunt correspondence, which, long as the letters are, ought to be introduced here. He is still painting in Jerusalem, and still thinking about religious matters; but he is becoming tinged with a morbid distrust of his own great powers, and also with doubts of his friends at home. He is evidently shut up too much by himself, and working too hard—confined too much to one subject. This first letter is dated 20th February 1871.

MY DEAR SCOTT—I was glad to hear from you at last. Your letter came by our latest post. Your long silence had not led me to think that you were bitten with the fever which so many of my friends and acquaintances seem to suffer from, making them conclude I am a monstrously over-rated person, and that it is their particular duty to let me know this important fact as distinctly as their several natures will allow. After exhausting the surmises of accidental hindrances, the danger was that I should jump to this conclusion; but my constant experience of your extremely broad principles in estimating art and character forbade me to take such a leap as I might have done with others. But there are not many of the band who used to treat me as their authority, who have not lately indulged in a conscientious avowal of their recognition of my demerits! Thus the wind blows towards the sun!

I hope, after all your trouble in the old house you have taken [Bellevue House, Chelsea], you will find it a comfortable haven of rest. I remember looking at and talking of it with friends many times as an inviting one for an artist. Chelsea I have always liked; but when in England last I was obliged to avoid all proximity to the Thames from having the Syrian ague in my blood. This guest would probably be no quieter from my second residence here, which has given me two or three fresh attacks of it; so if I ever come to live in London, I shall still have to choose Kensington, Hampstead, or Highgate as my place of torture from organ-grinders, halfpenny (?) postmen, tax-collectors, etc.

We are going to be still farther apart, it seems, in the next life! You are going into the Elysian fields with all the genius of the age, while I am to make myself as comfortable as circumstances will permit with greasy methodists and spick-and-span orthodox parsons in the commonplace heaven; but I have not Dante's assurance in claiming Paradise for my home. I don't pretend to know what my deserts may be—but it will be said that I am rather too fast here, counting too much on my host where no host may be found, seeing God Almighty does not exist at all. Here was a truth to discover! Hitherto men of worldly wealth only delighted in the thought; I think no one of intellect in any century before ours could have done it: an inspiration—no, that's not the word—a conception, in all the majesty of the big-boy style, at first by Shelley, not held proudly by him later, but now by other combinations of poetic atoms, even more newly moulded from earth, but now published as settled with omniscient penetration of mind that can reach within the innermost veil of all, and discover there is nothing, where poets before them have dreaded even to peep, lest an awful majesty should revenge itself. Thus foolish generations have died in the hope of reward for their awe at least. Unhappy slaves were these who without the eternal halo of genius round their names are lost in the world to come. I have no idea of the grim sublimity: it seems to me that in this day the eternal powers I recognise have a great sense of fun, and that were they such as we, they might be in some danger of convulsions just now.[1]

You say true, that I have had no experience whatever of (professional) spiritualism of a kind to justify me in believing in any celestial guidance of the affairs of the world, and that I have no arguments to offer in proof of the possibility of facts such as those recorded in the Testament. But in my own experience I have had occasional presentiments and other psychological consciousnesses, of a nature that forbid me the conclusion that we are mere burning bonfires, to cease with the consumption of the fuel. These experiences, of course, would only serve to my own conviction, and so they need not be cited; from the conclusions they suggest to me, however, it is an easy transition to the best religious revelation I can find. I thought perhaps your own consciousness had given you something not less indicative of post-terrestrial vitality than I had experienced; every man must be guided by his own light: if I can find any that suits me more than that I see by at present, so much the better.

I hope you will not give up painting, but am glad you are writing on art. There is a temperance and an insight at the same time that practical men have, wanting in the criticisms of those who have no means of testing and refining their groping ideas and theories. The fault practical men are in danger of, in writing for the public, is the adoption of a spirit of severity and exclusiveness necessary for the studio, where we must settle upon one particular treatment only. No man that I know is freer from this peril than you.

As yet I have no confidence that I shall get my

---

[1] I cannot now remember in the least what could have called forth this astounding tirade. It must have been some report or statement in my letter Hunt had just then received. In copying this out, at first I began by combing the entangled sentences a little smooth, but soon gave that process up. He seems to have been in such a state of excitement that his language flew in tatters. The reader must puzzle out the intention of his harangue.

picture done. Much depends on the weather; lately it has been so wet and windy I have not been able to get out of doors to paint. Unless there is a break I have no chance whatever. Fortunately there is a prospect of this, but at the best I am in doubt. If I come home it will be about the end of April; should I be too late for this I shall probably stay here another year, and thus get enough done to be able to move to another part of the world for future work. . . . I am glad to hear there is a chance of England doing something in art after all! The discouraging fact I saw was that men were getting into the way of doing *annuals*, a certain number for every season. At the Paris Exhibition of 1856 I was much struck by the insignificance of certain pictures that had been great stars on their first appearance in Trafalgar Square. The French, with what seemed to me decidedly lower painting talent, were doing better things, showing the particular qualities we had in such perfection up to about thirty years ago in Wilkie, in Turner, and even in Leslie—freedom from pose-plastique or theatrical character. We seemed to have lost and the French to have gained this, but without the poetry and beauty, and it struck me we had got in exchange qualities that would not wear very well: but the evil may correct itself. Certainly as years go on in one's life they teach us that many things one looked to to give life interest are mere bubbles; one's occupation of time becomes even more sacred. In this way I feel the most intense desire that our country should be glorious in art, at least in painting, in which it has certainly done enough to give hope were there architectural patronage.—Yours ever truly,

W. HOLMAN HUNT.

*P.S.*—I add a postscript and a bit of maidenhair fern, from Nazareth, for your wife. I collected it myself from a cave there, so I know it is genuine, which will make her value it the more.

Ah, the war! I of course have not had the details

that every one in London has devoured, but it has been a subject of exciting interest to us all: the poor French connected with the Consulate seem to have lost all their life. Ordinarily all Europeans come out at five or six for a promenade, the Consuls attended by kawasses (constables with long silver batons); but after the reverses of their army the French postponed their walk until dark, when all but myself had abandoned the road, and latterly, since the greater distresses, they have hidden themselves altogether. When by chance one was met he nearly always had red eyelids, and had lost all his national gaiety. There is one very nice fellow here, a concelleria to the Consul, who recently, having absolutely disappeared till then, came and called upon me, perhaps because he heard that I avoided every other soul in the place, and I have made an exception with him, and enjoy seeing him. It is more fortunate that I happen to have anti-Prussian feelings of late, this because I feel persuaded that Bismarck played the whole game of bringing on the war at his own foolish time, managing so to irritate L. N. and the French nation, that they saved him from the appearance of being its author. When the Prince of Prussia was here, without seeking the honour, I had the privilege of talking with him and some of his suite, and they impressed me as such superior people, that the success of their army has not surprised me. I believe it is, where other things are equal, personal morality tells in an army. What could be expected from a set of immoral braggarts like the French soldiers against a set of vigorous husbands and healthy lads with honest sweethearts behind them — as the Prussians are? I dislike the Prussians only because they seem to be at this juncture Machiavellian-led, and are believing in craft for national policy, and are successful in this for the time.

I was here when the Crimean War was going on there. I could not understand how people in England could think, as they seemed to do, of anything else. When I heard of a man marrying it struck me as being against all natural feeling: I was wrong of course, but remembering that time I am now rather surprised and pleased to see how much England seems stirred at the misery of this war. Is the world getting softer-hearted? I hate war, but sometimes reading of it I feel a fury urging me to rush into its midst and spill my life, in desperation to have done with a world in which I can see no place for peace and hope.  W. H. H.

JERUSALEM, 30*th September* 1871.

MY DEAR OLD SCOTT—I should never have let so long a time go by without acknowledging and answering your last letter, but, indeed, this picture of mine treats me so severely that I am a miserable slave, with no time for anything but just the attempt to sustain life and strength enough to wrestle with my work, which plays the part of a tenacious foe. I have engaged myself in a very difficult struggle, and I have been unwise in many ways in the battle. Do you remember Herodotus's account of Scythian warriors, who being absent on a long campaign, came back to find that their impatient wives, anticipating widowhood, had elevated their hewers of wood and drawers of water into the position of second husbands, and that these their successors came out armed to do battle, and indeed did valiantly contend with the veteran warriors, until one old Ulysses said in council, "What do we? We are treating our slaves like equals, and so they are inflated with courage to fight with us; but now follow me, and we will soon vanquish them." So saying he took a whip, and with this rushed into the ranks of the impudent servants, and thus put the ignoble rabble to rout. Now, you see, I change my relative position to show the application of this. I am now in my psychical entity one of the Scythian warriors. My picture in its conceived perfection is the disputed plane of the eternal earth, or part of it. My happiness and ease are my wife (or wives, for I may be a polygamist in my art loves). I have too long left the dwelling-place of comfort, and now my paints, my brushes, my tools, my aids, the sun, morning, evening, working time and resting time, the wind, the clouds—all my helpers in proper place have risen with my peace of mind, long since unfaithful to me, to oppose my resumption of my rights. And here I recognise the wisdom of the old Scythian's counsel—too long unacted upon because I have been impatient, and too anxious to take vengeance upon my slaves. If I had treated them from the beginning more contemptuously I might long ago have vanquished them. To speak prosaically and plainly, I have grappled with the difficulties of this picture so seriously and slavishly for so long that I suffer now in my capacity for completing it from want of that elasticity of mind so essential to one for triumphing over the final difficulties of a picture. But, indeed, in this case there was no choice, for the work had and has peculiar obstacles, which could only be confronted by extra and even unlimited steadiness. Without this I should have had to give up my work, and with it the question is whether I shall not then be like a warrior who, in conquering, has desolated the country and made it worthless; *nous verrons*. Looking at it in my dejection, I am apt too much to trust the cheerless view of the end; however, rest may give me a better idea of it. I have no loving eyes to cheer me such as I hoped to have ever with me when I left England. I shall enjoy the opportunity of showing it to you whatever its prospects may be, for to have come to an end with it, and to be free to do another picture, will in itself be a comfort.

Do you know—not in a manner of speaking, but in sober earnestness—I thought in the middle of the summer it would be the death of me. I got but about four hours' sleep each day, and these were scarcely rest, for my feverish anxiety went on through the night, and I dreamed of nothing but newly-discovered faults—of paint drying before it could be blended, of wind blowing down my picture and breaking it, etc.—until my eyes sank so deep into my head, and I became green, and my body seemed such a heavy, stiff, and unelastic corpse that I thought the next stage must be coffinward. And now that it is past, people here tell me they thought me a doomed man. Had I got a fever or any illness, I daresay I should have made my way to the place, whichever it is, reserved for me—either the meeting with all that are dear and gone or, if you will, the dreamless sleep, which alternatives Socrates regards even at the lowest as enviable, and he had children and friends too. His interest in the next world or no world had grown into such a curiosity that nothing was so dear to him as the opportunity of satisfying it. I can imagine too he reasoned about his children thus :—If there were tutelar gods, these would look after them ; if none, it mattered nothing what course they took, only let the cock be paid to Esculapius, for that is a debt. As I grow older I have enough of this feeling to make me, in the possibility of death, unusually careless ; and thus during the time I speak of I did not take a step to change my fate, for my life has not often been a joyful one.

I think my rides out on Sunday saved me. As I lay out on the hillside taking my lunch and watching the horse graze, I felt like a sponge sucking in ease and health at every breath, and this restored me for the week. There is a man here whom I have made into a model, and who was a notorious highway robber. I did not know of his wild side at first. He has become very much attached to me, and when I want to find out-of-the-way places I take him with me on excursions at times. He rides like a Centaur, but with his knees up to the horse's shoulders, as all Arabs do ; and as his old character is still accredited to him, we strike a wholesome dread into all the country wherever we go ; but we are very harmless, although armed to the teeth, which is necessary since, owing to the tameness of our present improved views of Government in England, Englishmen are without any civil means of redress for injuries done to them. Thieves, if caught, are kept in hand until they or their friends pay a good bribe to the Cady, the Pasha's secretary, and the Consul's dragoman, and then they are discharged to repay themselves by other robberies. Just within the last three weeks a party of Arabs, who murdered an English subject here about fourteen years ago, have been liberated. They were apprehended on the evidence of an eye-witness, who gave evidence about three months past. They got off, it is declared, at an expense of £200, divided between the above-mentioned worthies. I would confer with the Consul about it, and publish the facts in England, but I have no time to get into another row. My correspondence with the bishop about a certain rascal whom he was protecting sixteen years ago cost me too much time to allow me to venture expressions of moral indignation for public good. The gentleman in question, too, at that time tried to murder me with his gang of housebreakers, but found me too wary, which I might not be again against a similar attempt. Soon after he was apprehended, sentenced to have his right hand cut off, and to be imprisoned for life. But last Sunday when alone I met him on the road, he having escaped both evils by becoming convinced of the exclusive orthodoxy of the Latin Church! Thus he gained the protection of the French Consul, who liberated him for fresh villainies. He politely recognised me in passing, but if he had thought of avenging himself thus late, he deferred it out of respect to a double-barrel breech-loader gun which I held slightly raised on my saddle, and which his pistol would scarcely have been a match for.

You refer with much surprise to the idea I expressed that I had some enemies of a less outlawry character in England, and you prove to me that I have many friends, which I rejoice to acknowledge. I would, however, give you some instances on the other hand, which might serve to raise laughter as much as grief; yet the balance in my account just now would be of the painful sort, so I will not rake up the question any more.

I am sorry to believe your assurance that you are amongst the unhappy ones of the earth. I had always regarded you as one who had made peace, as well as a truce, with life ; but the bitterness is not felt least by those who show it least. My trust is only in the ultimate loving goodness of the Great Father ; without this I should lose all patience. You gave me the news of the engagement of Miss Y———. X——— is a lucky fellow to get such a wife. I wonder all the unmarried men in London, with anything approaching a Roman nose, from little Tom to big Z———, did not engage in a series of combats for her. My crotchet is that no fellow without an aquiline profile should marry a girl deficient thus, so I should never have engaged in the contest. Y——— *père* deserves no commiseration, for I heard that when the young lady once wanted to marry the beautiful Lord ———, he was not even then satisfied with the proposed son-in-law. My story may be all wrong : anyhow the father was not pleased. Kind regards to Mrs. Scott.—Yours ever,

W. HOLMAN HUNT.

# CHAPTER VIII

1868 TO 1870—MY *KING'S QUAIR* PICTURES AT PENKILL FINISHED—D. G. R. SPENDS AUTUMNS 1868-69 THERE WITH US—RECOMMENCES HIS POETIC STUDIES— THE FRANCO-GERMAN WAR—MY REMOVAL TO 92 CHEYNE WALK, SEPTEMBER 1870.

FOR three years or so before the summer of 1868 I had been largely employed on the windows in the South Kensington Keramic Gallery. Intensely-coloured windows were found demoralising in a museum, and will be so found, I affirm, everywhere on a somewhat wider experience of their result in destroying the adequate effect on the eye of all objects seen by their light. My instruction from Mr. Cole was to represent a pictorial history of the Keramic arts in a medium that would obscure the prospect through the windows, and prevent the sunshine being offensive, without blinding the spectator by the violent colours of "pot-metal," as the glass-painters call glass on which the colours are flushed in the making. After many breakages I succeeded in giving the designs in *graffito*, painted on burnt umber ground in silica, making a true picture like a great etching, only partially picked out ornamentally in bright yellow. The long series of windows were now finished, as also were my staircase pictures at Penkill from James I.'s poem *The King's Quair*.

It was now midsummer, and Æ.B., finding D. G. R. in a depression of mind from the idea that his eyes were failing, prevailed upon him to accompany me to Ayrshire for an autumn vacation. He did so; we were a party of four—Miss Boyd's cousin, Miss Losh of Ravenside, being a visitor at that time. This old lady—she was about seventy years of age—had somehow or other taken a jealous dislike to me, thinking I had too much influence over her younger cousin, who entertained me so much and who lived with us in London in the winter. She had therefore looked forward to Rossetti's appearance, fully intending to play him off against me, which accordingly she did in the most fantastic way, without in the least knowing anything of the fearful skeletons in his closet, that were every night, when the ladies had gone, brought out for his relief and my recreation. These skeletons, which were also made to dance along the mountain highroad during our long walks, would have surprised the old lady not a little. They shall not be interviewed here, and without them we got on pretty well, although his talk continually turned upon his chance of blindness and the question, why then should he live? "Live for your poetry," said I. Strangely enough, this seemed never to have occurred to him as a possible interest or resource. Live for your poetry was echoed by the ladies.[1]

We determined to follow up the suggestion, little as we believed in the seriousness of his monomania about blindness. One day, when Miss Boyd was with us on a walk up Penkill Hill, we persuaded him to recall such of his poems as he could recollect, and he repeated *The Song of the Bower*, perhaps the most perfect of all his early verses in harmony between sound and sense, cadence and sentiment. I understood because I knew the history of this *pagan* poem; Æ. did not, having neither heard nor read any of his verses, except such as were published in the *Germ*, or in the *Oxford and Cambridge Magazine*. She could scarcely speak, so moved she was, and I confess that I was almost for the first time conscious of the full value of his faculty. Lifted to a rhetorical moment I said much, affirming that the value of his paintings lay in their poetry, that he was a poet by birthright, not a painter. After this I found there was established in his mind a new prevailing idea, able

---

[1] [In the preface to his "Illustrations of the King's Quair," privately printed in 1887, Mr. Scott refers as follows to this incident: "Miss Boyd and I found it no easy matter to change the bias of these late years during which he had become quite successful as a painter. Rossetti was a poet before he was a painter, and will probably retain his place as a poet when his pictures are mainly remembered by their poetic suggestions in design. We recalled him so strenuously to his early love, making him repeat the poems he remembered, that at last suddenly, like a dying man with a new life transfused into his veins, he became absorbed in the desire to have them all written out and printed."—ED.]

to contend with the monomania, and when we left for London at the end of September he had begun to write out many of his lost poems, his memory being so good. Many loose poems he also had by him in manuscript, and by and by he began to send them to the printer.

Before this return to town, however, the old lady's admiration had culminated in an offer of a loan of money to any amount to prevent him using his eyes in painting or in any other trying occupation; he would get better and repay her, but till then he might depend on her. This generous offer was made one morning. He never got up till near midday, my difficulty every evening being to leave him after we had emptied endless tumblers of the wine of the country in the shape of whisky-toddy. This morning she had him all to herself, and her daily delight was to see him smashing his eggs on the plate, to the loss of half of them, and making innumerable impressions of his tea-cup on the damask table-cloth. "You see, Alice dear," she would say to /B., "he is not like one of us, he is a great man, can't attend to trifles, is always occupied with great ideas!" so she was often left to enjoy the sight all by herself at that hour of the day. She intended indeed that this plan should be a secret one between them, but no sooner had we started on our daily constitutional than he entrusted it to me, with much effusion and gratitude, at the same time protesting he would never think of availing himself of her kindness. This determination I strenuously encouraged, and we heard no more of the matter until after the old lady's death, when the evidences to the contrary were all too clear.

Rossetti returned with me to Penkill next summer. A great part of my occupation in the intervening winter had been preparing my *Life and Works of Albert Dürer*, not a bad book at the time, as, strange to say, there was no such work previously published, even in Germany, to my knowledge. The difficulty with me was the translation of Dürer's own letters and journal, which were spelt phonetically and rendered archaic by the three centuries and a half that had passed since they were written. At that time, at Girvan, there lived a priest who had been educated at the Scotch (originally Irish) college at Ratisbon, so I took my materials down, as I had done the previous season, and he kindly assisted me. As to Rossetti, he was more hypochondriacal than ever, and our nightly sederunts more prolonged, so I did not do much, and Mr. Reid, the priest in question, had rather a holiday. Neither B. nor I saw or heard anything of chloral; we have therefore come to the conclusion that no such habit as that which was so injurious to him after his severe and too real illness had then been contracted. Miss Losh was not at Penkill that season, so Miss Boyd sometimes drove us about the country, instead of leaving us to take those long walks I found so trying in the previous year.

One day she took us to the Lady's Glen, a romantic ravine in which the stream falls into a black pool round which the surrounding vertical rocks have been worn by thousands of years of rotating flood into a circular basin called, as many such have been designated, the Devil's Punch-Bowl. We all descended to the overhanging margin of the superincumbent rock; but never shall I forget the expression of Gabriel's face when he bent over the precipice peering into the unfathomed water dark as ink, in which sundry waifs flew round and round like lost souls in hell. In no natural spectacle had I ever known him to take any visible interest; the expression on his pale face did not indicate such interest; it said, as both Miss Boyd and I at the same moment interpreted it, "One step forward and I am free!" But his daily talk of suicide had not given him courage; the chance so suddenly and unexpectedly brought within his grasp paralysed him. I advanced to him, trembling I confess, for I could not speak. I could not have saved him; we were standing on a surface, slippery as glass by the wet green lichen. Suddenly he turned round, and put his hand in mine, an action which showed he was losing self-command and that fear was mastering him. When we were safely away we all sat down together without a word, but with faces too conscious of each other's thoughts.

So for that time we escaped, and after all I did continue to be his keeper, or at least his companion. We encountered no such danger again, but on the very next day, I think it was, occurred an adventure more extraordinary than any I have ever heard of in connection with a man writing his best poetry, painting his best pictures, and exercising a daily shrewdness of business habits, the wonder and admiration of all who were in any way connected with him. The feeble-minded English law declares the suicide to be of unsound mind, whereas he is anything but that; it is the privilege of man alone, the only reasoning suicidal creature in the world.

But the circumstance I am now to relate, indicating the subversion of reason itself, it appears to me highly desirable to place on record. It is a problem for doctors and psychologists alike. Mounting the ascending road towards Barr, we observed a small bird, a chaffinch, exactly in our path. We advanced: it did not fly but remained quite still, continuing so till he stooped down and lifted it. He held it in his hand: it manifested no alarm. "What is the meaning of this?" I heard him say to himself, and I observed his hand was shaking with emotion. "Oh," I said, "put the pretty creature down again. It is strange certainly: it must be very young, perhaps a tame one escaped from a cage." "Nonsense!" was his reply, still speaking *sotto voce*, "you are always against me, Scott. I can tell you what it is, it is my wife, the spirit of my wife, the soul of her has taken this shape; something is going to happen to me." To this I had nothing to reply, but when we reached home in silence, by a chance which often takes place in life, incidents of similar kinds falling together, Miss Boyd hailed us with the news that the household had had a surprise —the house bell, which takes a strong pull to ring it, had been rung, and rung by nobody! Rossetti inquired when this had taken place, and finding it must have been just about the time when we met the bird, he turned his curiously ferocious look upon me, asking what I thought now?—a question as perplexing as the conviction under which he laboured! But I observed he did not relate the story of the bird to Miss Boyd with the same confidence he had shown at first, and when he saw she was altogether averse to entertain it, he shut up at once. Nothing more was said at the time, but we have thought of it often since, trying in vain to understand him.[1] He had brought a mass of "proofs," and nearly every day brought him more. But besides he was writing better than in the earlier days: both *Eden Bower* and *Troy Town* were elaborated now. Almost every day he would seclude himself in the glen. Here I used to find him face to the wall lying in a shallow cave that went by the name of a seventeenth-century Covenanter. Bennan's Cave, working out with much elaboration and little inspiration, *The*

---

[1] [In the "Illustrations" already quoted, Mr. Scott says of Rossetti: "His whole nature destined him to have a tragic, not a comic or placid background to his journey in this world. This, and his profound love of, and actual faith in, the marvellous, made him not only the dearest of friends before bad health overtook him, but the most interesting of men."—ED.]

*Stream's Secret.* After it was done he did not know what to call this poem, till reading over my series of sonnets called *The Old Scotch House*, and finding one called "The Stream's

Secret," he simply appropriated that name for his own performance. Nothing would restrain him: "No name in the world would suit me but that, it expresses what I want!" No doubt it did, but it also expressed what I wanted to say in my sonnet, which ended the octave with the words "passing away," and the sestet with the truth, but "never past away." A deadly quarrel I could not bear, so here, as always, he had his way.

One advantage he gained in these visits to Penkill was a knowledge of *The King's Quair, i.e.* book, *cahier*, or quire of paper, and an interest in the author's death, which afterwards germinated into *The King's Tragedy*. Perfectly acquainted with the early poetry of his own country, properly so called, he knew nothing of that of this country, and the perfectness of the scheme of *The King's Quair* struck him with wonder. Pity it was he injured his *King's Tragedy* by trying to quote some verses of the original turned into octo-syllabic metre very poorly.

My pictures, which had been finished the season before, though painted in a wax medium, impress me with the conviction of which Sir H. Cole was firmly convinced, that any wall-painting in this climate is a mistake. Part of the circular staircase was an outer wall, part was not. The last only has remained perfect, the picture on the outer wall had to be partly repainted, and partly lined with sheets of zinc.

But I must return to the story of my dear friend D. G. R.'s poetic studies. They led him out of one difficulty into another. Before he left us, he had a volume in print, thin indeed and with the prose story of his early days called *Hand and Soul* inserted at the end. But what then? He would not publish. There cropped up the fear of a public ordeal of miscellaneous criticism, which had prevented him from exhibiting his water-colour pictures, and had shut him up exclusively in his own studio. If he could not publish, what else would he do with the printed poems? Give them to his friends with a preface as a *privately printed* volume? Even for this, considering the whole question, I could not help agreeing with him, that the introduction of the prose tale was an exhibition of poverty not to be thought of. He suddenly determined to reclaim the MS. book buried with his wife. What he wanted most was the poem called "Jenny," written at the same time as he painted "Found." In a few days he was gone.

I have so repeatedly expressed my unbelief in all the vulgar or popular forms of supernaturalism that I feel a little hesitation in recording a circumstance resembling that class of things which began the very evening after his departure. I could now get a little peace to revise my Dürer Journal, and my German friend Mr. Reid, who had given me an hour, stayed to dinner. Rossetti's habit when composing or even correcting the press, was to retire after dinner to the room above, the drawing-room of the old house, to read aloud to himself, when by himself. This he did in a voice so loud that we in the dining-room beneath could almost hear his words. Well, as we were sitting after dinner, when he must have been approaching London in the train, what could it be we heard? The usual voice reading to itself in the usual place over our heads! I looked at *B.*, she was listening intently till she could bear it no longer, and left the room. Our learned priest found me, I fancy, to be rather *distrait*, so he rose saying it was about his time, and besides, he continued, " I hear Miss Boyd has some friend in the drawing-room, so I won't go up. Give her my goodbye and respects." I joined her at once, but of course we heard nothing in the room itself. Such is the circumstance as it took place. Mr. Reid, who knew nothing of the habit of D. G. R., hearing the voice as well as we did, although it sounded to him like talking rather than reading, was a sure evidence we were not deceiving ourselves. Next night it was the same, and so it went on till I left. When we tried to approach it was not audible, or when the doors of the drawing-room and its small ante-room communicating with the staircase were left open, we could make nothing of it. It gradually tapered off when Miss Boyd was left by herself; by and by the whole establishment was bolted and barred for the winter. Next season it had entirely ceased.

I may now return to my own affairs. My eighteen pictures from the ballad of *Chevy Chase* had been finished and placed in the beginning of 1870. Previous to this the long series of windows for the Keramic gallery, South Kensington Museum, done in *graffito* as I called it, were nearly complete. I determined on settling into a house of my own.

When we turn into the sixties, the battle of life ought to be a little relaxed in its severity: some indulgence in matters of taste may be allowed. A lovely old house close to the Chelsea end of the picturesque old wooden bridge to Battersea, a house built by the Adamses, with a garden buttressed up from the river, and a studio behind to be easily made out of a music-room, in which its first owner indulged himself and in which Handel's organ had stood in these former years. Early in 1870 I arranged the purchase to be completed in November, the requisite money being at the time invested in Berlin Water Work shares and Egyptian Bonds, going down shortly after in a confident frame of mind to our usual summer months at Penkill. A few weeks later we were driving through the town of Girvan to the coast, to enjoy a picnic by the multitudinous sea. What was it bringing people on the street and making the newspaper shops so attractive? Suddenly as an earthquake or a West Indian tornado, a European war had been declared —the French army was moving towards the Rhine! The invincible army of Austerlitz, with a Bonaparte —happily a degenerate one—at its head. An army of 200,000 without a button wanting on a gaiter! In one of his letters from Jerusalem, already given in a previous chapter, Holman Hunt spoke of this war as then likely to sweep away the Christians from that city. This letter was dated the 10th of August, but here the crisis was over by that time. A few weeks later Hunt had actually to fortify himself in his large house, provisioned for a siege, but here the death-grapple of Germany and France, the mastiff and the wolf, was already loosening; the throat of the more savage beast was already giving way under the irrevocable teeth of the nobler animal. But for a moment in the east a new complication seemed to threaten the world. Russia made a move as if to take advantage of the moment. It was this that had alarmed Jerusalem, and for another hour and day my position was an awkward one. At first my Berlin Water Work shares went down, down to zero: anon M'Mahon's carriages filled with ladies' attire were flying — the French Cavalry were worth nothing. The shares went up again day after day, till they were at their former premium. Russia quieted down too, and the Egyptian Bonds threatening to be unsaleable were higher than before. The Gallic cock ceased to crow: every mail brought greater and greater tidings of the total discomfiture of France.

These monetary interests no doubt intensified one's greater interest in this most rapid, most decisive, and most important war. The concealed anxiety of the papal party, and of all retrograde thinkers, increased the importance of every day's news. But without these helps the tremendous ability of Prussia, and the overwhelming punishment of the Beauharnais, as Swinburne used to call Louis Napoleon, made that autumn the most exciting in my life. Strange to say, the majority of Englishmen were in favour of France, although the ultimate triumph of

Italian unity was involved, and the suppression of papal encroachment, besides the rabid tendency of France to indulge in conquest if it had been successful. The vast mediocrity, literary or other, went in for France. An instance of this was afforded by Appleton, the editor and proprietor of the *Academy*, in which publication the Fine Art section was under my care at the time. The editor, who had some pretence to learning and philosophy, sent round a circular to his collaborateurs proposing that every one of us should sacrifice our pay for a certain period, allowing it to be sent over as a contribution to the war expenses of France. I gave him a bit of advice, my readers may be sure! Our own battles of life affect our sleep and our health, but this Franco-German war was exhilarating only. Living quietly at Penkill, I used to waylay the postman, take the daily morning paper into the garden, and in the summer-house read every word of the news. On the way I passed an immense Foxglove just beginning to bear its lowest bloom when the struggle began. Before its last blossom was shed the crowning destruction of the French army at Sedan was over. I afterwards commemorated this in two little poems, which I should like to reprint here in connection with the rest of my story.

# THE FOXGLOVE

## A REMINISCENCE OF THE WAR OF 1870

### I

That foxglove by the garden gate
The very day the war began
Opened its first, its lowest flower:
    The post that day was late,
Anxious I waited for the man
Then went into the wild-rose bower
And heard the warning voice of fate.

Week by week, even day by day,
Another petal opened fair,
Advancing up the long light stem:
    I counted them
    As I passed there,
While my heart was far away,
Listening early, listening late,
To the German march—the march of Fate.
    And when France lay
Quivering in the gory clay,
    The topmost bell
Rang a dirge before it fell.

### II

Oft throughout that deadly fight
We owned that might was right,
For from the steps of the Madeleine
Amid the trumpets' loud fanfare,
Years long ago we had seen there
Louis, triumphant from the South,
Hailed by the brutal popular mouth;
Along the streets where late the stain
Of blood lay, did his triumph fare;

>    I heard the cheer ;
>  While many said, the day must come,
>  When God with us, right shall be might :
>  Behold ! with cannon, trump and drum,
>    Now was it here !
>    The span of time
>  A foxglove bloom its stalks might climb,
>  He passed for ever from our sight.

When I got back to London and became an inhabitant of Chelsea, with the wide river flowing before the windows, I congratulated myself on having ably overcome one of the greatest evils of life—the necessity of periodical house-hunting and migration. The hermit crab had found a permanent shell, a better one than if he had grown it. Here was a room for my books, or two of them, and a room for my prints—the dear early Germans and Italians that had cost me so much trouble and money to collect, and that had been the exciting cause of my writing the books on Albert Dürer and the Little German Masters. I felt as if I too, as well as Marshal Moltke, was having a triumph, and I celebrated it in a sonnet, not for publication, but as it is in a way autobiographical, it may be added here.

### ON GOING TO LIVE IN BELLEVUE HOUSE, CHELSEA

*November* 1870.

>    Here, then, I am, to find my latest stage :
>    A good old home with elbow-room, I wis :
>      As if dame Fortune dealt her blindfold kiss
>    To one who had so often lost his wage,

A ruminant wandering creature, until Age
   Touched him upon the shoulder, and said, " So !
   Here we are, confrere, walking rather slow :
Strange your light barque should find such harbourage ! "

But sooth to say, two diligent nimble hands
   Oft save wool-gathering brains from bankruptcy,
For if we daily till the common lands
   That yield plain food, work out the tasks that lie
About us, serving thus the general hive,
The fates will let even a Poet thrive.

Yet, pleasant as it was to have found a *point d'appui* in life, at this very moment came a circumstance to make me contemplate returning altogether to Edinburgh. This was a chair of the Fine Arts being established in Edinburgh. The number of men combining literary and artistic powers of any value were so few that I was advised to offer myself for it. The only other man who had any equal chance was, it appeared to me, P. G. Hamerton, the clever etcher and writer on etching, who had, however, given up his chance of ever becoming a painter. I got into communication with the Senatus and their head, Sir A. Grant. I quickly came to the conclusion there was some bar in the way, and retired.

In the course of my short correspondence with Mr. Hamerton, I received a letter which may be worth preserving here.

Pré Charmoy, Autun, Saone et Loire,<br>
28<i>th</i> July 1871.

My dear Scott—During the war the postal service was so irregular, and even unsafe, that I thought it better to keep your prints[1] along with my own papers. I send them under a separate cover.

I am glad you have got a house to your liking at Chelsea. I remember houses there that seemed to me charming. You will have pleasant society within easy reach, which I rather envy you. In country places like this in France, although there are a few educated men, they are always divided by social or political demarcations. I had some thought of trying to found a club here. We have men enough, but their divisions render such a project Utopian.

I am practising just now, with great pleasure, my new positive process in etching, of which I sent an account to the *Portfolio*. I work out of doors, and see every stroke in *black on a white ground*, just when I do it, which avoids much of the deception in the old half-blind process. As the plate is in the acid all the time I have to mind to etch the blackest places first, and go by a careful calculated gradation to the palest; but I find that this sort of analysis becomes easy enough by practice. When the drawing with the etching-point is done, the plate is ready for printing, avoiding all the old bother of stopping-out. The new process is so agreeable that I could not go back to the old one now; besides, there is a great economy of time.

During the war I saw a battle from my study window, about 5000 men engaged on each side. I had a good telescope, and saw the men plainly enough. The cannonade went on from 2 P.M. till nightfall, and afterwards began again in the moonlight. We should have had the Prussians at our house most probably, if we had not been protected by a stream which was rather swollen, so they thought they could not cross it without leaving some of

---

[1] What the prints were that P. G. H. mentions in his letter I cannot now remember. My Collection, after having been very useful, ceased to retain their interest, and I sold them to a gentleman who promised to keep them together, but who last year brought them to the hammer at Sotheby's, July 1885. They brought £1260. I insert this note, September 1886.

their artillery in the mud. We were considerably anxious of course, but next day the Prussians retired. The only evil that has occurred to me during the war was a fortnight's illness brought on by an imprudence. On a very cold day in winter, acting as guide to a lot of Garibaldian cavalry, I had to lead them through a flooded river. I had the icy water up to my saddle-seat, and rode afterwards for several hours in wet clothes. The mortality in the (French) army here was terrible during the severity of the winter—I remain, yours very truly,

P. G. H.

# CHAPTER IX

LETTERS FROM D. G. ROSSETTI, AUTUMN 1871, AT KELMSCOTT—ON HIS OWN POETRY THEN IN PROGRESS—ALSO ON MINE.

WHEN D. G. Rossetti left us at Penkill, and recovered his buried MS. volume, he at once abandoned the *Privately Printed* volume he had already printed, which only exists since in two or at most three copies. The only really important poem recovered, except such as he had remembered, was "Jenny," which had its origin contemporaneously with the design for the promised etching to illustrate my poem first called "Rosabell." The two works had their origin together, when he visited me first in Newcastle, when I was in the act of arranging my first miscellaneous little volume sometimes called *Poems by a Painter*. However suggested, it was years on the anvil, and at last had a daring circumstance included in its story, which some friends tried in vain to get altered. "Jenny" bears the evidence of its derivation by being the only poem D. G. R. wrote on the morals or the period of our own day, and is really, notwithstanding its confessional character, one of the ablest of all his poems, even to the end of his life.  The others,[1] such as "Dante at Verona," "A Last Confession," are comparatively boyish and worthless, except, indeed, "Sister Helen," which he held in memory and afterwards improved.  However, he included all.

On the very successful reception of the volume by the public, his hypochondria about his eyes disappeared, along with the nervous fear about publishing. Still, however, he to the last moment *would* work the oracle, and get all his friends to prepare laudatory critical articles to fill all the leading journals.[2] Against this he would take no advice.  His brother especially offered him the wisest and kindest counsel.  "I often sadly reflect," as he said afterwards, "that I used to urge Gabriel not to go diplomatising (as I got to call it) to have his book reviewed in various papers by friends and henchmen, and that if he had taken this advice the soreness of outsiders would have been avoided."  How much reason had we all to wish he had denied himself "the jubilant proclamation of the merits of his poems."  And yet who can say?  No one could predict the effect adverse

---

[1] [Mr. Scott is speaking here of the poems recovered from Mrs. Rossetti's grave, and not contained in the privately printed volume, but included in the printed and published volume which was issued in 1870.—ED.]

[2] [A reader who should come upon this passage without knowing the strength and constancy of the autobiographer's friendship for Rossetti and admiration of his powers, might suspect him here of ill-naturedly disparaging his friend.  This would be entirely to mistake the spirit of the record, which is intended only to illustrate that morbid fear of criticism which was so paradoxical and so disastrous an element in Rossetti's character.—ED.]

criticism had upon him when it came; it was the morbid feeling in his own mind that made him work heaven and earth to render it impossible, as he thought, that such should reach him; and the very first, I should say the only, powerful attack upon his book knocked him over like the blow of the butcher's axe on the forehead of the ox. He had felt that such would be the effect of severe strictures, and feared them, else why the reluctance to publish, the desire to issue his privately printed volume when we had prevailed upon him to take up poetry again, and why the disagreeable expenditure of energy in working the oracle, to furnish all the ordinary channels of criticism with articles ready made under his own eye? The question is exactly similar to that of the habit and effect of the chloral he took. I had known him too long to believe it had much to do with either the mental or bodily peculiarities from which he latterly suffered. I asked Professor Marshall, his medical adviser, and his answer was that the chloral was merely a desperate attempt to cure his evils, not the cause of them. As to the article that troubled him so deeply, perhaps his anxiety to forestall criticism brought it upon him. The critic is the natural enemy of the poet, Gautier has said in a way sufficiently amusing though unquotable here, and critics who are themselves "literary poets" are the worst disposed of all.

Meantime, however, he was in excellent spirits, and an almost daily correspondence began to pass between us. I have none of my own letters, and never had the habit of copying them, but all his are with me still and deserve to be carefully printed, showing as they do the careful reconsideration he gave his poems.

Morris had at that time lighted upon a lovely ancient manor house, not the house of seven gables, but of ten, to be let near Lechlade. It was a house lying low, and sometimes surrounded by floods : the rooms, many and irregular ; the kitchens and sitting-rooms on the entrance floor, being lower than the ground outside, were not always safe from the inundation. Among the larger apartments above (the house properly speaking) was one hung with tapestry, the later tapestry with life-sized figures in Roman costume. This Rossetti, who joined for a time with Morris in renting the house, tried to make a studio, but found the draughts unbearable, the hanging waving about on all sides, making the room like a house attacked by vertigo. The first of the following letters was written shortly after he went thither, to me, then living at Penkill, a dwelling as thoroughly Scottish as Kelmscott was English, only of a century later.

D. G. R. to W. B. S. (I.)

THE MANOR HOUSE, KELMSCOTT,<br>LECHLADE, 17th July 1871.

DEAR SCOTUS—You see I write to you among surroundings new to me, but of such an old fashion in themselves that it is easy to identify one's own sense of use and habit with them, and to believe one has always known them. This is a wonderful old place which you must some day see, and of which I must get photos taken when I can, but photography is, I should think, unknown as yet in Kelmscott. The house and garden, with all their riverside fields and sleepy farm-buildings, make up a delicious picture to the eye and mind, and afford so much home variety that there is no need of seeking farther. When one does so, however, one is bound to confess that the country roads possess little interest, being so extremely flat that they may almost be said to present no objects at all ; and the solitude is as absolute as at Penkill, but not nearly so impressive in its natural features.  I am writing in my delightful sitting-room or studio, the walls of which are hung with tapestries which I suppose have been here since the house was built (by the same family who have only just left it). The subject of the tapestries is the history of Samson, which is carried through with that un-compromising uncomfortableness peculiar to this class of art manufacture. Indeed, I have come to the conclusion that a tapestried room should always be much dimmer than this one. These things constantly obtruded on one in a bright light become a persecution. However, it won't do to take them down, as they might get moth-eaten, and heaven knows what their value may not be in the eyes of their owners. We have got plenty of things into the house, and even a moderate amount of order by this time—Janey [Mrs. W. Morris] has been taking five and six mile walks without the least difficulty, and her children are the most darling little self-amusing machines that ever existed. The nearest town to this is Lechlade, some three miles off, a beautiful old place and not a station. I expect to be here for two months at least, though I may perhaps run back to London midway for a day or so to see what is doing in my studio, where a radical cure is to be effected in the light during my absence under Webb's directions, after which I shall have as good a studio as any one, I hope. I shall make a replica I have to do while here, and make some drawings besides, I hope. Whether writing will come of it I cannot yet tell. The weather is warm and genial at last here, and the same I hope with you. Have you really got Miss Losh at Penkill? Will you give my love to her (if there), as well as to Miss Boyd; and tell me whatever is to tell between one "haunt of ancient peace" and another. We have fallen back on Shakspeare here as at Penkill in the evenings, and are "doing" him religiously, sometimes indoors and sometimes out. A pretty fair supply of books has been got into the place, and the children, who are indefatigable readers, read about a volume of the Waverley Novels a day. Little May, the youngest, seems lovelier every day. I shall make drawings of both while I stay here—Allan and Emma [husband and wife, servants from London house] have come down with me; and we have besides the children's nurse and two native retainers. The garden is full of fat cut hedges that seem to purr and simmer in the sun, as do the farm buildings also on all sides. We shall have erelong to keep a trap of some sort as well as a cow and pig. Does Miss Boyd, I wonder, know anywhere of a highly desirable Ayrshire cow to be had? I am told that race is in demand, but the only question is whether the carriage would very vastly add to the expense. Otherwise the advantages of friendly selection out there, and security against cheating, would be good gains.—Do write to your affectionate         D. GABRIEL R.

*P.S.*—I suppose you know that mamma and Christina are at Hampstead.

In this first letter there seems nothing calling for any notice. The cow question opened up correspondence, which does not demand record here, although it filled many pages till it was found impracticable.

D. G. R. to W. B. S. (II.)

KELMSCOTT, LECHLADE,<br>*Wednesday.*

DEAREST SCOTUS—Your letter was very welcome, but did not reach me till to-day. However, let me go in at once for another, which I hope will not be so long on the way.

I send you a little ballad or song or something made in a punt on the river—not a very poetic style of locomotion. It's rather out of my usual way, rude aiming at the sort of popular view that Tennyson perhaps alone succeeds in taking. Not (I hope) that it's at all chargeable with imitation of Tennyson, but I mean that nobody but he tries to get within hail of general readers. But I fear, however much I might like to do so, that it's not my vocation except in such a trifle as this once in a way; and I daresay this would be voted obscure. I fancy it ought to be suited for music.

I have discovered some nice riverside walks now the floods have subsided, and there is a funny little island midway in one walk, which can be reached by a crazy bridge, and does very well as a half-way house to commit sonnets to paper going and coming. It may perhaps lead to further effusions. I got one sonnet out of it to-day. I daresay I shall get a fair stroke of painting work done here, as I have had all my things sent down together, with that picture of "Beatrice" to make a replica, and am also at work on a drawing for a small picture I mean to paint here to fit a beautiful old frame I have.

I also mean to make drawings of the children. The younger, Mary, is quite a beauty the more one knows her, and will be a lovely woman. She is very clever too, I think, and has a real turn for drawing when she gets a little less lazy. The older one buries herself in books, but is not so observant as the younger.

I got the *Academy* to-day, with an article on a German Dürerite, which smacks of the rival adept, though not unfair certainly. I shall want to see your article in *Fraser*, and must get the *Portfolio*, which I suppose is out now, containing that on Blake. I am extremely sorry to hear of Wallis's attack with his eyes, but seeing how completely he got over the first, I cannot suppose these attacks to be really dangerous in the worst sense. It is almost a pity he did not go with Top to Iceland. No news of the latter yet, though expected before this. I had a letter from Stillman, very loud of course in proclaiming his wife's enchantment with America and all American people and things. They are coming back, he says, this month by sailing-ship. I suppose you heard of their dreadful passage out.

I'm afraid I shan't do much poetry here, as my walks are seldom taken alone, Janey having developed a most triumphant pedestrian faculty; licks you hollow, I can tell you. We are doing a good deal in papering and painting here, as well as other repairs. So time does not run to seed.

If I were at Penkill I know, as you say, that I should do something decided in poetry—to wit, "The Orchard Pits" poem, which I much want to do; but I find it almost impossible to write narrative poetry in scenery that does not help it, and so have little chance of setting to that here.

I was sorry to hear that you had not Miss Losh with you, and hope her health is not the cause of her being unable to join you.

How intensely stupid it was of me when I wrote before to forget that Letitia was with you now. I can only account for it by the fact that I was never at Penkill while she was there. Janey's love to her, and mine to all.—Ever your affectionate      D. G. R.


## THE RIVER'S RECORD

Between Holmscote and Hurstcote
   The river-reaches wind,
The whispering trees accept the breeze,
   The ripple's cool and kind:
With love low-whispered 'twixt the shores,
   With rippling laughters gay,
With white arms bared to ply the oars,
   On last year's first of May.

Between Holmscote and Hurstcote
    The river's brimmed with rain,
Through close-met banks and parted banks,
    Now near, now far again :
With parting tears caressed to smiles,
    With meeting promised soon,
With every sweet vow that beguiles,
    On last year's first of June.

Between Holmscote and Hurstcote
    The river's flecked with foam,
'Neath shuddering clouds that hang in shrouds
    And lost winds wild for home :
With infant wailings at the breast,
    With homeless steps astray,
With wanderings shuddering tow'rds one rest,
    On this year's first of May.

Between Holmscote and Hurstcote
    The summer river flows
With doubled flight of moons by night,
    And lilies' deep repose :
With lo ! beneath the moon's white stare
    A white face not the moon,
With lilies meshed in tangled hair
    On this year's first of June.

Between Holmscote and Hurstcote
    A troth was given and riven ;
From heart's trust grew one life to two,
    Two lost lives cry to Heaven :
With banks spread calm beneath the sky,
    With meadows newly mowed,
The harvest paths of glad July,
    The sweet school-children's road.

KELMSCOTT, *July* 1871.

The poem here given, " Between Holmscote and Hurstcote," or " The River's Record," I now forget

what I said of. It was not in D. G. R.'s way, as he
says, but still has its good qualities.

### D. G. R. to W. B. S. (III.)

KELMSCOTT, LECHLADE,
2nd August 1871.

DEAR SCOTUS—Your verdict on my popular rhymes
is more favourable than I looked for ; but I fear I have
no more the popular element than yourself.

Did I, in the fourth line of verse one, fail to put apostrophe in "ripples"? I don't otherwise see why you
consider the line "isolated" in character. "Cool" resulted
from experience, while writing of the impression produced.
As to the repetition of rippling, this seems necessary, as
you will observe that two epithets are interchanged in
each stanza between the landscape and the emotion. I've
no doubt your objection to the title is valid, though I suppose I meant *A record of* the river. Would "May and
June" be better ? So I called it at first, but this seemed
hardly incisive enough.[1]

Your sorrows in connection with that infernal word
"quaint" recall my own. Only quite lately I had it revived by a friendly critic on my work, though a lapse of
years had occurred since I last heard it in such relation,
and I had hoped it and I had parted company. However,
it will be "in at the death" with both of us. Good God,
I cannot see the faintest trace of this adjective in either
of your etchings which you mention, nor in the design of
your mantelpiece (the carrying out I have not seen) in
any objectionable sense, though I suppose, so far as it
differs from other mantelpieces, it might be described as
peculiar, if that is one meaning of the hellish "quaint."

By the bye, on this point I have always meant, and
always forgotten, to ask you if you noticed an astounding
controversy raised in *Notes and Queries* about a wretched
little daub of mine called "Greensleeves." Had the thing

---

[1] [The title finally adopted was "Down Stream."—ED.]

is, probably enough; but how it should suggest to any human mind the maniacal farrago conjured up in these letters is incomprehensible, except as revealing to one the degree to which the world considers oneself insane. On reading them my brain whirled, and I sent to Agnew for the thing, to see if it bore any internal explanation with it. It seemed a poor daub when examined, but certainly innocent of the special enormities charged to it. However, once having laid hands on it, I gave it a good daubing all over, and transmogrified it so completely (title and all) as to separate it for ever, I hope, from this Bedlam correspondence, which, by the bye, I find revived this week—to end God knows when or where!

I hope you get *Notes and Queries* regularly, as by my directions. If you don't, I'll see to the posting myself.

And now, Scotus, you may just return the compliment by posting to me the *Fraser* and *Portfolio* with your articles (if you have them by you), as otherwise I shall go to the expense for them, which you counsel me not to incur.

I am getting to work now, both on the replica of "Beatrice" (Cowper Temple's picture, which I borrowed and have here); on a small picture to fit a beautiful old frame I have, and to which I mean to put a view of the winding river for background; and on the drawings of the children.

A little sonnet-writing gets done too, and a ballad—of the Sister Helen kind rather—is floating paperwards on a slow brain-breeze enough. I wrote an Italian song the other day! But I do a deal of making up in my head before I put pen to paper.

It would really give me great pleasure to see that dear old barn which has been the bounding of so many pleasant walks and talks embodied in a picture of yours, and I really hope you'll do it, as it is just the sort of material which half does a picture to one's hand.

Midway with this letter, Janey shows me at last one from Top, who writes from some unpronounceable place in Iceland, and seems to have had much pleasurable experience already, though nothing much to report at second hand, except the delightful fact that a packet from the co-operative stores, opened eagerly for table delicacies, was found to contain Floriline and violet powder. However, I judge it was the only one, or it would not serve Top for an epistolary horse-laugh. An Iceland paper also came, in which the arrival of the travellers is reported, Top being described as a "Skald." He ought to go by no other name for the future, and "The Bard" be reserved for Swinburne.

Browning's poem, *Balaustion's Adventure*, looks alarming beforehand. I have written to have it sent me when out, which will not be till the 8th. I see what it all means: B. has been inveighing all his life against translations (when I sent him my *Italian Poets*, I remember he never answered at all!), and now having by some accident slipped a translation of *Alcestis*, he had to look about for a consistent plan for putting it into print, and has hit on this alarming scheme. However, no doubt there will be plenty to admire and enjoy. Browning seems likely to remain, with all his sins, the most original and varied mind, by long odds, which betakes itself to poetry in our time.

Brown and family, with Hüffer and Miss Blind, are, as perhaps you know, at Lynmouth, where Miss B. has unearthed an old woman who knew Shelley and Harriet when they were staying there. I may as well enclose you a letter of B.'s giving some particulars on this curious matter, though indeed it will swell this epistle to a most portentous size. By the bye, you might send me your International Report if you have it. I see the *Academy Journal* is a very dry stick this time.

What you tell me of Allingham is no worse than I am myself, so I mustn't wonder. I cannot sleep, except at the back of my house, for the noise, and require all sorts of usualnesses all round me to make life possible. Alas for flying years! One wonders if one was always so, and is reminded how far one is looking back by the difficulty of remembering.— Ever yours, and Miss Boyd's and Letitia's, if still with you, affectionately,

D. G. R.

I cannot recollect what the strange writing in *Notes and Queries* that troubled him so was. The *Fraser* and the *Portfolio* he wanted, with articles of mine, I duly sent him. I think he mentions them again. The *International* I also sent him. The article by me was one of the critical articles published as separate pamphlets, written by various selected people, on the great International Exhibition that year.

At the end of the letter the mention of Allingham was called forth by his taking the friendly offer of my house at Chelsea while my wife and I were in the North. He [A.] could not sleep in the bedroom he occupied; it was too near the street, and the occasional noise of passers-by was too much noise for him. This brings out a similar confession from D. G. R. as to his sleeplessness. This, written in August 1871, is the earliest allusion to the sleeplessness, etc., so severely felt by him after his return to town and severe illness at the end of this year.

The letter about Mrs. Blackmore, the old woman who had had Shelley and Harriet lodging in her house (or friend's house) at Lynmouth, contains nothing of any importance to make it worth preservation. Shelley lived a long time there, and as in every place where accidental record is found of his having stayed, he left without paying up, so there still remained an unpaid balance. They used to play about like children, Mrs. Blackmore with them. . . . After reading every word in Dowden's immense life, I believe it will at last be found that his dislike to Harriet began when she had begun to treat with laughter his folly in thinking to reform the world with his paper-boats and fire-balloons.

D. G. R. to W. B. S. (IV.)

### COMMANDMENTS

Let no man ask you of anything
Not yearborn between Spring and Spring.
More of all worlds than he can know
Each day the single sun doth show:
A trustier gloss than you can give
From all wise scrolls demonstrative,
The sea doth sigh and the wind sing.

Let no lord awe you on any height
Of earthly kingship's mouldering might.
The dust his heel holds meet for your brow
Has all of it been what both are now:
And he and you may plague together
A beggar's eyes in some dusty weather
When none that is now knows sound or sight.

Let no priest tell you of any home
Unseen above the sky's blue dome.
To have played in childhood by the sea,
Or to have been young in Italy,
Or anywhere in the sun or rain;
To have loved and been beloved again,
Is nearer Heaven than he can come.

## SUNSET WINGS

To-night this sunset spreads two golden wings
    Cleaving the western sky ;
Winged too with wind it is, and winnowings
Of birds ; as if the day's last hour in rings
    Of strenuous flight must die.

Sun-steeped in fire, the homeward pinions sway
    Above the dovecote-tops ;
And clouds of starlings, ere they rest with day,
Sink, clamorous like mill-waters at wild play
    By turns in every copse :

Each tree heart-deep the wrangling rout receives,
    Save for the whirr within,
You could not tell the starlings from the leaves ;
Then one great puff of wings, and the swarm heaves
    Away with all its din—

Even thus Hope's hours, in ever-eddying flight,
    To many a refuge tend :
With the first light she laughed, and the last light
Glows round her still ; who natheless in the night
    At length must make an end.

And now the mustering rooks innumerable
    Together sail and soar,
While for the day's death, like a tolling knell,
Unto the heart they seem to cry farewell,
    No more, farewell, no more !

Is Hope not plumed, as 'twere a fiery dart ?
    Therefore, O dying day,
Even as thou goest must she too depart,
And sorrow fold such pinions on the heart
    As will not fly away ?

These two poems came without commentary. They have fine things in them, but are imperfect. He says in another letter he has now thirty new sonnets to add to the *House of Life*, since printing last year. I had just published a Christmas book on *Belgian Art*, and he wishes to see it. He sends "Through Death to Love," "The Lover's Walk," "The Dark Glass," and "Heart's Haven," also the first version of "Cloud Confines."

D. G. R. to W. B. S. (V.)

KELMSCOTT, 13*th August* '71.

DEAREST SCOTUS—I send back the *Fraser* and the Kensington papers. The first contains in your article an exhaustive summary, sure to be very valuable one day, of this year's art, which, owing to continental events, has assumed in England a very unusual aspect. It was a much better plan to do this than to retrace the circle of the Academy walls.

Your own paper among the *Reports* is of course solid good work, and Pollen's shows signs of something besides amateurishness. The others that I have looked at are mere pretentious vapouring, such as in England floats uppermost in all enterprises.

I have sent you two missives within the last day or two—first, a poem not long but meant to deal with important matters, and second, Browning's new book, of an extremely irritating structure—it is so absolutely everything that Greek ideas are not. Still there is much good work, and even pure simple diction in the translated part, and Browning is too great a man already to make it matter much what one thinks of a leisure work like this.

I ordered and got the last *Portfolio* and find to my vexation that Blake's Flea, etc., must have been in the July one. I don't know whether I shall try again now—

it is so provoking. I just this minute ask Emma about
*N. and Q.* She says they have gone to you regularly,
the only one in the house now being to-day's. This
seems strange. It would really be worth your while one
day, if you keep *N. and Q.*, to look back at the first
of these Greensleeves letters; it would enlarge your ideas
as to the gaping astonishment and perverse misconstruc-
tion of which we were writing lately. As my name was
in the heading, I wonder it did not catch your eye.

I send you another little poem (done from nature)
with this, and may perhaps soon muster energy to copy a
few sonnets, only they seem such lackadaisical things
to send about. I have now thirty new ones in MS. for
the *House of Life* since printing last year; I suppose
several of the last must have been unseen by you. I
should like greatly to see what you have written on the
*Belgians*. Pray send it. I hope, being clear of it now,
you will at any rate find some sonnets lurking in you,
and, above all, collect and print your poetry ere long. Do
you see the *Athenæum* gossip about my intentions this
week? Who ever conceives and then condenses such
inventions? I saw the paragraph about my father, and
had heard of the matter before at home. My own view
was quite yours—viz. that it ought to be done; but I
know nothing would induce my mother to consent.
[This was the removal of his father's remains to Italy.]

It appears from something I see written by Knight
that there has been a very obtuse review of Swinburne
in the *Edinburgh*—done, I suppose, by the same puny
Scotch hand which scribbled about Morris lately.

I am quite rejoiced to hear of Wallis's improvement
and pedestrian labours. It would be a real treat to
witness his first enjoyment of the beautiful glen. Pray
give him my love, and say how much I wish (if one could
be in two places at once) that I were making a fourth
stroller in the shelter of the glen slopes (hardly, however,
with much water-noise in one's ears now) from the sudden
heats we have come in for.

This place needs no Sunday to quiet it, so that I only identify the day by the trouble of having to send to the town for letters and papers. I am getting used a little now to the tapestry, though still the questions, Why a Philistine leader should have a panther's tail, or Delilah a spike sticking out of her head, or what Samson, standing over a heap of slain, has done with the ass's jaw-bone, will obtrude themselves at times between more abstract speculations. I have nearly finished my replica, which has gone wonderfully quick, and am getting on with the little picture with river background.

I suppose if Wallis is at all in working trim he will be sure to have an easel up in the glen before long, and you will not be behindhand with another, I should say. Here we read Shakspeare and Plutarch just as the first builders of the house might have done, and are on the whole Elizabethan enough. By the bye, there is one subject in Plutarch not done by Shakspeare and quite worthy of him—Pompey the Great. Some one should yet go in for it as a play.—With love, ever yours, D. G. R.


## THROUGH DEATH TO LOVE

Like labour-laden moon-clouds faint to flee
   From winds that sweep the winter-bitten wold,—
   Like multiform circumfluence manifold
Of night's flood-tide,—like terrors that agree
Of fire dumb-tongued and inarticulate sea,—
    Even such, within some glass dimmed by our breath,
    Our hearts discern wild images of Death,
Shadows and shoals that edge eternity.

Howbeit athwart Death's imminent shade doth soar
   One Power than flow of stream or flight of dove,
   Sweeter to glide around, to brood above.
Tell me, my heart,—what angle-greeted door
Or threshold of wing-winnowed threshing-floor
    Hath guest fire-fledged as thine, whose lord is love?

## THE LOVERS' WALK

Sweet twining hedge-flowers wind-stirred in no wise
   On this June day; and hand that clings in hand :—
   Still glades; and meeting faces scarcely fanned :—
An osier-odoured stream that draws the skies
Deep to its heart; and mirrored eyes in eyes :—
   Fresh hourly wonder o'er the summer land
   Of light and cloud; and two souls softly spanned
With one o'erarching heaven of smiles and sighs :—

Even such their path, whose bodies lean unto
   Each other's visible sweetness amorously,—
   Whose passionate hearts lean by Love's high decree
Together on his heart for ever true,
As the white-foaming firmamental blue
   Rests on the blue line of a foamless sea.


## THE DARK GLASS

Not I myself know all my love for thee :
   How should I reach so far, who cannot weigh
   To-morrow's dower by gage of yesterday?
Shall birth, and death, and all dark voids that be
As doors and windows bared to some loud sea,
   Lash deaf mine ears and blind my face with spray;
   And shall my sense pierce love,—the last relay
And ultimate outpost of eternity?

Lo! what am I to Love, the Lord of all?
   One murmuring shell he gathers from the sand,—
   One little heart-flame sheltered in his hand.
Yet through thine eyes he grants me clearest call
And veriest touch of powers primordial
   That any hour-girt life may understand.

## HEART'S HAVEN

Sometimes she is a child within mine arms,
   Cowering beneath dark wings that love must chase ;
   With still tears showering and averted face,
Inexplicably filled with faint alarms :
And oft from mine own spirit's hurtling harms
   I crave the refuge of her deep embrace,—
   Against all ill the fortified strong place
And sweet reserve of sovereign counter-charms.

And Love, our light at night and shade at noon,
   Lulls us to rest with songs, and turns away
   All shafts of shelterless, tumultuous day.
Like the moon's growth, his face gleams through his tune ;
And as soft waters warble to the moon,
   Our answering kisses chime one roundelay.


## THE CLOUD CONFINES

   The day is dark and the night
      To him that would search the heart ;
      No lips of cloud that will part
   Nor morning song in the light.
      Only, gazing alone,
      To him wild shadows are shown,
      Deep under deep unknown,
   And height above unknown height.
      Still we say as we go,—
      " Strange to think by the way,
      Whatever there is to know,
      That shall we know one day."

   The Past is over and fled ;
      Named new, we name it the old ;
      Thereof some tale hath been told,
   But no word comes from the dead ;

> Whether at all they be,
> Or whether as bond or free,
> Or whether they too were we,
> Or by what spell they have sped.
> > Still we say as we go,—
> > > "Strange to think by the way,
> > > Whatever there is to know,
> > > That shall we know one day."
>
> What of the heart of hate
> > That beats in thy breast, O Time ?—
> Red strife from the furthest prime
> And anguish of fierce debate ;
> > War that shatters her slain,
> > And peace that grinds them as grain,
> > And eyes fixed ever in vain
> On the pitiless eyes of Fate.
> > Still we say as we go,—
> > > "Strange to think by the way,
> > > Whatever there is to know,
> > > That shall we know one day."
>
> What of the heart of love
> > That bleeds in thy breast, O man ?—
> > Thy kisses snatched 'neath the ban
> Of fangs that mock them above ;
> > Thy bells prolonged unto knells,
> > Thy hope that a breath dispels,
> > Thy bitter, forlorn farewells,
> And the empty echoes thereof.
> > Still we say as we go,—
> > > "Strange to think by the way,
> > > Whatever there is to know,
> > > That shall we know one day."
>
> The sky leans dumb on the sea
> > Aweary with all its wings ;
> > And oh ! the song the sea sings
> Is dark everlastingly.

>     Our past is clean forgot,
>     Our present is and is not,
>     Our future's a sealed seed-plot,
>     And what betwixt them are we?
>         Atoms that nought can sever
>             From one world-circling will,—
>         To throb at its heart for ever,
>             Yet never to know it still.
>
> *9th August* 1871.

I must have been long in answering, for his next missive is nothing but this—

>     There's a Scotch correspondent named Scott
>     Thinks a penny for postage a lot ;
>         Books, verses, and letters
>         Too good for his betters
>     Cannot screw out an answer from Scott.

To this I answered—

>     It was not the penny or groat
>     That stuck in the Scotchman's throat ;
>         But, faith, he did lack
>         Nutcrackers to crack
>     Verses set his weak jaw on the rack.

[It would appear from the next letter in the series that a long letter about the said verses from the "Scotch correspondent" was on its way when the impatient remonstrance was penned.—ED.]

### D. G. R. to W. B. S. (VI.)

KELMSCOTT, *25th August* 1871.

DEAREST W. B.—I will generously consider our court of minstrelsy or bardic contest as closed with your rejoinder. I suppose you understood mine to have been written and sent before receipt of your later communications.

I may as well enclose the cutting from *Sunday Times*, though I suppose you have most likely seen it, and it is hardly an exhaustive treatment of the subject.

Many thanks for the Blake paper, which is full of interest. B.'s view about the flea is a muddle as far as expressed. One would suppose the figure, seen as you say, to be a sort of generic Eidolon of flea-hood, were it not for what the spectre is made to say of " I myself " as an individual. Perhaps it is not rightly reported by Varley. The etching is a valuable addition to Blake records, but I am uncertain whether you have rendered Milton's wife quite exactly. In yours there seems to me a certain *soupçon* of Miss Boyd! Can you or she see it? Perhaps, however, this may exist in the original (if indeed in yours), though I did not notice it.

I have read your Belgian book and find it thoroughly readable either for artist or layman. Your article on Leys takes, I think, quite the true view and is equal to its important theme. However, I am not sure that you dwell quite strongly enough on the fascination which L.'s intensity as antiquarian and colourist gives him even to the most ideal class of poetic minds, though, as you say, it be quite questionable whether there were any absolute poetry in his springs of action. I think you give Tadema his full dues, though perhaps not more. However, to many *dii Minores* I think you are far too lenient, having, I fancy, a leaning towards Belgians because at any rate they are not Frenchmen. Your placing Portaels by the side of Delaroche seems to me something like treason, I must say, and to me the leading and crying characteristic of Mr. Van Lerius is such wretched badness that *that* not being first executed, critique of such minor merits as he may possess appears irrelevant. I fancy some of the best Belgians are unrepresented with you, but might at least have been referred to. There is a family of De Braekeleer, one member, at least, of which is quite a remarkable realistic colourist and character-painter, and the late *International* contained a landscape by Lamorinière which struck me, on a rather cursory glance, as the only good Belgian picture there. Lastly, I am much concerned to find that you have alluded in no way whatever to Wiertz, whose works I never saw (with one large exception quite noteworthy enough to increase curiosity), but who, I am sure, must have been the greatest mental genius (except Lego in his very different walk) whom they have had yet. Your power of treating a critical subject lightly and yet thoroughly is as evident here as in the French volume. I am rather sorry, by the bye, that you have stated so positively that the death of Leys resulted from his alarm during a thunderstorm. I have heard this point spoken of by several who knew him and do not think it seems so certain, while it is a painful association one would wish away if possible.

I am very sorry I did not send the *Fraser* and other papers before Wallis left you, but had stupidly forgotten that such was your motive in wishing their speedy return. Another happy man, after all, seems to be Allingham, for all his want of "success." Nothing but the most absolute calm and enjoyment of outside nature could account for so much gadding hither and thither on the soles of his two feet. Fancy carrying about grasses for hours and days from the field where Burns ploughed up a daisy. Good God! if I found the daisy itself there, I would sooner swallow it than be troubled to carry it twenty yards.

In what you say of my sonnets I agree absolutely as to principles and partially as to application. For instance, I quite think with you that the two sonnets you prefer are better than the other two for the reason given; and I hardly ever do produce a sonnet except on some basis of special momentary emotion; but I think there is another class admissible also—and that is the only other I practise, viz. the class depending on a line or two clearly given you, you know not whence, and calling up a sequence of ideas. This also is a just *raison d'être* for a sonnet, and such are all mine when they do not in some sense belong to the "occasional" class. However, I cannot at all perceive that I have a habit of using images a second time, and think that any impression to that effect must result from hardly making due allowance for the general theme of the series. I do not know where you would find an instance in point, certainly it does not seem to me that there is any more than a generic likeness between the two called "The Dark Glass," "Through Death to Love," or any likeness in either to any sonnet previously written by me. Certainly there is a reference in both to love and death, but the keynote of one "Not I myself," etc., is a very special and quite individual theme, and I cannot see that the word "Glass" occurring in the title of the one and the body of the other is worth thinking about. What possible resemblance there can be between either of the other two and any former sonnet of mine I cannot conceive, though you seem to include these partially, if not so strongly, in the same objection. Moreover, Scotus, some of your verbal *cruces* remain quite dark to me. What particular fault can be found in the line "All shafts of shelterless, tumultuous day" I endeavour to trace but fail entirely; also to discover the weak point in the last word of "Cloud confines," which is "still." Can it be that you think it might seem ambiguous with its synonym meaning *quiet*? Surely not. Your remarks on the sunset poem baffled me too—moreover I seem to trace in the charge of being "fantastic" a covert form of the insidious "quaint." There, Scotus!! As for "Commandments," the three verses came into my head during a walk, and I think of carrying it further probably, only such like verses do not interest me much. I wish I could get some serious verse-writing done here, but begin to see that I shall not. In fact I cannot carry it on with painting to do also, at any rate not unless I am quite alone; and I had some painting task-work to do, and have set about a little not task-work also ; and these have kept me from the other Muse, who, I believe, after all is my true mistress. I am painting a little portrait of Janey for a beautiful old frame I have, and am getting into the background the leading features of Kelmscott, —the house, the picturesque old church, and the riverbanks. I think it will be pretty. I have made chalk-drawings, too, of the kids and of their mamma.

I am sorry you do not seem to see your way quite clearly about the Nativity at the old barn, but hope you will yet drop into it. I think you ought to do some painting again, for your own satisfaction above all, for I am sure when one has once got used to brush-work one cannot, somehow, do without it. I hope Miss Boyd is also at something, for I feel sure that her last efforts show great advance, and believe her to possess at least as much power in painting as any woman I know—even the best. Brown wrote to me from the Dark Blue for a poem which he was to illustrate, and I sent him that "Holmscote" thing now called "Down Stream," which removes your just objection to title.

The Stillmans are back and have brought me a Yankee Polly. Tell me if you want your loans (Mags. and Belgian book) back at once. With love—Yours,

D. G. R.

I hope all this palaver doesn't look as if I did not value your opinion, which I assure you I set great store by, and only call in question because it sets me thinking.

### D. G. R. to W. B. S. (VII.)

DEAR SCOTUS—Your three Burns Sonnets[1] are such as only yourself could produce, in their tension of relishing reality with an effortless command of thought. I have no doubt they are the very best things ever written about Burns in verse, or in any prose but Carlyle's. The first yields perhaps a little too much to momentary mood

---

[1] The sonnets are given later on, p. 164.

in its octave section, seeming a little hard to identify or localise, fresh and fine as it is. The last line of Sonnet I. *must*, I think, be altered. "I ween" is almost always a makeshift and moreover is essentially the same rhyme as "between." If the rest of the line remains as it is "now ours" will not do, will it, for sound? "Made ours" might mend it perhaps. In II. the first line of the sextet seems to have a sing-song quality by the placing of the words "tares" and "years"; the same is the case with the tallying sound of the first halves of lines 11 and 12; and surely the rhyme "man" and "one" will *not* do except Scottice—no pun meant! Might line 12 run—

"Die autumn-sounds, and lo! This man alone."

Not so forcible of course, but I fear me an unavoidable compromise. "Years" and "whirr," with their tallies come ill together as a combination of rhymes (of course I do not suppose them meant to rhyme with each other), but this it seems necessary to let be. Sonnet III. seems as satisfactory in form as in sense. I would only myself prefer the omission of the first "it" and the break in line 1; and in my copy there is an oversight in line 13, "beats" for "beat." I really think it will be a serious matter for regret if you do not go over everything you have by you carefully and bring out a volume again. I am sure it would be worth your while in every way. What a monstrous event is the rejection of *Lady Janet*!— but published in a volume it would take its place at once I have no doubt at all. I hope these three sonnets are to set you going again. What a very strange event seems the fall of Kilkerran occurring just in this little nook of time since my visit. I have often thought of it and the strange water-whirl near it.

. Brown is doing the cut for my verses, and I wanted him to come here (*en garçon*) for his background, but he seems not easy to move.

We did not expect to hear again from Morris till his return, as the steamer which took him brought the first letter we got on its passage back, and no other steamer would come thence till the one by which he will return— I believe about the 9th or 10th. However, a few days ago a letter did come (entrusted to some Danish merchantman sailing thence), and gave a very pleasant account, though not an elaborate one. He is enjoying himself thoroughly, finds the people so hospitable (when there are any) that his party has no lack of bearable provisions, and their rides consist of a cavalcade of no less than twenty-eight horses! Tent-sleeping they do not suffer from at all even in cold weather, as the cold is thoroughly excluded. He has seen all kinds of localities connected with the Sagas. He took sketching materials, but does not say if he has used them.

I have left no proper space to pulverise "criticasters" on behalf of my muse, so I will e'en leave her and them to their own respective devices. However, what do you think of this as a change in the last 4 lines of "Cloud Confines"?—

> Oh never from Thee to sever
> Who wast and shalt be and art.
> To throb at Thy heart for ever
> Yet never to know Thy heart.

Does this not seem as if it meant a personal God? I don't think it need do so.

I've done no more verses (hardly) except to begin a long ballad about a Magic Crystal—but I don't know when I may get it done.

My best love to Miss Boyd as well as to yourself. The Woodchuck has the same but (at Chelsea) wots not of it. Stillman, I hear, has brought me a green parrot.—Ever yours,  D. G. R.

### D. G. R. to W. B. S. (VIII.)

DEAREST SCOTUS—"Cloud Confines" again! One's "I" is obtrusive enough in *this* world at any rate.

I don't go with your objection to the wind-up as contradictory. It is *meant* as the possible answer to the question. I cannot suppose that any particle of life is *extinguished*, though its permanent individuality may be more than questionable. Absorption is not annihilation; and it is even a real retributive future for the special atom of life to be re-embodied (if so it were) in a world which its own former ideality had helped to fashion for pain or pleasure. Such is the theory conjectured here. But I believe I am of opinion with you, perhaps, that it is best not to try to squeeze the expression of it into so small a space, but rather to leave the question quite unanswered. When I sent you the change, however, it was a thought of the moment, and I have since made it fit better :—as thus—

(Last *five* lines.)

And what must our birthright be?
Oh, never from thee to sever,
Thou Will that shalt be and art,
To throb at thy heart for ever,
Yet never to know thy heart.

However, I now incline to reject this and adopt the other plan, only to wind up with the old refrain would hardly be either valuable or artistic. I should propose to end thus—

What words to say as we go?
What thoughts to think by the way?
What truth may there be to know?
And shall we know it one day?

Now about your Burns Sonnets.

I think your new last lines to Sonnet II. a great improvement, and of course much better than my suggestion, which, I said, was but a poor one. However, you've not removed the "eyes" and "dies," making a false rhyme at equal intervals—a great defect always, I think. Suppose we say "fails" for "dies." Since I wrote you last, a change for the first lines of Sonnet I. has occurred to me, which seems helpful in clearness, though it is rather venturesome to give it you. However, take it for what it may be worth—

"Out of the road, you ploughman clad in gray,
With hosen knitted by your mother's hand!"
(Methinks I hear some magnates of the land,)
"Stand from our carriage-wheels, you stop the way!"
Awed is he? etc.

*P.S.*—If you want to make Sonnet I. perfect, here I come bothering again. The form of apostrophe adopted seems too long in sequence, and rather inconsequent to the ear, though not in reality.

To me it would seem better if it merely said—

He keeps his happy way on foot between, etc.

Cheeky all this, but never mind!

*P.P.* etc. *S.*!
I almost forgot something.

The *Daily Telegraph* (!) has put a notion in my head, by an article on lithography. I should like to try and lithograph myself that big picture of mine, and see if one could make anything fit for publication, and what would come of it. I mean on the scale and style somewhat of the French organ-player subject. If one could do something of this sort with one's inventions (much the best quality I have as a painter) one might really get one's brain into print before one died, like Albert Dürer, and moreover be freed perhaps from slavery to "patrons" while one lived.

I fancy such a thing might be possible to my eyes if I could do it, but I always hear lithography cannot be done in England because of the climate or something or other. Do you know anything about it, or what is the best firm for printing such things?

### D. G. R. to W. B. S. (IX.)

KELMSCOTT, 15*th September* 1871.

DEAREST W. B.—I hope I shan't disgust you by saying that I miss the spirited start of Sonnet I. in your present version, though, of course, it elucidates the sense.

Moreover, the first line now seems of a Browningian ruggedness rather, and suggests a very rutty carriage-road. Also (alas!) I miss the original plan of bringing Burns and ourselves in contact in the last line. This seems a great loss.

Morris only stayed a few days here, but is coming back. He has kept a diary in Iceland, but not for publication, and his stories (as far as I have heard) are not so funny as I hoped. The best is to the effect that Faulkner and Magnusson, at one hospitable mansion which they visited, had their breeches deferentially removed by the lady of the house on retiring to refresh themselves and prepare for dinner! Of this national custom they had heard before starting, but it was only actually observed on this occasion. I do not know how Morris escaped, and he was silent on that point; but I should think most likely the evident imminence of a defensive bootjack flying through the air may have caused his kind hostess to think twice about this time-honoured tradition in his case. He seems to have been much the best traveller of the four, though he declares now that he feels no yearning towards a second experience of the same kind. One day he was here he went for a day's fishing in our punt, the chief result of which was a sketch I made, inscribed as follows:

> Enter Skald, moored in a punt,
> And Jacks and Tenches exeunt.

And this seemed to be the course of events.

My poem, "The Beryl Stone," has not a comic side, Scotus, or at least not an intentional one; indeed it is so consumedly tragic that I have been obliged to modify the intended course of the catastrophe to avoid an unmanageable heaping up of the agony. I have made a complete prose version beforehand, and so get on with it easily, and shall finish, I hope, before leaving here. I hope it is a good thing, but there is so much incident that it is necessarily much more of a regular narrative poem than is usual with me, and thus lacks the incisive concentration of such a piece as "Sister Helen." I have had to make three Parts of it, though the whole will not, I hope, now exceed 150 five-line stanzas. I shall be glad to make it less if possible, as this, I think, should be the great aim of all poetry which has not absolutely epic proportions. Nor should these be undertaken at all if avoidable.

Your suggestion about chiaroscuro engraving is one I should like to talk over. Two things sent me by Norton from Italy, and which I have stuck on my bedroom wall here, are, I think, of that class, done some hundred years ago perhaps. They are from Veronese and Tintoret, painters whom I have got to think simply detestable without their colour and handling. The Veronese is by an engraver named Jackson; the Tintoret I suppose to be Italian. I presume the line part in such work is wood-engraving, is it not? This at once calls in a hand not one's own, and I must confess the general effect seems to me wanting in depth and colour, though it might conceivably include both perhaps.

I am delighted to hear of the progress of the Nativity subject, from which I shall expect real results, and surprised to hear that the Burns picture has actually been accomplished. Howell is at Northend, I believe, and has actually got his *father* with him at last, as I hear! The Tademas will be lucky if they get the "Rainy Day," which, however, is rather an ominous wedding-present. The *Portfolio* you asked after is not worth sending, I think. With love to Miss Boyd, of whose work you tell me not, I am ever yours, D. G. R.

*P.S.*—Discontent again! I think the "and" before "lo!" in line 12, Sonnet II., is wanted. Could it not run:

Of stream and hoppers hushed; and lo! this one, etc.?

In this letter we hear of his getting well on with his longest mystical poem, "The Beryl Stone," which, however, he does not send me any portion of; in fact he never showed an incomplete work in poetry.

It is to be observed that he has made a *complete prose version* beforehand, a plan that he now began to practise, to the ruin of his impulse and invention. The subject "Orchard Pits," which he had planned before his departure from Penkill, and which I saw reason to think would have turned out his finest imaginative Ballad Poem, was ruined by his making a similar prose version. This being done had the effect of crippling his powers. The instant I read this preliminary piece of work, I felt the poem itself would never follow.

His idea of chiaroscuro prints was never tried. The things he mentions as being sent him by a Mr. Norton from Italy were detestable performances : attempts to revive the ancient chiaroscuros by early Germans and Italians, Da Carpi and many others, who, being themselves great artists, made admirable prints in a wild rough style of effect. All these I had among my collection, and still have many ; but Jackson was a very poor artist and his works are base. He tried his revival towards the middle of last century, and had some influence in rendering printed wall-papers the rival of stamped leather as interior humble decoration.

D. G. R. to W. B. S. (X.)

KELMSCOTT, *Friday* (1871).

DEAR SCOTUS—I have two only pieces of news I think ; let the worst come first.

Obiit Woodchuck

I have really felt very sad about him, poor dear.[1] Don't ask details of his decease, for I know none.

I really forget whether you or I be the epistolary debtor, but this news had to be told. The other news is that I have finished "Rose Mary," my magic poem—three parts making 160 stanzas. I hope it's a good 'un. It's no good thinking of sending it you, being too long to copy, and I want the one I have—moreover, shouldn't like to risk loss. It ought to have been done at Penkill, however, being a sort of Scotch or Border story. I found I could make it nothing else, though on this account I avoided setting about the long-delayed "Orchard Pits." I should like to do that and another now as soon as may be—and then with smaller things might perhaps make a fair volume again.

A brother Yankee sent me a queer account of Miller the other day cut from a New York paper. He seems to be known in the newspaper parlance as *The Wild Byron of the Untrammelled Plains.*—Perhaps there's a deal of lying about him.

I shall have to get back soon now, with less painting done than I hoped, as the poem clawed hold of me and had to be done. I hope your picture gets on.

Let's have a line from you. You're owing it now, whether or not you were before.—Ever yours,

D. G. R.

Hüffer has come to be our neighbour at 11 Cheyne Walk. He wrote me that a Tauchnitz volume of my things is to appear.

### D. G. R. to W. B. S. (XI.)

*Monday (2nd October* 1871).

Here comes my last Kelmscott letter, Scotus, and I'm blowed if I haven't been a better correspondent than

---

[1] The Woodchuck was one of the many favourites D. G. R. indulged in keeping. It was a curious creature; and should have lived for ever if the servants in his absence had attended to it.

you have—though I daresay I've done as much work too. I'm glad to hear you've got the barn painted, but view the proposal to leave it as barn simple, as a base one after my liberality in bestowing that splendid subject on you.

I fancy I shall be in town certainly before you, though I can't say exactly what day I leave here. They are all at Euston Square again, and Wm.'s news of Christina is that she is now much in her average state of health and spirits.

Morris has been here twice since his return, viz. for a few days at first, and just now for a week again. He is now back in London, and this place will be empty of all inmates by the end of this week, I think. M. has set to work with a will on a sort of masque called "Love is Enough," which he means to print as a moderate quarto, with woodcuts by Ned Jones and borders by himself, some of which he has done really very beautifully.

The poem is, I think, at a higher point of execution perhaps than anything that he has done—having a passionate lyric quality such as one found in his earliest work, and of course much more mature balance in carrying out. It will be a very fine work.

Of course I'm leaving here just as I was getting into the poetic groove, and I know were I to stay I should have a volume ready by the end of another three months. But it may not be. My title of "Rose Mary" is a compounded name, dedicatory to the Virgin, quite possible enough and useful to my scheme. The poem is much more plain-sailing narrative, I think, than any of mine hitherto; but one must not forget that when Browning finished "Sordello," he wrote to his friends from Italy that now at any rate he had done something which his worst enemies could not call obscure.

I see by advertisements I figure as the first victim in a series (I presume) under the title of the "Fleshly School of Poetry"[1] in the *Contemporary Review* for October, but

---

[1] This was the first notice of the blow that nearly lost him his life. Byron's impudent couplet—

haven't seen it yet. Brown's drawing to my verses (stanza 1) in the *Dark Blue* is a very fine one, I think—two indeed there are, and the minor one (stanza 4) also is very nice.—You ask me about America. My vol. was printed there at once, and I received through the publishers many reviews—some enthusiastic, others sulky or disparaging. All the author's percentage they have sent me is a beggarly £20,[1] and I don't believe the thing has had a popular success there.

Did you see in the *Pall Mall Gazette* a letter about a Communalist Benevolent Society in London? It interested me, as they seem really, poor fellows, to be helping each other in a very bad plight, and I sent a subscription to Colvin, asking him to get it conveyed through the *Pall Mall*, but have not heard from him. Poor old Courbet's escape was satisfactory, though after all it seems probable he may be stripped of all he possesses, being the only one, it seems, with any money to meet the joint liability of the prisoners for their expenses. It put me in a great rage all along to see the contempt with which this really meritorious man was treated by the press, as contrasted with the excitement about everything concerning so paltry an adventurer as * * *

I have read several of Scott's novels here, and been surprised both at their usual melodramatic absurdities of plot and their astounding command of character in the personages by whom all these improbabilities are enacted.

---

Strange that the soul, that very fiery particle,
Should let itself be snuffed out by an article

has been entirely denied as applied to Keats. There can be no doubt of its truth applied to D. G. R. He was saved from immediate death by Professor Marshall, but he never recovered his mental balance, even such as it had been for many years before.

[1] This puts me in mind of Emerson's answer, when I asked him on his last visit to England (he called twice on me at Chelsea) why the Americans had not taken to Rossetti as a poet. His answer included Christina's poetry as well, and showed the keenness of his critical incision. "Yes; we scarcely take to the Rossetti poetry; it does not come home to us; it is exotic; but we like Christina's religious pieces."

The novels are wonderful works with all their faults. *Guy Mannering* and *St. Ronan's Well*—neither of which I knew before—delighted me extremely. Another I read is the *Fair Maid of Perth*, which is on a level with the Victoria Drama in some respects, but in some points of conception and vivid reality in parts can only be compared to the greatest imaginative works existing.

I am sorry Miss Boyd is not to return with you, as it will thus be some time before we benefit by the society of Hüffer, Boyce, or our old friend Tacitus. Will you give her my love and believe me your affectionate

GABRIEL.

*P.S.*—I hear through William that the proposal to move our father's remains being negatived by my mother's objections, a memorial is to be erected to him in Santa Croce, Florence.

And so the one-sided correspondence ends. I may, however, make a finale by quoting a distich on his poor lost friend *the Woodchuck*, which I have somehow preserved, while losing the leaf of his last letter on which it must have been written. The title " Parted Love " is chaff directed to my Sonnets so called, which he held to the highest honour of any poems I had ever done.

### PARTED LOVE!

Oh, how the family affections combat
Within this heart, and each hour flings a bomb at
My burning soul ; neither from owl nor from bat
Can peace be to me now I've lost my Wombat!

But since I have given Rossetti's complimentary opinion as well as persevering criticism, showing both the fulness of his expression of friendly and favourable verdict, and his willingness to aid with advice, I think it necessary to give the reader the Sonnets about Burns themselves, that he may satisfy himself regarding the works calling forth so much notice from the author of such great performances as the "White Ship," and the "King's Tragedy."

### THREE SONNETS
#### ON VISITING BURNS'S COTTAGE AND MONUMENT

#### I

" You Ayrshire ploughman clad in homespun gray,
    And hosen knitted by your mother's hand—"
    (Methinks I hear some magnate of the land,
Loitering upon fashion's smooth highway),
" Step out and sing to pass our time away.
    We'll call thee Phœbus in his shepherd trim,
    Or eastern Bacchus with the wine in him.
Your song is done?  Good-night then, do not stay!"

But why now think of him except between
    The plough shafts, or with seed-corn in the spring,
Or by his native streams with loves unseen,
    Or where autumnal flowering hedgerows bring
    Odours and bees, and reaping lasses sing,
Whose brows now wear his myrtle ever green?

#### II

This is the cottage room as 'twas of old :
    The window four small panes, and in the wall
    The box-bed, where the first daylight did fall
Upon their new-born infant's narrow fold
And poor, when times were hard and winds were cold,

As they were still with him. Lo! now close by
Above Corinthian columns mounted high
The old Athenian Tripod shines in gold!

The lumbering carriages of these dull years
   Have passed away: their dust has ceased to whirr
About the footsore: silent to our ears
   Is that maelstrom of Scottish men; this son
Of all that age we count the kingliest one:
Such is Time's justice, Time the harvester.


### III

Could we but see the Future ere it comes,
   As gods must see effects in causes hid,—
   How calmly could we wait till we were bid!
Heroes would hear triumphal far-off drums,
   Would see fame's splendours ere the threads and
      thrums
Had formed it in to-morrow's living loom;
Would feel the honours round the marble tomb
   O'er the black fosse in which this life succumbs.

If it were so! but wiser fates take care
   That it is not so: passing mists and storm,
   The sunlight and the drifting clouds all form
A rent but triple veil 'gainst which the wings
Of crimson passion beat, a lock-fast gare,
Where, blinded nightingale, the poet sings.

It may be naturally asked why I did not print these three sonnets, which had received so much approbation from the greatest of our circle, and from others. The answer requires a little explanation. In my estimate of the poet's true mission in this

world, I hold that whatever he says should be the
vital truth in relation to the thing mentioned, man
or fact in story or nature, and I had come to the
conclusion that Burns's moral nature disqualified
him in my mind from receiving such eulogium.
Poetry without this absolutely critical sincerity and
truth may be beautiful, but its beauty is to me not
charming but offensive. It is as a Cyprian, to be
relegated to shores of Paphos and left there. At
this very time I had been engaged to edit the poetry
of the Ayrshire bard, to edit and illustrate, a task which
occupied a goodly share of study. This edition was
never published, although paid for by my publisher,
but it brought me into intimate correspondence with
Mr. Scott Douglas of Edinburgh, among others who
had dedicated themselves to the most elaborate and
careful examination of successive actions in the life
of the poet. Mr. Scott Douglas's subject was the
hitherto-considered lovely idyll of the swearing fealty
across the running stream, and giving Mary the
Bible with the same oath inscribed in it. By the
dates of various incidents and letters, Mr. Scott
Douglas established beyond doubt that Burns, immediately on Mary's leaving the neighbourhood to
visit her relatives before her expected marriage,
made up his old intimacy with Jean Armour. Had
Mary not died on her journey to meet him again,
she would have found his oath gone to the winds,
and Burns already married. The Bible may still be
seen in the Mausoleum at Dumfries, but with the
inscription carefully pasted over by the family of the

girl. This discovery with all its possibilities of treachery so disgusted me that I threw the sonnets aside; only converting the last of the three into a celebration of Keats, who died with the belief that he had written in water![1]

[1] [Sonnet II., however, was published in *The Poet's Harvest Home*, 1882, among the sonnets "Of Poets," p. 125.—ED.]

# CHAPTER X

1872—ROSSETTI'S ILLNESS—STOBHALL

OCTOBER of 1871 having begun and ended, all of us had returned to Cheyne Walk. D. G. R.'s vigour in all things, painting, poetry, and letter-writing—the tone of the latter showing a healthy elasticity—he had left never to find again. We recommenced our whist, sometimes with Boyce or Hüffer, and sometimes by ourselves with our classical friend Quartus Tacitus, but the article in the *Contemporary*, referred to in his last letter, was to him like a slow poison, till at last he could not follow the game, and used to throw down his cards.

A few words about ourselves. Miss Boyd had become heiress to a large share in a vast ironwork, and to a considerable share in the Tyne Main coal-mine. One of these great commercial undertakings became overhead in debt, cut out by other better-located iron companies, when none of them were very remunerative, and the water came into the Tyne Main pit! Whether the ancient family place would be lost to her was hanging in the balance, yet she showed no anxiety, but, like a heroine determined to meet her fate without closing her eyes, she waited the end, which was not so serious as it threatened to be. She had found, too, after her brother's death, that Penkill was mortgaged! I mention these things, which are not properly within the compact with myself in writing these notes, just to show the contrast in the trio thus meeting together in the attempt to make life pass pleasantly. One a lady able to bear herself equably on the verge of what she felt to be the greatest misfortune possible to befall her affairs; another, the man thought by his world (myself among the number) one of the greatest geniuses of the age, visibly breaking down under the paltry infliction of "an article." The third, an old boy, making himself contented at last to be a *pictor ignotus*, a *poet without recognition*, during the span-long time of his journey in the world; supported, it may be, by the belief that sooner or later, somehow or other, we all get some part of our deserts, and if we do not it matters little. I was, indeed, haunted by the consciousness of having missed my mark by following "all things by starts, and nothing long" —a habit that had become necessary to me; it was ruinous to me, in one way, but my salvation in another, assisting me in keeping up a naturally defective interest in life, and filling every moment with more than its due weight of occupation, my most efficient means of preventing the recurrent attacks of a species of nervous despair. This mental disease, although not mentioned before as far as I remember, had been all my life one of my most perplexing and dangerous enemies. I had gradually outlived it; and now, much the oldest of the three, I was able to sympathise with and to assist both.

Sir Henry Cole had committed to my hands a scheme for decorating the staircases to the two doors of the lecture theatre at the Museum of South Kensington. Had this been carried out it would, I believe, have affirmed my position in art, but the increase of the Museum made the accumulation of new objects swarm even up the staircases; at least the fear of that delayed the work till funds had to be otherwise applied. The drawings in small were deposited in the archives of the Museum, but here is a tracing of my design for one of the doors, representing The Genius of Art recording names in a *Libro d'Oro*, and on the pilasters on either side the apple boughs of Knowledge, with the serpent round the stems, modelled and cast in metal. Among the literary work of the passing day I wrote a Christmas book on the Venetian School, and one on the Spanish, which Sir W. Stirling Maxwell kindly read over in proofs. Others followed, on *English Sculptors*; *English Landscape Painters*; *Italian Masters, Lesser and Greater*, etc. These were better than they deserved to be, and only made me feel that I was throwing my time away, and was in danger of looking like a literary hack; so I did no more. When the scheme for paintings on the staircases collapsed, I said to Sir Henry

Cole how much I regretted the failure, adding that my *chances* somehow were always withdrawn. " Oh, we make our own chances," was his reply, which I have never forgotten, so true and yet so delusive, temperament having so much command over us. For myself the bias natural to me is to somnambulate, not to act; never to play first fiddle, rather to pay him; to reflect mainly, and to absorb amusement from my surroundings and friends.

At last midsummer of 1872 was drawing on. Æ. had left us for Penkill, and I was looking forward to following her. One day I had some friends to dinner; ten used to be my number, two or three times in the season before leaving town. On this particular day one of the friends was D. G. R.; we were loitering about the drawing-room waiting for the latest man, who was Gabriel himself. At last we heard a tremendous peal at the bell, and knocking, a great noise ascended the stair, and he burst in upon us, shouting out the name of Robert Buchanan, who, it appeared, he had discovered to be the writer of the article in the *Contemporary Review* which was so distracting him. He was too excited to observe or to care who were present, and all the evening he continued unable to contain himself, or to avoid shouting out the name of his enemy. I was glad when the sitting came to an end, and one after another left with a private word of inquiry regarding Rossetti. From this time he occupied himself in composing a long reply, which he read over a hundred times, till the lives of his friends became too heavy to bear. But in a very few weeks the crisis came.

One morning at an early hour W. M. R. came along to me—now living at hand, at No. 92—in a desponding state of mind. He wished me to accompany him at once. Swallowing a cup of tea, we hurried to No. 16, and found our friend in a condition painful to witness. Professor Marshall, and Dr. Hake, whose verses Rossetti had so admired and assisted—now doctoring his doctor in another art—were there, and agreed that the patient must change his surroundings. Where was he to go? Dr. Hake answered that question by offering to take him out with him to his house at Roehampton. A cab was brought at once; we all thought it strange to see him so willing to go, but that night it was too evident he wanted to be secluded, and for three days he lay as one dead, and only by a treatment, invented for the moment by Professor Marshall, was he cured. But as I was only at Roehampton on one visit, not to him, but to William, who was made seriously ill by his brother's state, it does not fall to me to give any further account of my friend's sad condition, till it was determined that he was not to return to Chelsea, but that a further change of scene would be necessary, and I volunteered to be a second with young George Hake, to take charge of him. His new retirement was to be far off, at Stobhall, near Perth, the shooting and fishing quarters of William Graham, M.P. for Glasgow, his most efficient

friend, and the greatest admirer of his art. Brown and George Hake took him down, and when I was free to leave town, just two days after, I released the former and stayed with him there for three long weeks.

The place where we lived, Stobhall, by the Tay near Perth, was, two centuries ago, one of the houses of the ancient family of the Drummonds, the head of which, the Duke of Perth, as the Jacobites called him, lost everything in the rebellion of 1715. It was originally a peel tower with a very uncommon appendage, a chapel of the same early date as the tower; and now it had one of the most charming old gardens I have ever seen, with Irish yews and hollies, trained by long years of careful shaping into straight columns 25 feet high, and roses almost reaching to the same height supported on poles. The part we lived in was more modern, but some of the small rooms in the early portion of the house were lovely in their rude but pure style. I painted a water-colour picture of the garden, and here is a sketch of a primitive fireplace, dated 1578, and recessed window in a small room. The chapel, I considered on careful examination, had been the earliest portion of the building. There is no other example of a *peel* or defensible square tower, incorporated with which is a chapel, and in this case the chapel occupies the ground, and the house has been built partly over it. After a time, the larger dwelling-house in which we lived, with its gateway and causewayed courtyard, had been added.

Of our lives these melancholy weeks I shall say little. He could not take much walking exercise, a partial lameness or paralysis of one side having resulted from the days of unconsciousness during which he had remained rigidly in one constrained position. He could not bear reading, nor would he join us in the old game. From all the letters I wrote at that time I make no extract. I have not hitherto used my own letters, the few I have access to, in this writing, and shall not do so now; it would be too painful; although, indeed, I cannot help feeling that his malady was unique—different from other maladies, as he himself was different from other men. His delusions had a fascination, like his personality.

Meanwhile his brother William had been so prostrated by anxiety, loving Gabriel much and fearing him not a little, that F. M. Brown took all business matters out of his hand. Gabriel's affairs were alarmingly out of order, and it was thought proper to have all his pictures, finished or in progress, removed elsewhere. They were accordingly taken to my house, which was conveniently near, among them the large "Dante's Dream." The blue china which he had collected, partially but very inadequately accounting for the exhaustion of his exchequer, was precipitately sold. This æsthetic passion, which would have excited the laughter of any other poet, except the most artificial man of the Hôtel Rambouillet, if such gentlemen of the full-bottomed wig and the clouded cane can be called poets, was still so strong upon him that when in a few months his amazing power of resuscitation brought him back to health, the loss of this china appeared to trouble him more than anything else! Perhaps it might be that the disposal, without his knowledge, of this assemblage of pots and dishes proved to him how ill he had been, as he still continued to assert that *we* were under delusions and not he himself, as to the number of his enemies, and it was difficult to make him own he had been ill at all.

I have spoken of the amazing bodily power of recovery our friend showed; week by week the cloud rose, and towards the end of September he insisted on leaving Scotland, and returning, not to Penkill, whither Miss Boyd had invited him, but to Kelmscott, which at that moment he could have all to himself.

From there he wrote to me in the beginning of October. "Here I am, as well as ever I was in my life. I passed the greater part of yesterday with my mother and sisters at Euston Square, and came on here to-day. Even my lameness seems a little better the last few days, and my voice is itself again. Your character as a correspondent is entirely gone. Are you ever going to give me news of yourself again? If I wanted to get possession of the large 'Dante's Dream' picture, now at your house, how am I to do so?" This inquiry showed he had returned to painting again! And so it was: I visited him, and found him hard at work, as if no break in the continuity of his habits had taken place! Anxious for some medical news of him before I went to Kelmscott, I wrote to Dr. Hake, and he answered that he heard very often of Rossetti, directly or indirectly, and found every account satisfactory in a high degree. "The past seems to be dwindling into a dream, and I cannot doubt but that it recurs to our gifted friend only in that light, though he will, to avoid a painful avowal, never return to the subject with his friends, and it is best perhaps that it should be treated as forgotten. His mind appears now to be in a state of healthy activity as regards painting, but I doubt if he will resume literature for some time to come, his poetry having produced him so painful an experience."

I was at this time (as I have already said) much occupied on a new edition of Burns, both as editor and illustrator, and Mr. Scott Douglas of Edinburgh, kindly assisting me, among other things sent me an unpublished letter of Burns, so exuberant in its flowers of speech, I sent a copy to amuse Rossetti, fearing I should not be able to have it printed, and not being able at once to visit him. This letter of the Ayrshire poet's delighted him immensely. He replies: "Many thanks for this wonderful epistle!—to what Corinthian, Galatian, or other, seems not to be known. It is Burns himself for once, instead of Burns trying as usual in his letters to be Addison, Pope, or any one else. Is it really possible that such a document should not get into print? It stands out among the mass of his correspondence and should absolutely be in print. If you could only get a few more such letters, your edition would supersede all other editions." Then he goes on to notice all the news of our friends current at the day, just as he used to do before his illness! Colvin's success and F. M. Brown's unsuccess at the Cambridge election of the first Slade Fine Arts professorship, and his own extraordinary activity in painting, having begun his "Proserpine" five distinct times on five canvases, and having at last brought it nearly to a close, after infinite pains making it his "best picture." He has been reading *Vasari, Benvenuto Cellini*, and among new books *Salammbo*, "a mighty and altogether new kind of French abomination, very wonderful and unsufferable." Besides, he has got together all the necessary books for the purpose of translating and editing M. Angelo's poems, which he is to set about at once in the evenings.

Here is this astounding letter of Burns's with an alteration :

MAUCHLINE, 3*d March* 1788.

MY DEAR AINSLIE—I have been through sore tribulation and under much buffeting of the wicked one since I came to this country. Jean I found banished like a martyr—forlorn, destitute, and friendless—all for the good cause. I have reconciled her to her fate ; I have reconciled her to her mother ; I have taken her a room ; I have taken her in my arms ; I have given her a mahogany bed ; I have given her a guinea, and I have kissed her till she rejoiced with joy unspeakable and full of glory. But—as I always am on every occasion—I have been prudent and cautious to an astonishing degree. I swore her privately and solemnly never to attempt any claim upon me as a husband, even though anybody should try to persuade her she had such a claim, which she had not, either during my life or after my death. She did all this like a good girl, and I kissed her again with a thundering kiss. Oh, what a peacemaker that is! It is the Mediator, the Guarantee, the Umpire, the Bond of Union, the Solemn League and Covenant, the Plenipotentiary, the Aaron's Rod, the Jacob's Staff, the Prophet Elisha's Pot of Oil, the Philosopher's Stone, the Horn of Plenty, and the Tree of Life between man and woman.

To Mr. ROBERT AINSLIE, at Mr. S. MITCHELSON, W.S., CARUBBER'S CLOSE, EDINBURGH.

When I did get down to Rossetti at Kelmscott the change upon him was a metamorphosis; it was like a miracle! A few months ago he was paralysed on one side of his body, and entirely out of his mind; now he was perfectly well, painting better than ever, and talking with his old incision! Young George Hake was still his wakeful attendant, though little necessary, and his father, the doctor himself, developing "the ideal" in solitude in the room below at the rate of about two lines a day. From the clearing away of breakfast there he sat by the fire, a pencil in one hand and a folded piece of paper in the other. On the table near him lay a little heap of other pieces of paper, his failures at the improvement of the same couplet in various transformations, sometimes expressing quite different meanings. The old gentleman in the character of a poet had interested all of us. He had retired from medicine determined to cultivate poetry. And he was really accomplishing his object by perseverance and determined study, utterly pooh-poohing the maxim that if a man has not made a good poem at twenty-five he never will.

I was not sanguine in considering that my dear friend now looked back on his former state as dreams. They were still to him realities. But here I stop; perhaps, indeed, finishing all I shall have to say of him. The habit of taking chloral for insomnia—the origin of which or the time of its commencement I am ignorant of, but of which I observed nothing at Penkill in 1868 or 1869—is fondly credited with all his evils by some of his intimate friends. But these evils were in fitful activity very long ago, and were really the cause of his resorting to chloral—not the effect of that in any way.

On the 19th of April 1874 I received these words by post: "MY DEAR SCOTUS—I am likely to be needing £200 in a few days, and happen unluckily at this moment to be run rather dry. Could you manage to lend it me? and if so, to oblige me with a cheque at once?" Knowing his affairs to be prosperous at the time, I could not view this request with composure. He was living quietly at Kelmscott; but I came to the conclusion that it was my duty as his friend to keep his mind easy. Accordingly by next post the cheque was despatched. By next again it came back to me in a note, saying he had "just received some money, and he returned my cheque no less thankfully than if he had needed it." He had by that time lost nearly every old friend save myself; did he now suspect that I was among his enemies, and had he done this to try me? I fear this semi-insane motive was the true one.

A very short time after he suddenly left Kelmscott for altogether, having got into a foundationless quarrel with some anglers by the river, unnecessary to describe. He sent for me. I found him quiet and taciturn; he only said the change would do him good. From that time till now that I write this he has lived within the house, never going even into the street, never seeing any one. Holman Hunt, Woolner, and other artists had left him long ago; now Swinburne and Morris were not to be seen there. Even Dr. Hake deserted him, feeling aggrieved by his patient and long-suffering son George having been driven away after several years' sacrifice. The old doctor would see him no more. Before his worst attack, a few days before Hake took him out to his house at Roehampton, Browning had sent him *Fifine at the Fair*, which obscure performance greatly aggravated Rossetti's state of mind; he believed it was entirely written about him, and against him, all the innuendoes and insinuations being aimed at him! Browning, as his manner was, had never acknowledged Rossetti's presentation copy of his poems, and now this confirmed him to be among the enemies. What did the book mean if it did not mean what Rossetti said? And in truth none of us could say at once what *Fifine at the Fair* did mean! Only two quite new men were now to be seen about him: one was William Sharp, a poet to be; the other Theodore Watts, who, being professionally a lawyer, managed everything for him, and who was just then beginning to write criticisms in the weekly papers, so was

looked upon by poor D. G. R. as doubly important.
Happily Watts has been invaluable since then in
many ways: fascinated by Rossetti, ill as he was, and
always ready and able to serve him. For myself,
Rossetti had been the last of a succession of men I
had loved and tried to make love me; for each of
them I could have given all but life, and I was
again defeated by destiny. Equal candour and
confidence he never had to give, but now his singular
manias made ordinary friendly intercourse impossible
to him. After having been both his banker and his
nurse I could not depend upon him either in action
or word. Still I remained faithful to the old tie,
and Miss Boyd agreed in doing so also. We continued our occasional visits, either morning or evening, the only two of all his old circle.

# CHAPTER XI

1873—MY LAST VISIT TO ITALY—DR. FRANZ HUEFFER
—F. M. BROWN

By 1873 our permanent settlement at Chelsea had attained to a tolerably perfect state of furnishing, and in that year I was for the first time appointed to assist in the examination of the annual works of Schools of Art at South Kensington. William Rossetti had recovered his composure of mind; all seemed settled into serenity. It was the time for a long holiday. William and I arranged for a visit to Rome by Genoa and Pisa, to take with us Miss Boyd (who had overcome the danger of having to part with her family place) and my wife. Neither of the ladies had hitherto been across the Alps. We proposed to go by Pisa, and return by Venice and St. Gothard. At the last moment F. M. Brown's daughter Lucy was added to our party, and our expedition had a pleasant sequel in a wedding celebrated soon after our return.

F. M. Brown was one of the few men of genius I knew, and I may here record some particulars of another addition to his family circle. To do this I must go back a year or two and introduce an amiable and a very charming man with all the talents of the *élite* of his native country Germany, who appeared just then in Brown's circle; universally learned and able in languages, yet unpretentious, and even regretting the ability to think in several tongues as a disadvantage, the habit being a distraction to a literary composer. He had also some of the defects of the German nature, at least as we think of it. With the determination of critical thoroughness he was lazy beyond any one I had ever known. Franz Hueffer was a youth of twenty-five, but being unseasonably stout and unseasonably bald, he looked like double his age; and when he made love to Brown's second and handsome daughter Cathy, who was in mind as well as body like a child, there seemed a little discrepancy in the intended union. However, he persevered, and feeling that he should have a profession he began his literary career. I tried to help him through my friend, Mr. William Longman. But he could not settle himself to the continuous hard work of writing a book; his mind was too much in suspense, and he became the most fidgety of white elephants.

Yet it happened that at that moment he rushed in upon me visibly in the happiest frame of mind, reporting that he had got an offer of a kind quite to his mind in his then happy state—an offer quite to his taste, which was this: he was to have £150 a year for doing nothing! His knowledge of both classic and modern languages was coming good to him; it had helped him to this! though, alas! it did not help him to an understanding of London literary life or business. I found on inquiry that he had been offered a directorship in the management of a new company. A number of literary men had bought the plant of a great printing-office, and formed themselves into a board of directors, with salaries of the sum named, and had invited him to join them, only he must sign the deed of transfer. I advised him to examine the whole matter first, but he repudiated that troublesome preliminary. They wanted some other good names on their prospectus; would I join?

I agreed at once; we sallied out to make inquiries. We went first to the great printing-office, which we found shut up under sequestration of bankruptcy; then to my bank, finding it to be the same named on their printed circular, which I produced to the manager. Here I found the new company had been warned not to use the name of the bank till further proof of validity! "Now," said I to him, "let's go to the meeting (the meeting whereat the deed of transfer was to be signed) if you are not yet satisfied." Thither we went, to find the men who were to have £150 a year for doing nothing anxiously waiting in the empty office of a solicitor in Chancery Lane. I could scarcely believe my senses when I saw Hueffer taking the pen in hand to sign; however, I immediately took the odious duty of reporting where we had been, and what we had seen and heard, and got him away. Even then he was inclined to continue in the delusion that I had stood in his way to fortune.

I left to go down to Stobhall to take charge of my sick friend when his wedding came off. Here is the intimation of the happy occasion :

FAIR LAWN, LOWER MERTON,<br>
30th August 1872.

MY DEAR SCOTUS—The above legend, simple as it may appear to the eye at first glance, is for me the symbol of a sea of past troubles and tribulations. I daresay you know what it is to hunt after a house for more than a fortnight, and afterwards to furnish it ; but you are luckily unaware of the unmitigated misery this idea conveys to a man who hitherto has not cared to know the difference between one piece of furniture and another. However! I have at last got landed in a delightful little cottage surrounded by countrified simplicities, and I hope the spare bedroom—which, by the way, has a delightful view—will soon shelter the illustrious sage, poet, and painter. What a pity you can't come to the wedding, my dearest Scotus. I shall miss you tremendously, as I have always considered you as my dearest friend.

So I am going to be "spliced" next Tuesday, and offer my bachelor liberty on the shrine of matrimony, as they say. I wonder what this clerical operation will feel like, which is to open the gates of happiness for life. Upon the whole, I am mystified, and much more happy and contented than Schopenhauer would approve of. But I still see distinctly that the grand foundation of matrimonial happiness is the principle of keeping the pot boiling, and with that view have enclosed the accompanying letter [here follow some business particulars]. Goodbye, dear Scotus. With kind regards to the fair chatelaine of Penkill, —I am ever your devoted friend, F. HUEFFER.

A little while after his honeymoon—only four months after our escape from getting £150 a year for doing nothing—reading the *Daily News* one idle morning, I fortunately observed the names of the directors of the proposed company we had met at that seductive gathering in Chancery Lane, in the police reports. It was a case of a dozen starving compositors and pressmen having the board of directors of a new printing company before the Marylebone magistrate for non-payment of wages! What made it more perfect was that the sitting magistrate asked the lawyer for an explanation. "Is it," he asked, "that these directors divide the profits among themselves?" whereon the attorney answered "that he could assure his honour that not one of the directors had received a penny!" I posted the paper to my friend Hueffer, with some chaff and a little advice, and here is his acknowledgment in the same spirit. At the same moment I received a letter from the Secretary of the Newcastle Literary Society, complaining that he had never answered an invitation to lecture there!

DEAREST SCOTUS—You have actually managed to bring forward in the three pages of your letter three distinct charges against poor me—(1) Imprudence ; (2) Unpunctuality ; (3) Neglect in answering letter. Your mixing up with this broth of defamation a monstrous amount of self-praise is, of course, in keeping with the tone of your letter, and your character in general, is it not? I have succeeded in cramming the essence of my indignation into the following verses, which I hope will silence you for some time to come :

> There's a grumpy old Scotchman called Bell Scott,
> Who deserves to be roasting in hell's cot,

> So he would be, forsooth,
> But for Lucifer's tooth,
> Which shuns the tough morsel of Bell Scott.

Perhaps you will think I have been assisted by some printer's devil of the "*London Printing and Publishing Company*," especially as I still send kindest regards. Even under the blast of your satire—Your "blooming shrub,"

F. H.

I enjoyed this fun of his, and asked him to dine with us on Christmas Day. In answer to the invitation arrived the following:

DEAREST SCOTUS—Ever so sorry we can't come and share your Christmas pudding, but the fact is, we have been engaged for a long time to eat our dinner *en famille*. Many thanks, also, for your forgiveness for my energetic utterances regarding his hellish majesty's dental faculties. I now subjoin another rhyme, which imperfectly expresses my later feelings:

> There's a darling old Scotchman called Scotus,
> Who, when fear and repentance had smote us,
>     Has nobly forgiven—
>     Sure he would be in heaven,
> But that earth cannot spare that dear Scotus.

The habit of making satirical rhymes like these was an outcome of the appearance of Lear's *Book of Nonsense*. D. G. R. began the habit with us, the difficulty of finding a rhyme for the name being often the sole inducement. Swinburne assisted him and all of us; and every day for a year or two they used to fly about. The dearest friends and most intimate acquaintances came in for the severest treatment; but as truth was the last thing intended—though sometimes slyly implied—nobody minded. Of course

I came in for a few. When I at once lost all my hair after a severe illness, he began one :

> There's that foolish old Scotchman called Scott,
> Who thinks he has hair, but has not.

Another about me has some sense in it; indeed I adopted the second line in beginning to write these notes, now extended to so many pages :

> There's a foolish old Scotchman called Scotus,
> Most justly a *Pictor ignotus*,
>  For what he best knew
>  He never would do,
> This stubborn donkey called Scotus.

This I revenged by the following on Gabriel himself :

> There's a painter his friends call G———,
> Whose pictures the public ne'er see ;
>  If you want to know why,
>  It's because he's so shy
> To show how funny they be.

The allusion to his determination never to exhibit did not please him ; but he made one on himself severe enough :

> There is a poor sneak called Rossetti,
> As a painter with many kicks met he—
>  With more as a man—
>  But sometimes he ran,
> And that saved the rump of Rossetti.

Here is one on our dear learned friend Hüffer, using a jocular pronunciation of the name current in our circle, which at last made him write his name Hueffer :

> There's a solid fat German called Hueffer,
> Who at anything funny's a duffer:
>     To proclaim Schopenhauer
>     From the top of a tower
> Will be the last effort of Hueffer.

One of the cleverest I remember was the following:

> There's the Irishman Arthur O'Shaughnessy,
> On the checkboard of poets a pawn is he,
>     Though bishop or king
>     Would be rather the thing
> To the fancy of Arthur O'Shaughnessy.

My notice of our dear friend Franz Hueffer has led me into a vortex of the nonsense verses of that day which used to afford us much amusement at that time, and so into a digression. But, indeed, my whole manuscript is digressive, and sometimes far from progressive.

To return to the family of Ford Madox Brown, of whom Hueffer was now a member. F. M. B. was one of the highest thinkers among the English artists, and one of the ablest painters; he was, in spite of singular caprices, one of the leaders of the new school, and one much beloved by many of us. Much beloved by all within the charmed circle of the P.R.B., he was respected by all artists, and by the world at large, holding a high character, which, however, never brought him fortune nor even fame. I have already given D. G. R.'s account of his first introduction to Madox, the beginning of a life-long friendship; but to make the reader understand further what manner of man he was, and why he was so late in life before taking the position in the art-world to which his powers entitled him, I shall relate another anecdote which comes into my memory at this moment. In doing so I am far from laughing at my friend, and indeed am conscious that I myself might be accused of very similar absurdities in moments of anger. Be that as it may, the anecdote was funny enough at the time.

Mr. Cole, afterwards Sir Henry, was then finishing the central saloon of the S. K. Museum by filling the top niches with figures of great artists, including workmen deserving the distinction. Many of the artists employed were entirely unconnected with the department, and among others he invited Madox Brown to do one, selecting for him Julio Clovio the miniaturist. Calling on my own affairs a few days later, Mr. Cole asked if my friend Brown had gone out of his head. On my replying with some surprise, he placed in my hand a letter, which I saw immediately was in Brown's writing—the absurdest thing of its kind I had ever seen. To make its absurdity understood, I must premise that the vast Department correspondence was, and probably is, facilitated by the use of a certain size (foolscap) paper, having printed on the top corners, right and left, forms containing a number appropriated to the document, and other directions to the correspondents —all this being printed within ruled and ornamental square enclosures.

F. M. B. had looked at this half-printed folio,

and not finding it anything he understood at the first moment, became furious, read it wrong, and replied in a moment by cutting a piece out of an old drawing-sheet, making some grotesque scribbles in the top corners, which had struck Mr. Cole as examples of lunacy, filling the paper below with a refusal to do any such thing as celebrate any such fool as Julio Romano, and posted his reply at once.

I was most curious to unravel the mystery, and took care not to be very long before calling on F. M. B., who seemed quite in his usual frame of mind. "My dear fellow," I said, "why did you repudiate the invitation to do one of the cartoons for the Museum?" The explanation was just what I have given above, only he had mistaken the name, and thought they had selected for him, not Julio Clovio, but his pet hatred among Italian artists, who happened to be Julio Romano!

# CHAPTER XII

## THE RISING GENERATION IN POETRY, 1875

SEVERAL new persons have been introduced to my little drama in these latter pages; there are more to follow. Poetry was the speciality of them all. Poets in outward form are numerous nowadays, and the British Museum abounds with them, although verse-writing and publishing proclivities are peremptorily discouraged by the heads of the departments there. Twenty-five years ago I had met the single poet of the establishment, Coventry Patmore, and since then his single successor had been Richard Garnett. Now they were impatiently hiding their productions at every desk, poets with whom new *forms* were everything; French verses, rondels, and rondeaux being the perfect thing with them; imagination, knowledge of life, insight, and power of thought, the motive or sentiment, were very well, but not to be had, so not to be required. English heroic verse was presumed by them to be dead and buried; ballad quatrains, blank verse, and so forth, were all spoken of with contempt; and Tennyson's line in a lately-published poem noting the danger to our poetical literature from the "poisonous honey brought from France," was the subject of mild but endless humour among them.

The first of these to come in my way was E. W. Gosse, who introduced himself by a note so long ago as March 1870, on the publication of my *Life and Works of Albert Dürer*—a book good for the English public at the time, but now antiquated by the rapidly-developed Dürer literature in Germany, which has culminated in the thoroughly-studied *Memoirs* by Dr. Thausing. I had omitted to mention the pictures by Patinier, or rather never had observed them in the National Gallery, and my new correspondent pointed them out to me and asked me whom I thought they were by, as they had somewhat attracted him, and he remembered a picture with this painter's name attached to it in some gallery at Antwerp. He apologised for trespassing on my time, but would be glad to hear from me. This note, dated from Tottenham, associated itself in my mind with an individual of the same name and address who had bought a picture by me from the Hogarth Club. The note of my new correspondent had all the *aplomb* of an amateur of long standing intimate with obscure early masters. It flashed into my mind that here was my old friend turning up again, and that perhaps he might be a purchaser once more. I accordingly invited him to call upon me some day to inspect my Dürer's prints, of which I had already a formidable collection, and to talk over old German art. Instead of my former patron, the portly gentleman of middle life, who should appear but a boy of nineteen! We took to him, however.

The next of the British Museum poets who came within my ken was Theodore Marzials, who had indeed published a volume, which he called *The Gallery of Pigeons*, half a year before, marked by surprising individuality and imaginative qualities, that ought to have given its author celebrity. Marzials had previously circulated as a pamphlet one of the poems in the volume called *Passionate Dowsabella*, which made us look for the coming book with curiosity. This was not disappointed. But he was of a restless, nervous nature, rushing into elevation or depression of spirits, and I have never ceased to regret that the reception his first volume met with has prevented him from persevering. Among discouraging letters D.G.R.'s seemed to have hurt him most. This letter passed through my hands, but I knew nothing of its contents till I had the following from Marzials:

MY DEAR MR. SCOTT—I have to thank you for so many things I hardly know with which to begin.—Your truly kind and sympathetic letter about my book I need not tell you how much I value. And for sending me Rossetti's letter—your intention has so flattered me, the deed could hardly have done it more. I mean "flattered" in the French sense—delighted and gratified. I think I am right, or rather was right, in taking Rossetti's criticism as a great kindness, since I feel that what he says is true, that my book is crude and immature, and, what to my mind is worse, trivial. But I may say in confidence to yourself that when one considers how every reader of only one line of mine becomes my critic and how very few, —some half-dozen, perhaps—there are in the world whose sympathy one can honestly care for—sympathy for one's aim, I mean—it is hard to lose it. Rossetti does not seem to see (by what he picks out to admire) what I am driving at; he praises my *imitations*, and not the *me*, in the book.

On asking D. G. R. what he had said in the letter that had so hurt a noble but eccentric man like Marzials, he was sorry for what he had written. "But," he added, "if work sent to me is weak, I prefer silence; but if it is not, I take it the author can only wish for one's real opinion either way. I have since dipped into some of the poems again, with the same result as before, except that I have been even more struck with the daintiness and fancy of the last poem. It is so much more a whole than almost any of the others, that I should suppose it to be the last written. [This was a mistake, it was an early one.] I must say the first in the book seems about the worst of all—quite irritating in its pettiness and absurdities." Unhappily, again, this was Marzials's last and best, according to his own ideas; the one representing himself. It was full of surprising beauties, but expressed in the most wilful way. Rossetti's criticism was not perspicuous, though in a measure intelligent, resembling those on the appearance of Keats's poem *Endymion*, which Marzials's workmanship closely resembled.

The third of the British Museum youths to be mentioned here, but really the eldest, the most accomplished, and the earliest lover of the Muses—

"the last shall be first"—is Arthur O'Shaughnessy, a man with the most sensitive temperament, and the strongest artistic faculty among them, though with less literary facility. He did not, however, touch one with any lively interest, although he had some surrounding of admirers, one of whom, Nettleship, an artist by determination, in spite of the lateness of his beginning, illustrated his friend's first volume with remarkable inventions showing distinct imaginative power. Nettleship had published a book on Browning's poetry, an enthusiastic eulogium, the first evidence that the difficulties of Browning's style and scheme of writing, as well as thinking, would at last tell in his favour. The first time I met Nettleship was by invitation, with others, to inspect a portfolio of his drawings, some of which were very extraordinary attempts to represent supernatural and *unrepresentable* ideas. Two of these were life-size heads of the Jupiter Olympius type, with the mighty envelope of hair, only not adequately drawn; one of these was smiling blandly, the other with great tears like solid marbles such as gods may shed—only they never weep—rolling down his cheeks from closed eyes. These were, he said in a jaunty, off-hand voice, "the Almighty rejoicing he had created the world, and the Almighty weeping over the existence of evil, despite himself." It was astounding to find a man drawn to apply himself to painting dealing with such subjects; one could not resist respecting him, at the same time having to warn him off metaphysics, as Thornton Hunt warned myself when I told him I was reading in that quasi-science, about the time I first visited his father.

Nettleship's speciality was really wild animals. D. G. R. gave him a commission, paying him well beforehand; but the way in which he performed it was as extraordinary as the drawings of the Creator, which I shrewdly guessed were inspired by the anthropomorphism of Blake. A year and a half after the commission was given a child of the "Marchioness" species left with Mr. Nettleship's compliments a roll of dirty paper cut into by the string that tied it and dog-eared at the corners—a disreputable roll it appeared, for I was present when it happened to arrive. This being undone, disclosed to view a rude water-colour of two lions lashing about enormous tails and grinning at each other as if they were laughing—presumably at D. G. R., who had commissioned the drawing.

Another aspirant belonging to the O'Shaughnessy choir was John Payne, an able man in various ways, whose Gallicanism was as pronounced as that of the B. M. set. It was, however, independent of Swinburnian example and influence, his knowledge of early French poetry being as intimate as his acquaintance with Musset, Baudelaire, and others whose heavy odours charmed those young men who spent their innocent lives between the office desk in the B. M. and the quiet lodging in a neighbouring street. If they were not fast in practice they could at least be fast in literary tastes. Another jaunty tenet they all held was *art for art's sake*; what matters the sense, motive, or morals of a poem, if it is beautiful? Art above everything! One of them called the year of the Franco-German war (that war that changed the face of Europe, reversed the position of the two countries, ensured the independence and unity of Italy, and broke the power of the Papacy) "the year when Regnault died." To return to Payne. I thought him at once one of those who develop. I do not mean that Payne will rise into the highest regions of poetry, but that he will show an intellectual advance through life, perhaps even of a surprising kind.

Entirely unconnected with this coterie, if I may so call them, there came within my knowledge at this time several other men more worthy of a leaf of the laurel—

The rod of marvellous growth, the laurel bough.

The first was perhaps Austin Dobson, in his nature one of the most amiable of men, and consequently most charming of friends. By a natural bias, however, giving himself up to the celebration of the eighteenth century, and to the writing of *vers de société*, he is sure not only of popularity, but of celebrity, every one of his little poems being so perfect of its kind. Another was Philip Bourke Marston, an able sonnet-writer; a boy of the class we speak of as born to do some wonderful thing,· had not Providence made him blind from his birth. But the more I mention, the more I ought to name. Verse-writing and the study of poetry, not only our own of the beginning of the century, and of the generation now gradually passing away, but of the classic and the early poetry of the world, has spread rapidly of late years. The vast advance begun by Wordsworth and Coleridge, and varied by so many developments up to about 1825, has not ceased for a single year. My own contemporaries, the stars of the first magnitude among whom are so often mentioned in these pages, were and are much more learned than those leaders at the opening of the century, and now at the present writing, every little writer of verse is a more expert critic than any editor of a century ago. Imagine Coleridge in his early little book publishing a dozen sonnets or so under the name of *Effusions* and applying to Lloyd or to Charles Lamb for help to fill up his meagre volume. This increase of educated ability is indeed not confined to poetry, it has spread over all literature, as every leader in every penny newspaper can prove; but in other fields it is nearly unmixed gain, while in poetry the case is altogether different. The more knowing the aspirant is, the more imitative he is, and the less he depends on original powers, invention, and knowledge of life. The form becomes all-important to him, and there is no form of verse native or exotic, however artificial and silly, but it will find adherents, men or women who have nothing to say. This has therefore become the age of literary poets, every year giving out innumerable green 12mos, perfectly well done in the eyes of their authors, but without vitality or any *raison d'être.* To be sympathetic human creatures with eyes in their heads and hearts in their bosoms, to do and to feel, to know something of the men and women about them, is not necessary to them. What is necessary is only to read and write; reading and immediately writing is the amusement, and in great measure the work of all of us, and writing, without something urgently requiring to be said, ends in imitation, restoration, selection. The important question becomes, How is it to be done? Is it to be a sonnet?—Is the verse to be anapæstic?—What will the schoolmaster say?

The ladies as yet have not come out so strongly in verse as might have been expected, considering the novel-writing powers they exhibit, but that may be because the publication of poems is not very remunerative; still I know whole households competing with each other. A pretty sight, but not so safe as bézique to short tempers, nor so economical, if the desire to appeal to the public supervenes as it generally does, keeping up the large annual amount of money thrown to the printer's devil.

In Dr. Lonsdale's honest little *Life of Wordsworth*, in the fourth volume of the *Worthies of Cumberland*, we find him quoting a letter of the poet to Archdeacon Wrangham, wherein he says "he had not spent five shillings on new books for five years." How would our numerous decorative poets of 1879 get along under similar privations, being left, in short, to the imaginative faculties God has allotted them? This cultivation from without has given us a new critical term, whereby to distinguish classes, and we speak of the " Literary Poet," without the offence implied by the word poetaster.

This popular extension of knowledge of the forms of poetry has another result, altogether satisfactory. If poets have become more numerous, their audience has still more greatly extended. The " Literary poet " is the professional critic, and a better informed auditory happily makes his verdict of less effect : the majority of his readers have or presume they have as much knowledge of the matter as he has himself. Thus we see *The Light of Asia*, and Lang's *Helen of Troy*, and other able works, have taken their important places without the presumptive help of dailies or weeklies, as far as I have observed, but simply from their intrinsic value.

# CHAPTER XIII

MY POEMS PUBLISHED 1875—ALMA TADEMA—MY
*DEDICATIO POSTICA*

FINDING an expectation on the part of my friends, old and new, that I would print my poems old and new, and so give some evidence of my powers, little or great, in that now so popular art and mystery, I began to think such a thing reasonable. The younger men knew me only by hearsay as a poet at all, so I began preparing the book ultimately issued in the beginning of 1875, illustrated by Alma Tadema and myself. I find in a letter from D. G. R., about the end of 1873, some allusion to this intended publication. What I tell him of my present stagnation surprises him, he says, as he has always been used to view me as beating him hollow in constant occupation, which is much less his plan of work than mine. However, he thinks something is coming of it before long.

At any rate such a moment is the very one for such a piece of work as doing justice to your poetical chances once for all; thus a moment when regular occupation is slackened may be made quite as seriously serviceable as any other to the mass of your life's productiveness. I think there is no doubt whatever that the thing to do is to collect old and new poems together. As to vignettes, the plan you name is much the prettiest as in those Stothard and Turner books of Rogers's, and would really be worth doing, but liable to delay matters perhaps. I think there is nothing so uncomfortable as thick separate plates in a book of poetry, which should be easy handling. That last splendid ballad (*Lady Janet May Jean*) should not lie idle, but should be got out. It should, I think, stand first in your volume, unless you think some pleasanter subject more attractive to open with.

Having amused myself by preparing some designs, I held by the intention to publish my poems as an illustrated book. This was, I am sorry to say, a mistake, as it narrowed the number of buyers very certainly, and changed their character. However, having set my affections on making a set of small etchings, I once more missed my aim, lured away by another fancy. These etchings I finished in the studio at Penkill in the summer of '74, when Tadema and his wife, the amiable Laura, joined our party. He was a little hipped with hard work, and wanted repose, which he found in *The Old Scotch House* and its glen and garden. I had brought down with me sixteen little plates, and was etching the first one when he arrived and made his first appearance in our new studio, when he offered to do some if I would help him in the technique, in which I had already in London given him a forenoon's lesson. He went into the task in the most friendly spirit, working in his impetuous way while I sat with him revising the text, and Laura made pen-and-ink sketches of us. He did his best, but partly by being new to the process, and partly by a difficulty in understanding poetry in English,—and to say the truth, I was never sure that he quite made out what any of the poems was about,—his aid was not so efficient as it might have been ; and alas, my amiable critics attributed the appearance of that highly popular artist in my book to a desire on my part to bolster up my now inadequate powers of pleasing. At the eleventh hour also I conceived the idea of making the book record my attachment to the three friends with whom I had been for some years most intimate, and with whose poetical successes I had most sympathy ; and to do this I added a dedicatory sonnet at the end, inscribed to Swinburne, Rossetti, and Morris, which was similarly interpreted. To say the truth, I printed this sonnet in a purely friendly spirit, and not by any means to imply any inferiority either poetically or socially, but to express the fact that I had published nothing for upwards of twenty years. But it pleased my critics to understand it differently.

The helpful Tadema was not long about his friendly aid ; his health, too, was quickly restored, and he became the loudest and most overpowering of housemates. It was of as little use to protest against his robustness as to advise him about his designs ; his vigour became boundless, and his good humour endless. He was up long before anybody else in the house, was heard struggling with the great door, and after a cessation of all sound for half an hour or so, during which he had had a bath under a waterfall twenty feet high, his voice was heard calling on his wife and every other person to look alive. I suppose this was his habit at home. In the evening we finished up by whist, which he now played for the first time in his life, though he soon began to lay down the law to the others, who knew the game pretty well. He made a number of rapid little pictures, leaving a space for the figure which was to give them value; and the certainty of hand so exhibited, and the unerring instinct, were delightful to see.

I call it instinct, because Tadema really does fortunate things in his works without consciously intending them beforehand. Such is the artist by nature, *nascitur non fit*, endowed with another sense as it were. A sound mind in a sound body, troubled by no metaphysic, believing in no intellect or more soul than can look out of the actor's eyes, he is the most successful man in the world, and in some sense the happiest. A functionary for all the world and for all times alike is the painter, the giver of pleasure to those to whom thinking is repulsive. This sphere, that of representing life by externals, is narrowed the more our education advances. The more scientific and analytical our education becomes, common life conforms the more to great regularity of habit, rejecting on the one hand ideals, on the other picturesqueness, in both of which the painter delights. These are left at last to him to deal with only on canvas.

When the Tademas left Penkill, Miss Boyd and I accompanied them to Edinburgh. He was greatly pleased with some of the pictures in the National Gallery there, especially those by living artists of the Scottish School. Noel Paton's "Oberon and Titania," and George Harvey's "Columbus," on the first sight of the New Continent at the moment of revolt among his marines, pleased him immensely. This last picture represented Columbus, not as a splendid, heroical Guy, but as buff-coated manhood, hardy enough for anything. Sir G. Harvey was one of my oldest friends, and Sir Noel Paton one of my newest, so we called upon both. The first was then President of the R. S. A. We found him broken down by long illness, but still genial and pleasant; the other was absent from town. We also visited James Ballantine, who had sat beside me drawing from the antique forty-five years ago, and who had also attained now an ample material success, visible in the carriage standing at his door, in which he had just returned from church, the day being Sunday. When I introduced Tadema, it was evident Ballantine had never heard of him, which made the visit not so great a success as it might have been, but this *faux pas* over, we stayed and lunched, the addition of four guests not incommoding the ample family table. These two visits I was afterwards truly glad to have accomplished, if even in an accidental way; very shortly afterwards both of my old friends died. Both of them were men, not simulacra of men; they had taken a strong grip of life as well as of art in their several ways. Harvey's Covenanter pictures showed his conscientious sympathies, and opened a new page of history which his audience throughout Scotland thoroughly rejoiced in; and Ballantine, in the *Gaberlunzie's Wallet*, which Lord Cockburn says in his *Life of Jeffrey*, " Robert Burns would not have been anxious to disown," added to the literature of the country.

We parted from Tadema and his dear wife at the railway, they taking their places to Newcastle to visit my friend, James Leathart, and see his collection, and we returning to Penkill. The next day took place that singular dynamite explosion on board a boat on the Regent's Canal opposite their house. The boat was lying under a stone bridge, which was blown utterly out of existence, and the line of houses, of which Tadema's was one, were all more or less wrecked and shattered. This house had employed his powers of ornament for a number of years, and had gradually been transformed from an ordinary citizen's habitation into a sort of miniature palace, or if you like it better, a "make-up of trumpery," as G. E. Street characterised it when called into consultation as to its repair. Here is the note in which Tadema informs us of his misfortune, which, however, does not prevent his trying his powers at punning on my initials W. B.

Townsend House, 5*th October* 1874.

My dear Bubble-you-D—I am sure you and Miss Boyd especially must be anxious to hear from us. How conceited this sounds; but never mind, I am conceited and half-ruined. Not in health, you know, as Miss Boyd's and my nymph's hospitality [the nymph of the waterfall where he took his morning bath] have saved me in that way, but in material possessions. Luckily bones and pictures are safe, though doors and windows and roof are gone. We received the news in Newcastle, where we enjoyed your friend's hospitality. We enjoyed the castle too and Durham, which is nice, but not paintably so.

The mob here is mad, for they all sing the new song of the "Poor Creatures of the Explosion" of Regent Park. Thousands of people come and go; cabs and carriages without end. We are rather badly housed, as every door and window is barred with boards. The children are at Devonshire Street, and the governess brings them every morning to stop the day with us. The scene of desolation is a very wide one, the disaster extending at least for several miles. How we are not more hurt I cannot understand. Of course our blue china is singularly diminished. The ceilings are dropping, and marked a great deal. And now I will direct this to Miss Boyd in case you are gone; that kind lady will have news of us at least.—Ever yours, L. A. T.

Mrs. Tadema appended a nice little note:

I must squeeze in a few words to say, dear Miss B., that really our delightful visit to your castle has made my husband so strong and well able to endure our sad trouble. It would have been too much for him two months ago.— So much love and so many thanks from yours affectionately, LAURA.

My volume of poems, with etchings by myself and four by Tadema, was published in 1875. Its *Dedicatio Postica* to the three poets and most intimate friends mentioned so often in these pages brought them to me in a way curiously characteristic of each. Rossetti wrote me at once, with much earnestness, showing a careful perusal, pointing out critically things good and bad and such poems as he most esteemed. The letter is dated from 16 Cheyne Walk, 3rd May 1875. To make his amusing commentary on the dedicatory verses fully intelligible, I had better copy the sonnet here:

### DEDICATIO POSTICA

Now many years ago in life's midday,
   I laid the pen aside and rested still,
   Like one barefooted on a shingly hill:
Three poets then came past, each young as May,
Year after year upon their upward way,
   And each one reached his hand out as he passed,
   And over me his friendship's mantle cast,
And went on singing every one his lay.

Which was the earliest? Methinks 'twas he
   Who from the Southern laurels fresh leaves brought,
     Then he who from the North learned Scaldic power,
   And last the youngest, with the rainbow wrought
     About his head, a symbol and a dower—
But I can't choose between these brethren three.

### From D. G. R.

MY DEAR SCOTT—I have got into a habit of acknowledging welcome poetry by letter, which should not be foregone because we are likely soon to be meeting. Your book is welcome and goodly beyond others—the real result of native unforced powers, struggling manfully and successfully through every fissure of a rocky life. I have read old and new with equal pleasure, and I had no idea till now (when the whole spread before one gives a clear view) of what extraordinary beauty exists in some of your earliest pieces, even when open to fault-finding. The *Ode to Keats* is well worthy of him; that to *Shelley* second to it, but still good; the *Fable* is a little masterpiece in its way, and the piece called *Midnight* admirable, though here I recognise (perhaps) its finest passage as an addition. The *Four Acts of St. Cuthbert* delighted me greatly on re-reading. All these pieces are replete with wellbeing, clear-breathing youth ; one is glad to see such work not lost at last. I never knew that *Anthony* belonged to the same early period. It is among your finest things, in spite of an unkempt quality which (as it seems to me) might easily have been called to order. This same matter, I must confess, disturbs me somewhat throughout the volume, though much less in the sonnets and other sustained metres than where greater irregularity of structure requires one to keep one's eye on the ruts, and guard against a jolt. When you come to a second edition I should like, if you thought it worth while, to glance with you over my copy, in which I have marked some of the more decided instances. A trifle here and there might be registered as actual errata. . . . Many alterations in old poems seem to me questionable—more than questionable some of those in *Morning Sleep* and the *Monody*, the former of which I think much injured. Of the "Studies from Nature" the finest are *Midnight* and *Sunday Morning Alone*, the latter not to be surpassed in its way. The *Duke's Funeral* is quite equal on its own grounds, though necessarily less poetical. The *Requiem* too must not be forgotten, and here the changes seem beneficial. . . . Among the Ballads the one which, to my mind, stands out from all the others as a very piece of your Scotchest self, is the *Witch's Ballad*. This I admired absolutely from the first, and I believe it is now even better. There is here a truer sum of the quintessential qualities which really make Burns's humour what it is, than could be found in any direct follower of his ; and the much that there is besides makes the piece utterly your own, and I suspect unique in the language. *Lady Janet May Jean* strikes me as things do when they are intricate in their nature, and have never before been seen properly, but only heard or hastily deciphered in MS. I think it could hardly be understood at a first reading, if thoroughly even at a last ; but I fancy if some decisive explanatory touches—putting the reader on the track of the dream-structure of the poem—were introduced with a firm hand in one or two stanzas following stanza 1, and some slight alterations (which melody as well as clearness renders most advisable) made here and there throughout, this objection might be removed. [Here follows much analytical criticism of great value to me if I ever print the poem again.] I see I have been dwelling at some length on—I will not say objections, but critical impeachments not passing the point of query. You know what I think of the vigour and originality of the theme and its treatment, and of the extraordinary beauty of many among the varied burdens.

Among the Sonnets the speculative ones are still, on the whole, the finest, I think, and probably are unrivalled on their own ground. I must not forget the *Dedicatio Postica*, an adjective, by the bye, on which Latinity seems to cast a rather lurid light! Regarding this sonnet I would almost venture to suggest that line 9 appears hardly in a final state. If chronological doubt hovers round its subject, I think that—

Who earliest? I should rather think 'twas he, etc.,

or else—

Who earliest? On the whole perhaps 'twas he, etc.,

might be a racier form ; but if, on the other hand, some certainty could be arrived at, it might even be safe to say—

Who earliest? By nine years or so, 'twas he, etc.,

only it is true that thus the initials of the heading would seem rather out of their natural sequence.

Pardon a moment's chaff, my dear Scotus. Thanks warmly for my share in your generous dedication—as good a title to goodwill assuredly, as my poor memory will have to show—and one which you have bestowed at the pretty certain risk of some responsive bespatterings from the scavengers of the *press*-gang. However, yours is a book which has its place, and cannot be robbed of it.—Ever affectionately yours, D. G. ROSSETTI.

I had, indeed, somehow or other placed the initials of the youngest (A. C. S.) first, and so given rise to this last reflection. Swinburne was in bed when the book reached him, by the hand of a friend, who found him unwell. In a few hours, however, his cab drives up at my house, and I hear his voice on the stairs: "Where is he? Let me see him. I want to speak to him at once." I was unwell myself, lying on two chairs in the library, when in rushes Swinburne. "Tell me now, *mon cher*, tell me exactly what you alluded to as the rainbow wrought about my head!" "Well," I said, "you know you are hailing in the new time hopefully; you are assisting the advent of the brighter day; you are writing *Songs before Sunrise*." "Ah! is that all? I was in hopes you meant the glory of my hair, that used to be so splendid, you know!"

The last of the three, William Morris, was in no such hurry, but after a few days came the following:

HORRINGTON HOUSE, *6th May* 1875.

MY DEAR SCOTT—I must ask you to forgive me for letting a week go by without taking any notice of the gift of your book; but I do think you remember that I am a bad letter-writer even on ordinary matters, and often on extraordinary ones a helpless shamefacedness holds me back till I find I have committed an act of rudeness as now, which I am very far from meaning. I trust to your good nature to understand that, and to forgive me.

I was very glad to see your book, with the poems that I first found so sympathetic when I came up to London years ago, when I was pretty much a boy; and also that there were others that seemed to me as good, of which I have heard nothing meanwhile. Pray believe that I was touched and delighted by the affectionate inscription in the beginning, and though not more so (in some sense) by my share of the dedication at the end, yet as much, amidst my surprise at the honour of it; for indeed, I did not suppose you would have put me in the same place with A. C. S. and D. G. R., both of whom I consider for the most part as "passed masters" over me in the art.

I am sorry we have seen but little of each other for so long. I was thinking of coming in one morning next week to see if you would come over here some evening soon, and meet Ned Jones. I was very vexed that my Welsh engagement kept me from coming to you that evening you asked me. . . . With hearty thanks for your book and its dedication.—I am, yours affectionately,

WILLIAM MORRIS.

Having thus recommenced quoting the letters of friends, I may add something of an interesting one Rossetti wrote to Miss Boyd half a year later from Bognor, where he was living under the care of George Hake and Theo. Watts in a state of health which has been represented to me by these gentlemen as even alarming, but of which there appears not the slightest symptom in the letter, which was dated at Aldwick Lodge, Bognor, Sussex, 3rd November 1875. They had been for some little time here, he says, hitherto chiefly idle after getting through a new picture in London. He has taken the house they are inhabiting for an indefinite time, and will possibly keep it till the end of the year. It is within one minute's walk of the sea-beach, which is a fine one; the sands like a carpet at low water; and he has been meaning to write Miss Boyd a line ever since he had an opportunity of showing her picture of "Taliessen" to his friends in London, who admired it greatly. (This picture of Æ.'s, her *chef d'œuvre* perhaps, had been sent to the studio from the Dudley Gallery, where it was exhibited. It represented the tradition of the Welsh bard hearing his deceased master's harp playing by itself as it hung on the wall.) Of course Rossetti reckons on going on with his work here, getting both the "Venus Astarte" done, and the "Blessed Damozel," for Mr. Graham. His delay in leaving town had had the good result of keeping him for a visit from an appreciative amateur, who had given him the commission for this "Venus Astarte," at the price of 2000 guineas, so that he starts fair with the painting. He is, however, first finishing a new work for Mr. Leyland, from Coleridge's lines—

> A damsel with a dulcimer
> In a vision once I saw.

As to poetry, it seemed to have fled from him, and indeed "it has no such nourishing savour about it as painting can boast of, but is rather a hungry affair to follow." Nevertheless he means to write some more poems yet, and good ones too. He says he was greatly pleased to hear from Moncure Conway that the Yankees have got an edition of W. B. S. as well as the Britons, and asks if they have adopted the etchings also. (This was a mistake, I am sorry to say. There was no American edition of my poems.) Towards the end of his letter he says he has sat with poised pen for a minute or two, thinking whether more news were in the air or not; but no breath responds. They see almost no one, and when they do they learn nothing worth report. He will take much interest one day seeing Miss Boyd's portrait of Scotus. "Poor Maggie" (his sister Maria, who was then entering an Anglican Sisterhood, and who died about a year and a half later) "is parting with her grayish hair next Sunday, and annexing the kingdom of heaven for good."

In a postscript, nevertheless, he says he is forced to reopen his letter to tell what he designates a wondrous tale. Some four years ago G. F. Watts (R.A.) painted a head of him for which he only gave that artist two sittings, and which remained unfinished. His impression of it was appalling, though possibly from the exactness of its likeness, and people have ever since kept telling him it was horrible. Accordingly he executed a *coup de main*. He finished a spare chalk drawing, and sent Dunn with it to Little Holland House, sending also a note saying that he should be very much obliged if Watts would make an exchange, as he wanted the picture, not for himself; and that the bearer would call next day at same time for it to save trouble. "This resulted," he continues, "in my getting the picture next day, though Watts's note with it showed plainly that it was even as a tooth out of his jaws. Now that I have got it, I really think it very fine, and am quite ashamed to have played him such a trick.—D. G. R."

After our return to town in 1875, the Tademas left for Rome, whence he wrote me some letters amusing and interesting in some degree, and filled with the exuberant spirits that distinguished himself. He was now elected an Associate of the Royal Academy, and in reply to my congratulation says, "Of course for the honour I feel greatly obliged, but I feel more so when friends tell me they believe in the schools there my experience can be of some use for the coming generation." This he has certainly proved. His mastery over the difficulties of art is greater than that of any other man I have known. His command over the palette is like a miracle, yet his powers only give him pleasure when extrinsic evidences are awarded him. Now he could make a necklet of orders and crosses for his wife, and still wants more. The other men of great power in art I have known have never thought in this way. One day I asked Burne-Jones if he had been awarded a *Medaille d'Honneur*, as I had heard. His reply was: "What does it matter, my dear Scotus, whether they give one a medal or not, if one can't do what one tries or wishes to do; and I can only come near what I wish, and am unhappy in consequence."

Thinking over this and other observations, all going to prove how much we inherit our mental and moral individualities, and following out this train of thought, I may add my conviction that it is essentially vain for the most of us to labour to accomplish what we cannot do by natural endowment; in short, to aspire after artistic excellences as objects of ambition. Anything really worth doing in the arts, including poetry, must be in absolute harmony with ourselves, and come easy to us. I remember Tadema passing sentence on an aspirant highly recommended to him. On my asking him why he thought he would never do great things, " Because," he replied, " he had no awe of me, showing he had no respect for art." This was the moral aspect of the same question. I must say, I have always from the first seen what every one of my acquaintances would or could do, and, if he lived for a thousand years, would continue to do. In the spirit of his work, I mean—the essentials. " Diligence and perseverance accomplish everything," as Reynolds says; but I would add, " in what can be acquired"; they ensure *comparative* success, and a good share of turtle soup; they fill professorships and academies; but if any whose endowments are these, and no other, is troubled by " the last infirmity of noble minds," he will find they do nothing for him. Time will most certainly disclose the difference between the real and the automatic, between inherited and acquired mental possessions.

This conviction of the ultimate uselessness of *endeavouring* to do greater things than one is bound to do—of learning and acquiring from without by ambitious labour—is detrimental to success in life, of course; it is a great hindrance, it makes a man more a spectator than an actor, especially if he is indifferent to the *vox populi*. But the part of spectator, however pleasant, is dangerous besides. Bacon has said that in this universe of life "it is only for God and His angels to be spectators"; and in all that conduces to material well-being, or to the fulfilment of a man's duties to the world or to his family, he may be clearly right—diligence and perseverance being the wings that carry us forward in all improvement; and what would come of history without the continuous advancement in civilisation? But confining myself to personality, I have another conviction, resulting from temperament, no doubt, which makes me question Bacon's aphorism, and limits my respect for perseverance in one exclusive path.

This other practical virtue I would discredit, or rather limit, in the conduct of life is not perseverance pure and simple, but that negative kind of it constantly recommended under the form of the proverb, "Let the shoemaker stick to his last,"—the avoidance, in short, of dispersing one's forces by following various attractions. If the shoemaker sticks to his last he may, it is to be hoped, make good shoes; but will he, after all, make the best possible shoes? Further, if he never tires of his last, his soul must have had originally, or must have contracted, some affinity with it—must be more or less a foot-shaped and ligneous soul, and what can come of that? To all his eternity—that is to the end of his consciousness—he will be nothing but a shoemaker. So it is with all specialists. If shoes are wanted in the world where all are spectators, he will be welcome. But possibly the angel-spectators may not need shoes, and in that case will not care about the society of the man who has exclusively *stuck to his last*. Perhaps the spectator class here below are qualifying themselves to become angels! The clever practical fellows about us generally hate reflection, which is the food of the spectator. Thoreau the American, we are told, invented or perfected some valuable improvement in the trade to which he was apprenticed. Thereupon all his friends said, "Now Thoreau will make his fortune"; but Thoreau said to himself, "Now I leave this manufacture off: I have done all that can be made of it: I need not do the same thing over again," or something to that effect. He would not go round and round. None of us have too much time for culture and discipline; he turned to cogitation and found his life more harmonious.

It is this sticking to the LAST, this limitation, that makes a strong man within a narrow sphere: the smith's arm is strong, but then it is the strongest part of him, and he is a hireling, a poor devil, whatever amount of money he may accumulate, and though he is made baronet or lord. What if our performance, by concentration of our abilities, is the best that can be done in that way? Is the performer wiser, better, or more beautiful? Yet common prudence is always howling against turning from one study to another, from one love to another, from one form of art to another. It may be few can do this without losing their way, coming to grief; it requires tact to hold half a dozen lines without allowing them to tangle, or to ride six horses as they do in the circus. Trying to sit on two stools is thought to be likely to land one on the ground; and I am far from supposing that a certain amount of success is not necessary to peace of mind and well-being, or that a wise man should die poor. Carlyle—than whom no able shoemaker ever stuck more closely to his last—once thought he would like some routine post, and applied for the appointment of Astronomer for Scotland, as if that was one! In his account of the transaction he acknowledges that he never had looked through a telescope in his life. Nay, he affirms that he is sure he could do anything or everything he chose to do, from making a hut to building a palace! One wonders what he would have set about on being elected Astronomer for Scotland. By concentration and limitation he was great, but on meeting him closely we found him almost a monomaniac; and there is this to be added, he enjoyed life less than most men. For myself, spectator and even somnambule as I am, had I to re-live twenty or thirty years of the past, I would say with the pedantic gentleman in an old play trying to make love by teaching astronomy, "Let us turn round the celestial globe once more!" Then, I own, I believed in myself as poetically *nascitur non fit*!

# CHAPTER XIV

HOLMAN HUNT'S PICTURE "THE FLIGHT INTO EGYPT,"
NOW CALLED "THE TRIUMPH OF THE INNOCENTS"

AFTER all this wisdom, deduced from my experiences of life and perceptions of my own character, I may return to my friends. Holman Hunt returned from Jerusalem with his wife and son, and his new picture of the "Flight into Egypt," or "Triumph of the Innocents," in the spring of 1877; and I went to lunch with them one Sunday after they had got partially settled. The dear, serious, successful, and yet in some degree disappointed man I found, after his long absence, the same as ever. No change could possibly take place either on his art or himself, except the change of years: on myself I could not detect the effect of advancing age, but I saw it on all my friends; and they generally told me they were surprised they did not see it on me. I suppose the cause of this immobility was that I now took all things easy, having reached a table-land, and contented myself with the before-mentioned character of Spectator. With Hunt it was not so. He was more than ever an anxious man—spoke of going again for a month or two to the East to finish his picture; meanwhile he had taken a studio here, and begun struggling with certain difficulties resulting from the canvas, a Syrian cloth, on which he unfortunately began his picture.

Among others, Millais dropped in with his two daughters, his eldest and youngest—the eldest now close on twenty, very handsome, as might have been expected. I had not met him for many years, except once, and that was at the funeral of John Leech, where he was one of the pall-bearers, with manly tears filling his reddened eyes; and in him now it was easy to recognise the old nature, always happy and at ease, but with a great development into the affirmation of success and worldly wisdom. In me he professed to see no change! I asked him who the young lady was—was she really his daughter? "Yes, she is one of my girls—the eldest; did you think she was my wife?" he answered in his old chaffy way. "She is going over with me to Paris to speak French for me: I can't parley-vous at all now." When he first appeared in London, he and his parents had come from the Channel Islands, and he was bi-lingual; but having little care for conversation or reading—liking, indeed, everything else better, such as going out with Leech to the meetings of hounds, or shooting, or whist—he must have lost his French—if he had really lost it—from disuse.

He did not say so—perhaps was generously afraid Hunt might feel that he too should have been included in a similar compliment—but I heard afterwards that he was only going to Paris, the International Exhibition being open, because of an invitation from a party of artists who proposed to present him with an honorary memorial of some sort. He had had Carlyle for two sittings to paint his portrait. The philosopher of Chelsea turned round upon him on the stair of his new house, which is said to be quite a *scala dei giganti*, and inquired, " Has paint done all this, Mr. Millais ? " On being answered, with a laugh, in the affirmative, Carlyle continued, " Ah, well, it shows what a number of fools there are in the world! " A very amusing anecdote of Millais was told me by F. B. B., worth record because it is about as characteristic of the painter as the other is of Carlyle. A Frenchman, who had caught sight of a handsome cook Mrs. Millais had, became troublesome in his persevering attentions. The cook complained, as well as Mrs. M., and Millais warned him off the premises. The Frenchman could not comprehend, bowed himself away, but immediately reappeared, just as they were all sitting down to dinner. Millais caught sight of him ringing the area bell, rushed out of the room, collared the pertinacious offender, ran him up to the top of the street, and over against the railing of the new Natural History Museum to be, where a crowd immediately collected, the poor man volubly and breathlessly remonstrating. Millais retreated home, after explaining his position hastily to the crowd; but it was worse at home, where all the ladies of the household laughed him to scorn !

The next Sunday Hunt and I walked over to Battersea to find a model he wanted who lived there. On the way we talked of the old times of his struggle to be a painter, a time he was fond of dwelling upon; and I was pleased to find that but for Millais he would have given up the battle and gone, most probably, to be a farmer with his uncle. Both the old Millais explained to Hunt that their son John had told them how sorry he was to let Hunt abandon painting, and that they seconded their son to the full in the plan of lending W. H. H. money as long as he required it. At last they prevailed, and for a long time, about three years I think, till "The Light of the World" was finished, this generous scheme took effect. Even then his difficulties did not cease, of course not, as he was in debt and anxious to repay, and Gambart could scarcely be brought to give him £400 for that enormously successful picture, as he averred that sacred subjects would not pay in this country. The accomplishment of his first Eastern journey was again the cause of debt, and when he brought back the "Scape-goat," an eminent picture-dealer would not look at it. "You have no business to paint animals," said he; "the Scape-goat? I never heard of him, is he a Syrian creature? What will the public care for a Scape-goat?" Hunt explained that every one in Great Britain knew all about it, that the Scape-goat was a type of Christ, a kind of sacrifice of atonement, and that if Mr. —— had read the Bible he would have known that too. "Bible, Bible! well, well, there are two English ladies in the house ; I will call them in and we will see if they know anything about this Scapegoat." The conclusion of the interview was very amusingly told by Hunt. The ladies were not sure that they had heard about the Scape-goat, but at last the picture was bought for a moderate sum, and the publication succeeded in a way, but not so greatly as "The Light of the World," which Gambart in a court of justice declared had yielded him a thousand pounds a year for a series of years.

Hunt continued to struggle with his picture, which would not come right, and had in consequence a severe illness that reduced him to death's door, and forced him to take a long holiday. After this he began again. On the last day of the year 1879, having been all the intermediate time labouring fitfully and nervously with his bewitched canvas, he sent his man with a pencilled note in hand, requesting me to come to his studio in Manresa Road at hand in my neighbourhood to see the picture. I had never asked to see it, though I had heard it said that it had been secretly seen by some friends, and I immediately went there. My curiosity as to his treatment of the subject, and my growing anxiety as to the prolonged technical difficulty, were great.

I found him in a state of suspense and suppressed excitement, his temperament being one that showed no emotion in ordinary ; even when taken by surprise he would show no signs of such being the case. He is in fact one of the kind who seem to count twenty-five before replying to any unexpected interrogation. Now he said that I would see his work was far from finished, but he had determined to show it to me first of all, a compliment for which I thanked him. I was surprised to find he had stepped out of his usual form of invention altogether; not only leaving the realities of Oriental life, but introducing supernatural actors and appearances. He still indeed retained the Syrian costume on the Virgin and Joseph, and the ass on which she rode with the child in her arms was a Syrian ass, but he had surrounded the orthodox group with a running dance of many very elaborately-painted children, whose heads and bodies, and, to speak more exactly, their feet also, were surrounded with a bright phosphoric nimbus. There was something exceedingly charming in this rhythmic accompaniment of the Flight, in this very vividly and solidly painted troop of bright creatures wreathed with flowers, and carrying palms and lilies, of the same age as little Jesus. Besides, they seemed there for His amusement and delectation. The treatment of the halo as an inborn phosphoric light shining outwards, which mesmerists have affirmed to be sometimes visible in real life, is here introduced with great effect. Little cherubs or *amorini* employed in natural actions have been often brought into pictures of the Flight into Egypt by the old masters; and I accepted these supernaturals as such, although they had no wings. Some of them expressed joyful emotions, but others were represented with the flaccid helpless character of quite new-born things. The light and shade too of the whole picture struck me as a confusion between sunlight and moonlight. Up to the time of my present writing the picture has never been exhibited; but some day or other it is to be hoped it will be visible to all the world, so I shall not further describe it; I have only done so so far as to explain the correspondence which followed. He had also startled and grieved me by relating a preternatural incident, or something like one, that had happened to him a few days past, on Christmas Day. Reflecting on these matters, I wrote him next morning.

MY DEAR HUNT—I have thought a great deal about your picture and cannot help coming to the conclusion that it will be a perfect success. This is a very bad day, otherwise I would venture to call again and offer you, or press upon you, it might be, a criticism on the lighting of your picture, particularly of the angels (?). I want to speak more from a poetical point of view than as a question of pictorial treatment. You have lighted them not by any natural means, as they are brightly lit when the rest of the scene is in partial moonlight, lit in a preternatural way, receiving light as they would in their native region—heaven, I suppose,—"of such is the kingdom of heaven"; to fleck them with shadows as if from interrupted sunlight is not therefore allowable.

Thus I wrote, with more to the same effect, enlarging on the treatment in other respects. I ended with an allusion to the apparition, if I can so call it, when nothing was visible:

I have related your strange adventure on Christmas Day to the ladies here, my wife and Miss Boyd, and find them curiously interested. Would you mind writing me a few words to say how you *knew* no one was in the house at the time? What o'clock was it? Yours seems a common cast-metal stove; if riveted, it seems such stoves sometimes crack or throw out a rivet with a tremendous noise, if intensely heated.—My dear Hunt, ever yours,

W. B. S.

The picture had now been under his hand a long series of years refusing to come right. In his frame of mind he had come to believe not that the world was in league as his enemy, but that the devil himself was fighting against him. In two days I received a painfully interesting answer to my note, recounting the incident at length. I was wrong in my precipitate conclusion that the numerous charmingly-painted children were angels; he had a much more original idea than that stale one: they are the souls of the innocents massacred by the orders of Herod. I must insert his letter, which enters fully into both subjects, and is, indeed, one of the most interesting and charming letters I have ever received.

2 WARWICK GARDENS, KENSINGTON, W.,<br>
5*th January* 1880.

MY DEAR SCOTT—It was very good of you to write to explain your impressions of the points in my picture which invite reconsideration.

The first question about the light on the supernatural figures I debate thus: The children must be so treated that they shall not be mistaken for infantine angels of heaven or amoretti, which previous illustrations of the subject would lead people to expect to find them to be. The beings I want to represent really differ in this, that they have only just left this life instead of having got altogether established as celestial creatures. Some of them, if not all, may indeed scarcely have altogether lost the last warmth of mortal life. It seems desirable, therefore, to avoid a treatment which would make them like the angels who regard the face of our Father in heaven. A support to this view I find also in the desirability of avoiding to distinctly pronounce the figures to be either subjective or objective. I wish to avoid positively declaring them to be more than a vision to the Virgin conjured up by her maternal love for her own child, the Saviour, who is to be calling her attention to them. Having got so far in my reading of the conception, I rely for the next step upon what, to use a presumptuous phrase, I will call my experience of the embodiment of ideal personages. These develop in solidity and brightness by degrees, and I imagine the Virgin to have seen these children at first, scarcely discerning that they were not natural figures under the natural light which illuminates the other surrounding objects, until, with longer examination and recognition of the individuals as the neighbouring babies of Bethlehem, the more distinctive parts of each figure become lighted up with the fullest light, and as a full consolation, she sees the glory of their new birth. The division of the two—the natural and the supernatural illumination —cannot be avoided, but when the picture is completed, I think the light on the duller parts will be more ethereal in effect, and therefore less separated from the brighter. The criticism about the immature development of the ankles I will attend to in some way when I get to these parts again.

The story about the unaccountable noise, you will remember, I gave as an illustration of the degree to which the difficulty with my picture has distressed me. For four years this torment has been going on, wasting my life, and health, and powers, just when I believe they should be at the best, all through a stupid bit of temper on the part of a good friend. I don't like to hold him responsible, although his agency caused the beginning of my difficulties, but I have got into the way of thinking that it is one of many troubles during these seven years (balanced by much joy of my last four years) which the Father of Mischief himself only could contrive. What I told you is only a good story, as my impressions give the experience. It is not evidence, remember, one way or the other, although I give the exact truth. I was on Christmas Day induced to go and work at the studio because I had prepared a new plan of curing the twisted surface, and, till I could find it to be a practicable one, it was useless to turn to work which I had engagements to take up on the following days. When I arrived it was so dark that it was possible to do nothing, except with a candle held in my hand along with the palette. I laboured thus from about eleven. On getting to work I noticed the unusual quietness of the whole establishment, and I accounted for it by the fact that all other artists were with their families and friends. I alone was there at the group of studios because of this terrible and doubtful struggle with the devil, which, one year before, had brought me to the very portals of death; indeed, almost, I may say, beyond these, during my delirium. Many days and nights too, till past midnight, at times in my large, dark studio in Jerusalem, had I stood with a candle, hoping to surmount the evil each hour, and the next day I had found all had fallen into disorder again, as though I had been vainly striving against destiny. The plan I was trying this Christmas morning I had never thought of before the current week, but it might be that even this also would fail. As I groaned over the thoughts of my pains, which were interwoven with my calculations of the result of the coming work over my fresh preparation of the ground, I gradually saw reason to think that it promised better, and I bent all my energies to advance my work to see what the later crucial touches would do. I hung back to look at my picture. I felt assured that I should succeed. I said to myself half aloud, "I think I have beaten the devil!" and stepped down, when the whole building shook with a convulsion, seemingly immediately behind my easel, as if a great creature were shaking itself and running between me and the door. I called out, "What is it?" but there was no answer, and the noise ceased. I then looked about; it was between half-past one and two, and perfectly like night, only darker; for ordinarily the lamps in the square show themselves after sunset, and on this occasion the fog hid everything. I went to the door, which was locked as I had left it, and I noticed that there was no sign of human or other creature being about. I went back to my work really rather cheered by the grotesque suggestion that came into my mind that the commotion was the evil one departing, and it was for this I told you the circumstance on the day of your visit. I do not pretend that this experience could be taken as evidence to support the doctrine of supernatural dealings with man. There might have been some disturbance of the building at that moment that caused the noise which I could not trace; indeed, I did not take pains to do this. Half an hour afterwards I heard an artist, who works two studios past mine, come up the stair, and before he arrived by my door he said to some one with him, " It is no use going in, it is as dark as pitch," and they went down again. This was the only being that came to my floor during my whole stay, which was till 3.30. I perhaps should have taken more pains to explain the riddle, but while I quite accept the theory of gradual development in creation, I believe that there is a "divinity that shapes our ends" every day and every hour. So the question to me is not whether there *was* a devil or not, but whether that noise was opportune, for I still hope that the wicked one was defeated on Christmas morning about half-past one. Thus, you see what a child I am!—Yours truly, W. HOLMAN HUNT.

To me the state of mind here indicated, though I respect it so much, is so foreign as to be impossible as an experience; but in this, again, I recognise our mental conformations are inherited even like our family likeness. I consider humanity as an organised portion of nature, only with the power of self-contemplation which separates it from all other organisms and places us over the rest of the physical world, so that life is to the human creature a preordained fight with every object we meet from adolescence to the grave. This fight is for self-preservation and for self-advancement. I hold that progress, mental and bodily aggrandisement, and ultimate victory in the course of time in this world, is a law of the nature of a being with self-conscious powers. Religion gives us ideals; science gives us command; morals give us justice; arts, beauty; medicine preserves and improves the body; civil law defends us against ourselves. But out of or beyond this controlling egoistic order of advancement there is no good thing; out of or beyond nature there is nothing at all but God, space, and time.

Does this end in a platitude? Let me try to explain myself, and save my attempted wisdom from so appearing. Our latest acquisitions of knowledge go to show us that the farthest star is like this world we live in, chemically and elementally, and subject to the same necessities and activities. Life, therefore, throughout creation is presumably physical, and only possible by the same means as with us. And in the second place, all attainment of an organic sort is a performance perfected by processes requiring millions of years by progressive steps. Many millions before vegetation covers the earth as grass;

many, again, before any kinds of four-footed creatures live by eating other kinds. We see that the tentacle after millions of years becomes a fin associated with a spine; and that is clothed with feathers as a wing; and again with hair and claws as a forefoot; and again the articulation is freed into fingers, and the hand of man with all his upright anatomy results at last—a result which must have been preordained before the manifold transformations began, in or by some Divine force. But in all this—the scheme of nature, which is a scheme of life—there is clearly no room for a devil or a ghost till we ascend to *the intellect*. Out of the intellect only they can come; they are therefore not entities, but ideas. This scheme of progressive or creative energy we call Nature; outside or beyond this we can predicate nothing save the Divine force we name God, Space, and Time.

Since that time, January 1880, I have seen him many times. He has abandoned the so troublesome canvas, and copied the whole picture on a fresh one; but still the difficulties in his way follow him, even on the new and sound English double canvas. The good friend he alludes to in his letter was his friend of many long years, F. G. Stephens, who had simply made the mistake of using too large a box, which he jocularly called Goliath. This large box could not travel by any means of transit known to the stony roads in Palestine; its address and key had both been lost, and it was laid away at the seaport till by accident Hunt saw it after nearly a year.

The "joy" he mentions experiencing during the latest four years of the seven was doubtless his second marriage, which has really been his salvation by the amiability and helpfulness of the noblest of women.

On one of my latest visits I determined to say what I had long thought, that his difficulties were imaginary, not caused by the canvas, but in his own overworked or over-anxious brain. He took the remonstrance in good part, answering with a gentle smile that he knew too well all the different causes of the trouble, and alluded in a distant way to the incident of Christmas Day, acknowledging that the influence, of whatever kind it was, had not yet been fairly banished. Very shortly after this, I must add, his brow cleared; his picture went all right; it was finished; both pictures were finished admirably!

# CHAPTER XV

### SPIRITUALISM

THE unpleasant subject of mesmerism, table-rapping, or spiritualism, *quid sit nomen?* has turned up in these pages now and then; ugly enough I may describe it, like one of the misshapen things in the Dutch Temptations of St. Anthony, yet I would like finally to introduce it again after the interesting relation of the preceding chapter, and the faith in it held by D. G. R. and others already noted. The incident in Hunt's studio was somewhat similar to asserted phenomena among spiritualists, but it was totally different, inasmuch as my dear friend Hunt is a sincerely orthodox believer, whereas the so-called spiritualists have neither faith nor philosophy worth inquiring about. The absurdity of men who do not believe in any hereafter calling up the dead is so great that it needs only to be mentioned to be laughed at, and it is clear that if the visitation of the souls of the deceased can be credited, it must be as a belief dependent upon other dogmas, and resulting from faith in new life endowed with full consciousness and memory of the life here. A new revelation would be necessary to give authority to any scheme of future existence supporting this vulgar, sensuous intercourse! However, putting all absurdities out of the question, the direct power of one mind over another is very great and obscure; there may be much yet unknown within the ordinary bounds of human nature.

Twenty-five or thirty years ago, when my series of pictures from the *History of the English Border* was in progress, a young relative of Sir Walter Trevelyan returned from India, sold out of the army, and was much with us both at Wallington and at Newcastle. He was a clever and amusing addition to the circle. He was bitten by the evidence of great fortunes being made in the iron trade in these parts; lost *his* fortune at once by investing it in a failing concern; and on our migration to London we saw him from year to year, finding him always promulgating astounding schemes for retrieving himself. He went to South America to catch wild horses, a scheme he kept to himself till his return after failure. Next he came in for a family legacy, and left us, again disappearing for a series of years.

In the summer of 1878, when preparing to leave town, a card was brought to me with his name in a new form, the maternal name being incorporated in full with his own, and beneath it, instead of an address, the words, *Universal Republic. Without the danger-signal.* I immediately rushed from my library to meet him, and found the tall handsome man standing in the middle of the room, perfectly self-possessed, but literally in rags. Even in this disguise the maid-servant had had the perception that he was a gentleman, and treated him accordingly. I received him after a moment's surprise as if nothing peculiar was observable. He talked as of old, told me he had been to America, and gave me without reserve his experiences of the continent from New York to the Great Salt Lake. At first he had been in society of the best cultivation, as a descendant on both sides from two of the most ancient houses in the old country; he had also associated with several kinds of new-light sets of people, especially with magnetists and spiritualists; sometimes he had laboured in the fields; he had been told he ought to do so, and he did; we all ought; why should we let others do what we thought beneath ourselves. At last he fulfilled his apprenticeship, so to say, and came home; but as he had spent all his money, he worked his passage over. There again he conformed to the law of human equality, and learned something besides. He had no reservation; he perfectly believed in spiritual supervision, but he objected to the danger-signal! On inquiring into this, and wishing an explanation, he would scarcely believe I could have lived so long without being consciously aware oftentimes that impulses or warnings were conveyed into the mind in a moment from some outward power. In his case this definite impression from without, which, as he described it, closely resembled what my dear Quaker friend called in her pious way having a line of action or conviction " pressed in upon her," was accompanied by a smart pain. To this he objected. "And you see," he added, pointing to his card still lying on the table, " I have said that I do not practise, and wish to be without this momentary pain." To all this I utterly objected, and he politely received my objections as natural on my part, if I had experienced nothing.

He dined with us, criticised the wine, and now I ventured to speak of his habiliments, and I asked him where he lived. This he took frankly and in the best way, owning that he would have better clothes if he had any money to buy them; but, after all, why should he? He had been told that all his family and his old friends were in the opposite camp; he, belonging to the *Universal Republic*, knew this. He found, however, that *I* was not objected to; so he had called on me. "But the weather is warm; one can live on amazingly little. I have no place of abode; this is my house, my library, and my bed." With that he opened his great ragged wrapper of a coat, showing absence of shirt, but with the pockets filled with books and loose printed papers. Seeing books, curiosity got the better of me. I said I should like to know what they were; he pulled out two, left them with me, and disappeared.

These books were American productions by women-authors—creatures, I think I may say, bent upon distinguishing themselves by a mixture of imposture (conscious or unconscious) and egotism, relying upon ignorance to overrule reason and make them received as peculiarly gifted. One of them was an *Essay on Symbolism*, the symbols having been revealed to the authoress as a medium, and illustrated by coloured designs of the maddest meaning. One of them was called *Christ without Hands*, followed by another called *Christ the Female*. These meant that doing, working, using the human fin in any way was of no avail, but that the reign of the higher nature, *i.e.* the female, is about to begin! Man has the power of the genus Bos, and the equine qualities; he has had his day, the nobler spiritualism and weaker bodily qualities of the woman are to succeed; the time is ripe; she is to carry human nature into the divine sphere. The male organism is only the servant of the female, and once at least in the history of the world its service has been dispensed with already: the product of the woman alone was the Christ! There is a daring, if not very charming, heterodoxy about this that indicates a new era indeed, and spiritualism, of which women are generally the cleverest media, is the key to open it!

A year after this, the desire to hear something of my friend increased to such an extent that I made inquiry by writing Sir Walter, a step I had long meditated. No direct answer arrived, but, shortly after, the father of my friend, whom I had not hitherto seen, called upon me. No tidings of the wanderer had been heard for a long time; I had been the latest to see him on the visit I have recorded, but just a few weeks before my note of inquiry reached Sir Walter, my friend's brother, passing up Regent Street, suddenly recognised him selling flowers at the curbstone! His brother had rushed forward and tried to embrace him, begging him to come home to his chambers. This the wanderer peremptorily refused to do. His brother would then buy his flowers. "Take them," said my friend; "I paid half-a-crown for them this morning; take them for a shilling." A half-crown was placed in his hand in exchange for the flowers, but he threw it down, and fled. The result of this dreadful meeting was to increase the alarm of the family to such an extent that they took a house in town, and so the father had been able to call. He thought, as I seemed less tabooed by his son, that I might be able to assist in finding him; but I had no clue. His only plan now was to be always everywhere about, on the chance of meeting him. The world of London is large, but exhaustible. Walking with little hope in one of the parks in that June weather he saw his son sitting on one of the seats; he could not be mistaken! Cautiously he advanced, and cautiously addressed him; a singular meeting, the second indeed in the short history, and this one had a better result than that in Regent Street. He promised to see his mother, and to do so consented to go to the tailor first. Me he has never called upon again, and I have never ventured to ask for information, his state so nearly resembled madness. I only know that his father had placed a sum of money in a bank known to his son, to which he could apply. He was like a madman, yet he was not mad; his whole nature was changed by spiritualism. He had impressed me as a modern John the Baptist.

The difference between persistent enthusiasm and monomania is often extremely slight, and difficult to define. In the East Holman Hunt met a man in whom they were very closely combined, who followed him to England, where Hunt took so great a liking to him that he took charge of him for years. Monk was this old man's name, a rather handsome, innocent, large, white-bearded man. While Monk lived with Hunt he painted the enthusiast's portrait, calling it "The Prophet." Monk did not pretend to that character, but devoted his whole life to the formation of a new society of the Faithful, which was to own and inhabit the Holy Land; this was like forming a rope of sand. The first time I saw Hunt after the correspondence about the great noise behind the picture, he asked me if I remembered Monk, and produced a letter from him, now in the East again, or rather a circular, requiring all who received it to give up to the writer a tenth of their entire property to form a fund for the purchase of the sacred soil. Hunt had declined this fanciful proposal, and spoke of old Monk with a clear enough perception of the true nature of the character; but he had just had a visit from Ruskin, who had received a similar letter, which he had signed with an intention to conform to the demand. I have never heard that he did so.

About the same time Alfred and Anna Mary Watts came to live in Cheyne Walk, and so joined our Chelsea society. Mrs. Watts—Anna Mary Howitt of the old time—was now a neat little elderly lady with plenty of white hair, as pretty and vivacious—what people call *bright*—as ever, and both were as much attached to spiritualism as before. She had become vegetarian, and so closely adhered to her programme that she objected even to eggs. This, she believed, made her less bound by the body, more free of the physical trammel, and she had given up painting a long time, though she still had some of her little water-colour drawings, inspired by the spirits, hanging on the walls. Mrs. Lynn Linton told me a curious anecdote of the old Mrs. Watts, who died a year or two ago. One forenoon she found the old lady spinning a top on the large dining-room table. At first Mrs. Linton came to the conclusion that the poor soul had lost her wits, but Mrs. Watts turned upon her saying: " Do you wonder why I am spinning a top? But of course you do. I am only amusing the dear little children; the room is full of them, and they like nothing so much as to see me spin the top!"

It was instructive to see the enthusiastic girl who went to Munich to study painting, and wrote the *Art-Student in Munich*, changed into the idle-handed, passive woman of fifty-five, with all the sweetness and gentleness still left, listening not so much to you as to the empty air. I found her one evening sitting by the drawing-room fire alone, looking at the flames; not a book or newspaper, or fancy work, or piano, in the apartment. Suddenly, however, I found the inherited literary ability in both her and her husband, as vivid as ever, by their book of poems called *Aurora*.

This little volume with the significant name is, to my mind, the best outcome as yet of the spiritualism of the day, full of beautiful things beautifully said, though the light in it is the moonlight giving sharp, but doubtful visions, in which the true colours of material things are lost.

But enough of this: it would not have appeared in these notes at all, but that so many times I have had this spiritualism or kindred states of mind forced upon my attention, even by some of the ablest men mentioned in my story.

# CHAPTER XVI

DEATH OF G. H. LEWES AND GEORGE ELIOT—OF
R. N. WORNUM—OF SIR WALTER TREVELYAN AND
LADY PAULINE.

THE years 1878-80 have furnished me with a great many recollections, and I must still recur to them; they were the most fatal to my friends of all the years of my life. Lewes and Wornum, Sir Walter Trevelyan, Thomas Dixon of Sunderland—Carlyle at the beginning of 1881—and many others, not to be mentioned here, all passed away. All these have already appeared in these pages; to carry out my principle, preserving my interest to the last in all the friends whose intimacy has been dear to me, I must place them again on my record, and close the story of each.

On the last day of November 1878 Miss Edith Simcox—*Lawrenny* as she signed herself in the *Academy* and other journals—thinking, very kindly, that she ought to be the first to inform me, wrote to my wife that Lewes was dead. She and George Eliot (Mrs. Lewes) had become inseparably attached; she had been at their house, the Priory, daily. I was his oldest literary friend now living, she said. The feeling that I was much to blame living so apart from him, took possession of me. He is nearly the only man among all my friends who has never ceased to advance. At first he was only the clever fellow, but at a very early time he became the literary adept, then the able investigator, and lastly, the scientific thinker and philosopher, one of the most trenchant and advanced minds in the science of this country. The day was an aguish drizzle characteristic of the season, but in a sad frame of mind I went to leave a card at North Bank, and returned not the better of my excursion.

We use the word *genius* in a very loose way. It has a meaning always comparative, yet we use it as if its signification was definitive and fixed. To Lewes we would not apply it, and yet his mental powers were inherent, not cultivated. He set about learning any language necessary, or any science he chose, and never missed an experiment, never forgot a word or a proposition. This was partly or primarily no doubt because his memory was retentive, but no sooner did he possess himself of a science or language than he used his knowledge in such a manner that the men who had been all their lives occupied with that single subject, acknowledged him their comrade. At the time of his death I had not seen him for many months, a year perhaps it might be. They had then called together; it was the first time George Eliot had been in my house; she was evidently occupied at the moment with houses and furnishing; they had just got possession of their new place in the country, and she was much interested in our new abode, with its many reception-rooms. He was so too; there was the sort of self-complacent feeling between us of two old fellows who had not stuck in the world, but had made some considerable way since we used to meet in my first studio, which was a room up two stairs in Edward Street, Hampstead Road, where we talked well into the night, as youngsters do, but on the wisest and most recondite subjects.

It was remarkable that only a few weeks before I had made an etching from a pencil sketch done in Leigh Hunt's house in Cheyne Row, I think, one evening when he and I met there, nearly forty years ago. The pencil sketch was slight, but it conveyed the bodily semblance and characteristic action of both Hunt and Lewes—Hunt, with his face well raised, with a quantity of hair he continued to part in the middle, that made him look a large-headed man, as indeed he was, having found other men's hats, including those of Shelley and Byron, would not go on his head; and Lewes, a fidgety little fellow, stooping forward in an inquisitive, interrogating attitude. The only other person in the sketch, besides myself, was Vincent Hunt, then a boy, whose death was a grievous blow to Hunt in his later years. I now wish I had shown this etching to Lewes. His advancement in learning and position was carried out by advancement also in temper and person; he would have been pleased probably with this memorandum of the old time, and so might George Eliot, but I was not sure enough of this to venture placing it in his hand. The reason I did not was that he used to be called the ugliest man in London, and his poor little wife of that day was one of the prettiest. My etching, however, does not exhibit his plainness particularly. They had been buying a billiard table for their country residence—not, as he explained in a doubtful accent, to play himself, but for guests on a rainy day. Now I am the only one in this sketch remaining in the land of the living.

George Eliot did not forget the impression she carried away of our house, and the view of the Thames we had. Not long after the death of Lewes she took the mansion at the other end of Cheyne Walk, in which Daniel Maclise painted his latest picture, and we congratulated ourselves on having her added to the Chelsea circle of friends as Mrs. Cross. By this time we had been about ten years inhabitants of that locality, and very much attached to it, finding it in many respects like a quiet country town, although it is an integral part of the busiest and greatest of cities. Old-fashioned shops are the rule, many of them kept by the same families for several generations. Everybody knows something of everybody else; there are coteries without the exclusive feeling, great people like the son of Shelley, and the grandson of Byron, settled near each other, and the esoteric junto of the privileged, artists and literati. There were also the public characters of a country town. The old woman who called watercresses; the groggy old gentleman whom the boys waylaid, and induced to chase them with his brandished stick; and the ancient barber, too, who actually still had daily customers whom he shaved, was to be met on his beat, with brush, comb, etc., peeping out of the pocket of his snow-white apron. On Monday mornings my wife witnesses a different indication of provincial habits. Calling on the grocer with a list of household items wanted, she finds the incumbent of the old parish church (the charming old church where the great Bible is still to be seen chained on its reading-desk, as ordered by Henry VIII. for the use of the public) with piles of copper money before him, which he and his parishioners count out into shillings on the counter, getting silver instead, and expatiating on the fact that there were two half-crowns and a five-shilling piece in the plate yesterday! Is it not charming that in London we are still in this idyllic life?—But Mrs. Cross was not to enjoy it.

After her death some of the daily writers, who produced the overstrained notices of her career and genius, omitted all mention of Lewes. She was said to be great in philosophy, and wise beyond measure, but the mention of her instructor was not to be tolerated for the sake of propriety. An amusing revelation of the difference between the conventional style of the printed eulogium and the private verdict, is afforded by a reported conversation with Carlyle on the adoption of George Eliot by the ignored Lewes long years ago. "Ah! *George Eliot is a female writer of books like myself and himself. I got one of them and tried to read it, but it would not do. Poor Lewes! Poor fellow!*" were the words with which the "philosopher of Chelsea" eased his mind.

With Ralph Wornum the close amity of the early day when he, Tom Sibson, and I spent every Saturday night together over a male life study of an hour and a half, and a glass of toddy or punch after it, was never disturbed. He became lecturer to the Government Schools of Design, and on his visits to Newcastle was my guest. On one occasion he found me painting the trial of Sir William Wallace as rebel at Westminster, and gave me a study from his own Herculean arms and chest, and I found him possessed of a nearly perfect human form, only a little too fleshy. My picture was a rather imaginary piece of British history, but I afterwards discovered a subject from the same story of a sublimely dramatic character. The execution of the hero took place on a day of the Fair of St. Bartholomew in Smithfield, so that the hurdle with the doomed patriot, the executioner, and a little John Bull of an officiating sheriff, passed along among the zanies and quacks and dumb heads of heifers. Another fine subject, of a quite different kind, I have often thought of, if the R. A. had ever treated my pictures with a grain of consideration. This was the marriage of dear Albert Dürer, and was suggested on my visit to

Nürnberg by the loveliest of backgrounds in the "Bride's Door" of St. Sebald's Church, with its decorative statuettes of the wise and foolish Virgins; Dürer having been married in the parish of St. Sebald. Imagine Agnes in her good and pretty young days, and the strangely interesting Albert himself, and old Wolgemut, and Albert the old, and the boy's godfather, the printer of the chronicle!

This muscular power and beauty of Ralph Wornum did not save him from a comparatively early break-up in his general health. One day I had my fellow-examiners from South Kensington to dinner, and Wornum came to meet them. He had long parted with the department for the position of Keeper and Secretary of the National Gallery, under Eastlake, who procured his appointment, so pleased was he with Wornum's solution of the difficulty that he, Professor Long, and some others, were at the moment troubling their heads about, whether Claud Lorraine was in boyhood a baker of pies or a painter of pies—*pistor* or *pictor*.

✻ ✻ ✻ ✻ ✻
✻ ✻ ✻ ✻ ✻

The night of that dinner-party, if I remember right, was one of the thickest fogs of the London season, so thick that no cab or carriage ventured out, and Wornum had to expose himself to it, refusing to remain with us all night, I am sorry to say, and was very ill on the way home. I only saw him once after, these being very busy years with me. He had long determined to write a life of St. Paul, placing, as he believed, the true character of the apostle of the Gentiles before the *literary* world for the first time. At last the voluntary labour was completed; a goodly volume, which had entailed late evening labour for years, now that Greek and other necessary acquirements for such a task were rather fading out of his mind, and it was published under the name of *Saul of Tarsus*. At the National Gallery I met him. Mrs. Wornum, his sustaining friend, had accompanied him from home and waited to take him back. The strong man was giving way. Supporting himself by leaning heavily on the barrier protecting the pictures in the great room, he told me he was gradually getting weaker. "I should have taken fewer tasks in hand," he said; "some of them will never see the light; *Saul of Tarsus* has conquered." This was very painful to me. Yes, it is fruitless to fight against convictions, the accretions of centuries. Here was my dear friend Wornum saying again with Julian, the philosopher and "apostate," *Vicisti, Galilæe*.

A few months after the death of Ralph Nicholson Wornum, Senator Schœlcher, who still retained his villa in the neighbouring street (Upper Cheyne Street, the street or road where Leigh Hunt lived when I knew him), although his time was now mainly spent in France attending on his political duties, presented me with a similar book. He had introduced himself to me as a brother print-collector. In his house the walls from cellar to garret were literally covered with framed engravings, from the time of

Schongauer to our day, his task being to find a specimen of every engraver or artist whose name is preserved in a dictionary, and his object in so doing was to present the collection at last to the École des Beaux Arts. He, too, had discovered that *Saul of Tarsus* was unworthy of his place in the calendar, and he had then (1879) published in Paris *Le Vrai Saint Paul, sa vie, sa morale* : a labour prompted by a conscientious desire to disclose the truth, which shared the same fate as Wornum's larger and completer criticism.

The prolonged winter of 1879-80 was sadly fatal to many old people. We counted eleven deaths within the radius of our coeval friends, and now, just as the cold was giving way to spring, though still at the end of March the snow recurred, and the icicles formed again as the snow ceased to melt, while the daffodil persisted in opening, tidings arrived of the disappearance of Sir Walter Trevelyan, whose acquaintance and employment made to me the most important milestone in my life journey, the *meta ultima* marking the end of the hard and harassed period of my uphill labours and family misfortunes, and the beginning of a continual excitement, and the pleasure of many years of success in the pictures for Wallington and other gifts of fortune. He was eighty-two—a good age to live up to and to die at, the age at which it is well to die ; and he died after one day's illness, which is also well. When I saw him, even for the first time, his aspect was that of indefinite age, and no change was visible upon him to the end. He was a man of the coolest temperament, yet constantly active in many minor pursuits that did not strain his intellect, only kept it occupied, avoiding excitement of every kind, preserving as a duty the normal equanimity of his pulse; always well in health, which he attributed to avoiding stimulants. Two years ago he fell by stepping on a frozen pool hidden under a thin carpet of snow, putting his shoulder out and endangering his life, and now on the last flying storm of the "sullen rear" of another winter he dies. Of the three charming places he owned, Nettlecombe Court in Somerset, a lovely Elizabethan mansion in an ancient deer park, full of comfortable warmth; Seaton-by-the-Sea in the genial climate of Devon, the property entered under the family name in Doomsday-book, he elected to live all the year round at Wallington in Northumberland, where the fierce weather killed him at last. Now and then he continued to write me, and to enclose a mass of printed papers of all sorts referring to the small reforms and benevolent objects always occupying him, and his last communication, exactly a month before his death, was very characteristic. He says, "This is the longest and severest winter I remember without any appearance yet of its ending;" and he encloses a paper by Combe "On Voluntary Distortions," reprinted from the *Phrenological Journal* of forty years ago, for distribution by Sir Walter; "Argument for a Popular Veto on the Liquor Traffic," by Sir Wilfrid Lawson; a reprint of Lady Pauline's review of my *Memoir* of my brother;

his own pamphlet "On the Alcohol and Opium Trades"; "Bishop Selwyn and the Maine Law"; "On the Purity of Beer and Cider"; "Correspondence with Thomas Bewick on Certain Birds"; and other things. All these were of the driest character. He had no humour; in this respect unlike his brother Arthur, whose tract in the shape of an advertisement of "Death and Company's Foreign and British Spirits," gave a glowing account of their deleterious qualities, ending with a "*Nota bene*—Sacramental wine always on hand!" When his nephew Alfred became Roman Catholic, much to the chagrin of the head of the house, one day Sir Walter was showing us some curiosities in his museum; among other things he drew out of a cedar-wood cabinet a drawer of human bones picked up in the Catacombs. The convert lifted them, drawer and all, to his nose, and called out, "Oh, they have the odour of sanctity! they are the bones of martyrs!" The face of Sir Walter, expressing impassivity struggling with suppressed derision, was a study, but at last he said, without any perceptible change of voice, "The odour is that of the cedar-wood drawer, my boy." I was glad to have the note I have mentioned, although it was loaded with such a mass of matter for the waste-basket, ending as it did with a hope that I would come to see him, and find "The Way to Wallington," thus quoting an old electioneering song of his father's time, when the intimation of his final departure came so soon after.

I like to preserve a record of the last of the noble

old patrician whose action on my life was so beneficial, and so shall transcribe a letter Captain Percival kindly wrote me on the occasion :

WALLINGTON, 1st April 1879.

DEAR MR. SCOTT—You will, I know, like to hear some particulars respecting the end of Sir Walter Trevelyan, of which event you have already heard. It appears he had caught cold about a week before ; but on the day before his death he was well enough to propose driving over to Hallington, and only put off so doing as he thought it might be too cold for his lady.

That night he had a shivering fit : Lady T. wished to send for the doctor, but he would not allow her. He went early to bed and slept a couple of hours, when he suddenly woke up and said, " Tumours are forming on the lungs." The doctor was immediately sent for. He came about eight on Sunday morning, found the pulse quiet, nothing wrong with the lungs, *he thought*, only a slight tendency to bronchitis, but not to cause alarm. He left declaring he saw no occasion to return that day.[1]

When the post arrived, after reading his letters, Sir Walter dictated an answer to one of them ; Lady T. left the room for only about five or six minutes to write this out ; when she returned he was gone ; his eyes were closed, his hands crossed on his chest, there was no sign of a struggle or a pang ; he appeared to have passed away in sleep. You will be sorry to hear that poor Lady T., who at first could not realise the fact, is now seriously ill, and from one cause or another has now congestion of the lungs.

The funeral took place at Cambo on Thursday, when he was carried to his grave by his tenants, of whom upwards of a hundred attended, in the face of a terrible

---

[1] It would have been highly interesting to have made a *post-mortem*, so as to ascertain whether the tumours had really formed. Perhaps at that moment Sir Walter, like the "Seeress of Prevorst," had internal vision.

snowstorm, which added a cruel wildness to the scene.  I remain here till Lady T. is quite out of danger.— Believe me to be yours sincerely,      G. R. PERCIVAL.

*P.S.*—2nd April, five o'clock P.M.—I regret to say the doctor, who has just gone, thinks the state of Lady T. very critical.

Evening.—I open this to say, all is *over*.

This was the second wife of Sir Walter, Laura Capel Lofft before marriage—not the dear and admirable chatelaine of the period of my intimacy with Wallington. How different they were, the first and the second ladies who reigned there! Pauline, my never-to-be-forgotten good angel; small, quick, with restless bright eye that nothing in heaven or earth or under the earth escaped; appreciative, yet trenchant; satirical, yet kindly; able to do whatever she took in hand, whether it was to please her father in Latin or Greek, or herself in painting and music; intensely amusing and interesting to the men she liked, understanding exactly how much she could trust them in conversation on dangerous subjects, or in how far she could show them she understood or estimated them. This was intensified by the want of humour and imagination in Sir Walter, which must have been a grievance, but was only perceptible as a secret amusement to her. When I knew her first I was not learned in the female character, my own wife being the most difficult of human creatures to understand. She soon saw through me, and was the best of friends. Always amiable and often complimentary to strangers, towards me she had the appearance of severity, rating me for pride, for ignorance of the world, for conceit in things below my mark, as she too kindly said, till at last her young niece, then called Kitten, remonstrated, thinking her more cruel to Mr. Scott, who was making so many pictures for the hall, than to any one else! She had been married at nineteen or less, had lived in Rome after marriage, and travelled on mule-back in Greece with her husband, the most self-centred, unaffected, high-intentioned man I ever knew; and she became in many respects in perfect harmony with him. She was a true woman, but without vanity, and very likely without the passion of love.

When Sir Walter died he had a volume nearly ready, called *Selections from the Literary and Artistic Remains of Pauline Jermyn Trevelyan*, one of the essays in which was the review of my *Memoir* of my brother, reprinted and enclosed in the last letter of Sir Walter to me, with so many other things. This book was edited by his secretary David Wooster; but it is to me a *caput mortuum*, so great is the difference often between the personality and the prepared productions of many individuals. Still let me copy out one of her poems that my pages may possess something by her:

### STREET MUSIC

It was a squalid street, in truth,
Where crime and misery cowered side by side,
Where wretched infancy and ruined youth
And helpless hopeless age, swam down the deathward tide.

Redly the sunset came
Flickering on high, far up the blackened walls,
Less like heaven's light than that unhallowed flame
Lit by exulting hands when some sad city falls.

All through the impure air
Came sounds of grief and wickedness and strife,
Sickness and childhood moaned unheeded there,
Drowned in the turmoil of discordant life.

When high above the din
Rang the shrill bagpipes of the mountaineer!
Strains born of pastoral glen and rock-pent linn
Had joined the meaner misery walled-up here.

Coarse was the hand that played,
Without one touch of feeling or of fire,
Yet by the rugged notes were strifes allayed,
And pallid children danced amid the mire.

Oh, brother mortals, hail!
Sinful and sorrowful, yet brethren still,
Come from your loathsome dens, your garments stale,
Our inmost souls meet in that music's thrill.

I mused and passed away
From that dark street to where sweet Avon flows,
'Midst gleaming rock, soft grass, and woodland spray,
And nature's primal voice on my tired ear arose.

Go ask yon mountain rill,
Why it makes unheard music to the woods—
Why do the wild-flowers paint the soulless hills,
And cloud and sunbeam play over the ocean's floods?

But what if angels' eyes
Are gazing downwards on those unknown streets?
Ah, what if angel melodies arise
Echoing those notes far off in heaven's retreats!

> For what can Art do more
> Than waken childhood's feelings by her voice;
> Make pure tears gush from founts long sealed before,
> And saddened hearts obey its summons to rejoice?

This is better in an intellectual than in a rhythmical point of view, and after all I think it not one of her best; and the pictorial portion of the publication is very inferior to what she accomplished in aiding the decoration of the hall. The extraordinary Will he left kept Sir Walter's name before the public for some time after his death. He left the authorities of the British Museum, National Gallery, and other public institutions, permission to select what they chose from his collections. The director of the latter institution went down to Wallington a few months later to see if he could avail himself of Sir Walter's offer. Here is Sir Frederick Burton's letter to me on his return:

43 ARGYLL ROAD, W., 21st August 1879.

MY DEAR SCOTT—I have been down to Wallington, and have been fortunate in two fine days there. Sir Charles and Lady Trevelyan have been very kind and hospitable. I enjoyed my visit, but came away empty-handed. There was nothing placed at our disposal (*i.e.* of the National Gallery) by the Will, which I felt in the least tempted to lay claim to.

The place, its contents, and its associations, strongly interested me. Above all, I was pleased to see again your compositions for the hall. They are as fresh as ever; and the imagination and thought manifested in them, the great excellence and fulness of the composition in each, their originality and variety, engaged me as much as when I saw them in London—it must be about twenty years ago. It is only to be regretted that the necessities of the case involved their being placed so low down ; for, although their horizon is no doubt calculated for that position, I think they would look better and be better seen if placed much higher. I have little doubt you would have made them fit the arches, but that, of course, a space to light the passages behind was indispensable. I was also interested in the twin portraits of yourself and your brother (these ought to be in the Scottish Academy). And again, in the early water-colour by Rossetti.

I had so often heard you and others speak of Sir Walter, and the whole place was so redolent of him as an individuality, that a strange feeling of sadness haunted me, as I, although for the first time, wandered about it, now in other hands, and likely to undergo some changes. They are going to make an alteration in the entrance, by pushing the hall and its pillars some feet forward, enlarging the entrance hall by throwing down the partition on the left, diminishing the size of the ante-room where the cases of porcelain are, and so opening a way from the door direct to the great central hall. This will be an improvement, and will admit of there being an inner glass door to keep out winter draughts. However, both Sir Charles and Lady T. seem anxious to make as few changes as possible.

The British Museum people took away a good many things from Wallington : porcelain, coins, etc. A residue of Sir Walter's museum goes to Newcastle. But the terms of the Will with its sixteen codicils are somewhat complicated. While there I slept in that delightful room lined and furnished with Miss Julia Calverly's work in embroidery. Bless the dear soul, her works give more pleasure than those of some of our contemporaries in art are likely to do one hundred and eighty years *hence* ! I hope to get off abroad towards the middle of September ; till then I am here.—Ever yours, F. W. BURTON.

The " twin portraits " mentioned are two cabinet-size pictures, one of my brother David by R. S.

Lauder, of the Scottish Academy, and the other of myself by Waite, both very well executed; they are now at Nettlecombe Court in Somerset. The elaborate Will referred to was unfortunate, suggesting actions at law, which were, however, gradually compromised; the most amusing item was the bequest of his immense cellar of wines to Dr. B. W. Richardson, a brother in temperance agitation, to be "employed for scientific purposes." This cellar contained perhaps the rarest collection in the world. Under Lady Pauline's rule wine was to be seen on the dinner-table; I remember a visitor on one occasion, after a glass of the port laid down by Sir Walter's father, offering to be a purchaser of the whole at a guinea a bottle. Sir Walter declined the transaction, quietly adding, "No, I mean to have the whole carried out some day and emptied into the Wansbeck!" Dr. Richardson told me when the lawyer's first letter arrived he believed it was an April trick, but the key followed, and confirmed the letter.

The lists sent him included nearly thirty kinds of wines and spirits, but a great proportion was lost by decay of the corks. Still from sixty to eighty dozen labelled and entered in a book appeared in London, affording a delightful subject to the daily papers, from one of which I preserved an extract which I may enter here:

These were the most precious contents of the cellar as Sir Walter Trevelyan found it thirty years ago, when he sold the common poisons, but kept these heirlooms even as another man might keep a bottle of *aqua tofana* which had been distilled by Réné, the Florentine, for Catherine de Medicis. Most of it was carefully dated, and the oldest liquid of all, the Tokay and St. George, both of 1752, were said to be bought of Edward Wortley, and may possibly have been fellows to wine tasted by Lady Mary herself. There were Magnums of Hock of 1777, an age, if we mistake not, hardly to be paralleled in the most famous cellars on the Rhine itself, where the operations of the French patriots were far from favourable to the conservation of vintages. There was Cyprus of 1762, which we are told M. Gennadius, the Greek minister, pronounces "superb." Sherry-sack, "of date unknown," may have been of a vintage consumed by Shakespeare himself for aught that we know; and Malmsey, also of unknown date, duly suggests to Dr. Richardson the Duke of Clarence. There was port of 1784, which we are rather surprised to find was also pronounced magnificent, though it is generally held that fifty or sixty years is the utmost life of drinkable port wine. Some Arrack of extraordinary age even made Dr. Richardson or somebody else write a poem of an anti-Bacchic but still panegyrical character. After these things dates with the figure 18 at their left seem quite modern and scarcely worth regarding.

All this wine inherited by Sir Walter recalls to my mind a saying of his, one night when his gout was so bad he had to ascend the stair on his knees. I, carrying the light, suggested that he might console himself by reflecting that he had not himself to blame. "No!" he rejoined, "my father and grandfather drank the port and I came in for the gout!"

I have mentioned the laudation of George Eliot which followed her death. That which followed on the demise of Carlyle was almost as great, till the direct honesty of speech in his *Reminiscences* turned the tide of praise into something like a howl of execration not altogether to be accounted for. I was on the committee to further the erection of Boehm's admirable statue. At first the subscriptions swarmed in : then the *Reminiscences* appeared, and there was no more money to be got!

# CHAPTER XVII

MORE DEATHS—THOMAS DIXON OF SUNDERLAND—
RICHARD BURCHETT—SOLOMON HART

THESE memorials sadly portending the winding up of my autobiographic notes, like the curfew to the parting day, will only be prolonged by the commemoration of one or perhaps two more of those friends whose names have appeared in the earlier pages. A few years after my undertaking the Government School of Design work in the North, I received a note from Sunderland, very queerly spelt but rather ably expressed, inquiring what steps were necessary to obtain an institution in that town similar to that I had inaugurated in Newcastle, and also expressing some hints that the writer was agitating for a Free Library on the plan then promulgated of a public penny tax. Similar letters had reached me before, to which I had replied with punctuality, as I now did to Sunderland. A deputation was immediately arranged, and I of course expected to find the mayor, or an alderman, or two shipbuilders, or other important worthies, ready to come forward with funds and influence, but instead of those, Thomas Dixon, the writer of the first letter, and three or four other working men presented themselves.

A little taken by surprise at first, I received them in the same spirit and with the same attention as if they had been the most important persons the town could show, and was very agreeably interested by their confessing that they were only carpenters, and that their leader Dixon was a cork-cutter. "Not that I could benefit by such an institution as we want," said that gentleman, "but I want to see my native town possess the great advantages of having a School of Art. I have no talent, but I know several who have, and I come to speak for them." This was another example of a power of self-dependence and unegotistic manhood I had met in the North, such as it would be vain to look for anywhere else in England. It had nothing to do with politics, there was neither pretence of their ability to carry such a scheme forward nor complaint against the magnates of the locality for not doing more. On the contrary they took up the common-sense position that people who could have expensive teaching, and had plenty of books in their own homes, did not need to care for public schools and libraries, but that they, the workmen, wanted to help themselves.

All these men I knew afterwards. One of them, Pickering by name, was not a carpenter but a printer, and had secretly practised design, with a view to illustration, showing an amount of power unaccountable in one who had no other teaching than what he could give himself by the purchase of a few books such as he could afford. But Dixon was the one who affected me most, and who continued for the rest of his life to look upon my occasional advice and entertainment of his ideas with a sort of proud gratitude, all the while he was effectually carrying out in a quiet unostentatious way schemes that made me feel my own deficiencies as an agitator. This letter-writing to every one who appeared to him worthy of admiration in any way brought him in contact and into correspondence with many illustrious and powerful people, who, I found afterwards, had waved aside the want of education so visible in his letters, and had received him as a friend and equal. Both the Free Library and the School of Art were established in Sunderland. I must not say through his activity, but had he not, day and night, I may say, kept these proposed institutions before the eyes of his own class as well as before the authorities, it is very doubtful whether Sunderland would have been so early in the field. Not only was a School of Art instituted but a local gallery of pictures, open to the public, established in connection therewith. He it was to whom Ruskin wrote the "Letters to a working man," afterwards published by him. Had he interleaved his own letters with those of his correspondent, as Dixon said he at first proposed to do, the book would have been more interesting and dramatic, if less egotistic.

Dixon had a constant habit of picking up curious things and books of a peculiar kind, and sending them to such of his friends as might, in his phrase, "make a better use of them than he could do." He knew instinctively what would interest certain men, and through his agency I have received several pieces of peculiar literary knowledge I might have otherwise missed. One of these books was Walt Whitman's *Leaves of Grass*. It was seen by him in some quantity in the stock of a sort of peddler-bookseller who had been in America. He sent it me; and I at once invested in other copies, one of which I sent to W. M. Rossetti, as has been mentioned previously in these notes, who after an interval of some years brought out the edition that made the new development known to the English public, and largely conduced to the changed position of Whitman in America.

About the beginning of 1879, seeing in one of the illustrated American magazines an article about the author of *Leaves of Grass* and his book, ignoring altogether the critical influence of England in respect to the fame of Walt, I conceived the idea of asking Dixon particularly how he got the copies I had from him. His answer is worth preserving:

> I will tell you willingly [he says] about the first copies of the *Leaves of Grass*, which are still dear to me from the association of the man who brought them here, and because I, at least, knew by whom Walt Whitman would be valued. There is a plan of dealing in books called hand-selling, which is selling by a kind of auction, the

dealers who adopt this plan not being lawfully-qualified auctioneers. The value (upset price) of a book is gradually reduced till somebody takes it. Say it starts at five shillings, then it is reduced less and less, till it comes to a shilling or sixpence. A man came here at that time (I think it must have been about the beginning of the year 1856), James Grindrod by name, following this trade, with a stock of books that had missed their market, or had never been rightly published at all. Long after this—long after the American War was finished—he came back again to Sunderland and recommenced the bookselling trade in the old way, but his wife (from whom he had separated, though he had left her in a comfortable way of business) being still here, made him soon leave the town again. I was very sorry for this, because he used to bring such lots of wonderful curious books—books you don't in a regular way see. Since then we have never had a man like him in this trade. He used to come and take tea with me on the Sunday afternoons, and then I found out he had been in the thick of the American Civil War as well as Whitman. He did not care to speak of his war experiences, only my sympathy used to draw him out, for I longed to hear how they had pulled through. He had joined one of the States regiments, and was most part of the time in the army led by General Sherman. He was with Sherman in all the fearful raids towards the end, and was often without food, and was many times compelled to eat almost anything, however loathsome, they could find during arduous marches in the wasted country; he saw many men drop down and die for want of food. "But when we did reach the depôts where food was, we were all taken very good care of and nursed; but I never in all my life experienced any trial like that want of food during these raids." He was with Sherman at the taking of Atlanta, and then he got his discharge with others of the men who had done the same hard service.

He would not remain in Sunderland, though he could sell his books. He travelled about, went into Lancashire, and there he met his death in a railway collision in a tunnel a year or two afterwards. So you now have the history of the book.

It will be remembered that the first edition, a large thin book with a small portrait of the author, had no publisher's name on its title-page, and was never seen on the counter nor in the list of any American bookseller. Emerson had written a singularly laudatory letter to Whitman privately, which the latter made public as far as he could, but only in the obscurest way; so that we may say that but for this travelling bookseller with his "hand-sale" of queer volumes that had scarcely ever seen the light of day, the *Leaves of Grass* might never have reached this country at all.

The last time we saw Dixon was in London, so lately as in July 1880. He had saved money, and felt himself to be independent of his trade, which he never liked, its patrons being mainly the public-houses and gin-palaces of the Tyne and Wear. He was forty-nine years of age, but his thin white face, with its rather noble profile, indicated a feeble body, contrasting with the large strong figure of his travelling companion, Skipsey the pitman, and author of a volume of poems possessing considerable charm from their expression of some features of the writer's daily life. One of the smaller poems of this class, called *Get Up!* was considerably quoted, and Burne-Jones, going out to stay a day or two with the Premier, Mr. Gladstone, took the book in his pocket and read this poem to Miss

Gladstone, which reading resulted in her father getting Skipsey placed on the Civil Pension List—for a very small sum, it is true, being only £10; but the honour was worth more to him. These two good men and true were well received and entertained by many illustrious persons besides Burne-Jones and his wife, who took Dixon to see the Grosvenor Gallery. He had just managed to make a beginning with the establishment of the Picture Gallery for Sunderland, in which several of us aided him. One evening he came on to Bellevue, having just left Carlyle, who had received him, though then, in the last twelve months of his long life, he habitually resisted the inroads of all visitors. Dixon sat down, looking tired and worn, and told me where he had been, going on thus: "Mr. Carlyle looked at me very sadly, and said, 'When a man lives to be as old as I am, you see, he is about ready to go, and willing to be done with all this turmoil about him here.' This was his speech to me, and I am sure his life is sad, and the words he spoke were sincere; he is a lonely man, and has been for long, maybe for all his life." Saying this, Dixon's eyes filled with tears; he, too, felt himself a lonely man. His wife died a good many years ago, leaving him two sons, to one of whom I stood godfather. The elder of these became a sailor, and was washed overboard in a storm; the other resisted the education his father wanted to give him and took himself off to Australia. I sympathised profoundly with this middle-aged man, old before his time, as well as with his friend Skipsey, able-bodied and slow, contented with his fate, feeling it in his own hand, happy with his crowd of children and the mild appreciation of a few friends more cultivated than himself.

He was to leave London next day, and in a week or so after he suddenly died—simply ceased to exist when the servant had left his bedside after giving him some breakfast. The information came to me from William Brockie, as admirable a man as either of these, and, it may be, abler; an Oriental scholar who has published some really comprehensive and enlightened short expositions of Hindoo philosophy, badly printed and unnoticed, their author living among men who take no note of such things. D. G. R. was much affected by the disappearance of the excellent Dixon. He wrote me on the occasion: "He was a good man if ever there was one. I fear poor Skipsey, who is of a tougher mould, will miss him very seriously. But much as I admire Skipsey, I feel it is of little use to speak of him as a poet; the metal is too coarse; it is not beaten, but cast." I assisted in getting a bust of this simple and true public servant executed for the Sunderland Picture Gallery by Boehm, and a portrait of him was placed without my aid in the Free Library. At the public meeting on the occasion of this portrait being presented, a letter from Max Müller was read, full of such loving admiration, I preserved it from the daily waste, and still further preserve an extract from it here:

You have indeed lost a good and brave man at Sunderland. I wish I could have seen and known more of him, but our life is so busy that we seldom find time for what is the greatest enjoyment of life, free interchange of thought with our fellow-men. You know that Thomas Dixon was not a learned man, but I can assure you that his letters, in spite of occasional mistakes in spelling, showed a clearer insight into the true objects of all my writings, and conveyed to me more useful criticism than many a review in the best weekly, monthly, or quarterly journals. How he found time to do all he did, and to read all he read, and to think out all that he thought out for himself, is still a riddle to me. Nothing gives me a stronger faith in the intellectual vigour and moral strength of the English people than that such a man as Thomas Dixon could have lived and passed away almost unknown, except to his friends and fellow-citizens. We must not judge England by its so-called head or capital city, which at present seems often very silly and crazy, but by its backbone, that runs through the provinces, and by its noble heart that beats so strongly in the breasts of such men as Thomas Dixon—a provincial cork-cutter, if you like—but a truer, nobler man than many a duke or marquis.

One or two more of the artistic order of social humanity, and I have done with my records of the dead. The first of these I shall name is Richard Burchett, an able, self-dependent actor in the affairs of life, yet one whose action was rarely to his own benefit, although largely to the benefit of those under him in his official position—that of Director of the Training Class, when Messrs. Cole and Redgrave determined to substitute certificated teachers for the artists previously elected in a haphazard manner by the Board of Trade as Masters of the Schools of

Design. Of these last I was one, and so entitled to a Civil Service pension in proportion to the length of service; others, the few whose names I can remember, were Zephaniah Bell, one of the gainers of prizes at the Westminster Hall Exhibition; W. C. Dobson, now member of the R. Academy; Young Mitchell, a portrait-painter of moderate ability; Hammersley, a landscape-painter; and Nursey, who had been assistant to Sir David Wilkie. Not one of us, I may say, knew anything of scholastic ornament, or of the application of art to any manufacture whatever. Our Director at Somerset House, who was accountable for everything, was Charles Heath Wilson, against whom the whole of the advanced students rose in a body under the leadership of Richard Burchett. A Parliamentary Committee of Examination carried the day against Wilson, and on the change of Schools of Design into a Department of Science and Art, which matured itself by degrees, Burchett had entrusted to him the organisation of a Training Class for future masters, every provincial centre being now (partly through the first great International Exhibition of 1851) intent upon having efficient education in art in their own localities. This he did with great intelligence, arranged a curriculum, and prepared text-books on Perspective Geometry, etc. At the same time, however, he, like poor little Collinson, the P.R.B., converted himself into Roman Catholicism, took to a sort of farming at considerable expense, and gave himself up to historical painting on a rather large scale—just the kind of art which English taste and the R. Academy as the mediocre exponent of the same would like to crush out of existence. He began to get into deep water, and into the hands of 20 per cent money-lenders. Still he fought bravely with his difficulties, and even when his large salary was placed under trustees, he went on with his historic subjects. An anecdote regarding one of these I must give, as showing how a picture, like an action in actual life, is capable of even opposite interpretations. At this time Mr. Peter Stewart, shipowner, of Liverpool, realising a vast fortune, had built a great gallery for pictures, and visited Burchett to see his latest work. Stewart was an extreme Radical in religious and political creeds, a companion of my dear friend W. J. Linton in the benevolent action of securing food and lodging for a whole shipload of Polish refugees. The subject of Burchett's picture was the priest bearing the sacred elements, thus barring the way and preventing the conquerors after the Battle of Tewkesbury from invading the church, sword in hand, where their discomfited enemies were sheltered. Burchett had chosen the subject as a glorious example of the power of the Church and the faith of the prince at that blessed period in Merry England. Stewart looked a long time at the picture, admired the armour and the priest's cope and the monstrance he held, and at last spoke out. "I admire the picture, Mr. Burchett, it is excellently painted, and I like it for its subject; these men in full armour won't go in, they won't end the day completely after risking all their lives, because of that old priest with the jack-in-the-box! Superstition, you see, turns them into caitiffs!" This knocked over poor Burchett so much, the transaction came to nothing. Indeed, everything went amiss with him, and he died in what should have been the middle of his career.

The other artist I have to mention here is a contrast to Richard Burchett. Much associated with him in the examination of the works of the Provincial schools, not at all in private life, I never looked upon him as an artist. This was Solomon Hart, whose two great successes were his election into the Academy, and into the Athenæum Club, where he dined every day and only went home to bed. He, too, had tried the large historic canvas. His subject, the "Execution of Lady Jane Grey," I remember very long ago,—it must have been, I think, when, as a boy, I drew a few months in the British Museum. It was not at all like Burchett's works, capable of suggesting anything to anybody; it was only a row of beef-eaters, larger than life, in red loose jerkins, and above them, on a high shelf, a young woman in black, with a bishop in white lawn, and an executioner. He never tried the large historic again, but somehow the Royal Academy rewarded him by adoption. He was very learned in the prices English artists had been in the habit of receiving, amazingly small until our own day; he assured me that neither Stothard, nor any of his contemporaries, nor any earlier artist up to Richard

Wilson, inclusive—except the two great portrait-painters—made more than, or so much as, three hundred pounds a year. I have found a place for dear old Solomon Hart here, in spite of his continual habit of punning, even scheming to introduce a pun for half an hour, and after all our having politely to laugh at it for the twentieth time. My reason for doing so is that at his funeral in the Hebrew Cemetery I discovered the origin of the words *Requiescat in Pace*, still used by the Roman Catholic Church in the obituaries, and on gravestones of the faithful, a form of record on a Christian grave which has all my life been a puzzle to me. On every upright gravestone—and every grave had a similar upright stone—I observed three Hebrew words inserted towards the end of every inscription, the rest being in English. These words, my informant, who was a Hebrew, told me, were only translatable "May he rest in peace," exactly the same as the Romanist inscription "Requiescat in Pace," and they had been in use he said, time out of mind by the Chosen People. Why should this remain still in use with us Christians, whose boast it is that "Immortality has been brought to light through the Gospel," to whom, therefore, death is the opposite of eternal sleep, an awakening to a higher life? The truth seems to be, that the earliest Christians in Rome were Jews, whose graves in the catacombs continued to be so inscribed, and these again were imitated by later converts; and so the form of inscription continued to be ignorantly followed afterwards by the Church, even down to this nineteenth century! Such is the tenacity of life in religious usages, when they have once become authoritative.

# CHAPTER XVIII

### ARTISTIC INQUIRIES, 1879-80

I MAY enter here, a better opportunity being wanting, certain speculations of more or less artistic interest, which came in my way in these late days of literary loitering. One of the most inventive and superb designs of Hans Sebald Beham is the large woodcut representing the "Fountain of Rejuvenescence." A picture by Lucas Cranach, at Berlin, has long been a point of attraction to imaginative visitors; in both of these works the old people totter along or are carried to the bath or Fountain, which in Beham's print—a woodcut of about four feet long—is a large water surrounded by a grand Renaissance colonnade, under which the renovated men and women, active and handsome in the prime of middle life, sport together. In writing about the Little Masters I tried to find the origin of this myth in mediæval times, but Dr. Littledale assured me it was not at all an old fable, but one brought home from the Caribbean Sea by mariners following the discoveries in the New World. In all histories of these wonderful discoveries we find the account of Juan Ponce de Leon spending years vainly looking for the problematic island called Bimini, where the equally problematic fountain of youth existed. But then Ponce was only contemporary with the Little Masters, and Sir Frederick Burton told me he believed there was a picture attributed to Dirk Stuerbout, who died in 1475, of this subject, and I found in Passavant a print described under the heading "Le maitre de 1464," representing a hexagonal bason in which are men and women; men being seen carrying their wives towards the bason, and one throwing his wife into it. Behind the side of the bason is a man standing in complete armour, and on the ground at his feet are the words *Hic est fons juventutis.* The same print is entered by Bartsch under the heading "Anonymes du XV Siècle." Sir Frederick was so much interested in the inquiry that he followed it out to some extent, as the following letter indicates.

43 ARGYLL ROAD, 30*th December* 1879.

MY DEAR SCOTT—That question about the "Fountain of Youth" is a curious one, and it would be pleasant to see it cleared up. It may be that Dr. Littledale has substantial grounds for his statement. I mean, that it is not founded upon *negative* conclusions merely. But one would like to know what those grounds are. Considering the remote antiquity and the universality of the attribution (often well-founded) to springs and fountains of curative and renovating virtues—and the superstitions which amongst every people have sprung out of this belief, with myths and legends of all sorts connected with them, the one extraordinary thing would be to find no notion of a fountain which not only healed diseases, but restored youth to the decrepit. Such a notion would seem the most natural possible in legendary fancies and in myth-making times.

Yet I must confess that I have in vain searched in Grimm ("Deutsche Mythologie") and in Preller, as well as in Herodotus, for any myth or story of the sort. Nor do I find one amongst the Irish legendary lore, although we might easily suspect a Celtic origin for the notion.

It might very well arise amongst a notoriously pleasure-loving race such as the West Indian Islanders (not Caribs) are reported to have been, whose greatest horror must have been the approach of a period of life when they could no longer enjoy—and whose dreams might well have suggested the hope of an eternal renewal of youth. Yet I cannot help suspecting that the story published by the Spaniards, and which set Ponce de Leon off on his sagacious quest, arose from a mistake. Ignorant as they were of the languages of the Indians, save such vocables as they picked up, their chief communication with the natives must have been conducted by means of signs. They heard of a fountain which had healing properties; a wonderful spring that cured all maladies and "made people young again"—a figure of speech not unknown to us either. Ready to believe anything of those marvellous new-found lands, where almost everything differed from the old world, the Spaniards left their own imagination free play—and themselves invented more than they heard—so that not only their ears, but their very eyes deceived them. I think it was Ponce's companions, who, coming upon the huts of the Floridians, which were rough-cast with an extremely white stucco that glittered in the sunshine, at once came to the conclusion that they were cased in silver. They would only have to slaughter the natives (having first offered them Christianity) and then peel off the precious metal by the ton. However, even if the Spaniards were mistaken as to what they heard, and unwittingly invented the story of the magic fountain themselves, it does not, of course, alter the complexion of Dr. Littledale's statement, or in any way invalidate it. It is enough if the Spaniards can be shown to have been the disseminators of the story in Europe, and to have brought it with them, however acquired, from the New World. That is the question one would like to see set at rest, and that can only be done by finding some traces of the story in Europe or the East earlier than A.D. 1492, or some years after.

The daughters of Pelias we know tried to boil their father young again. But we are not told that they used the water of any particular fountain in cooking him; and so it is not a case in point—especially as the poor old gentleman was none the better of the operation.—Yours ever, F. W. BURTON.

This suggested my stating these earlier dates to my learned friend Dr. Littledale, but he still held by the story of Ponce de Leon as the origin of the fable in Europe, at the same time suggesting the possibility of its being a materialistic symbolisation of the Christian doctrine of regeneration by baptism. " This is quite likely," he adds, " to have arisen in highly literalist minds, but I have never met with any documentary evidence of this. All sorts of wild notions were flying about in the fifteenth century." In this case the figure in full armour might be St. George or the angel Michael.

The suggestion of a symbolisation of regeneration by baptism is, I must think, the origin of the *fons juventutis*, the subtilties of that period being most curious and recondite. In art this took the form of allegorical figures, a pedantic tendency gathering strength from every successive development of the

Renaissance till it became effete. As it appears in the hand of Giotto and others in the Arena chapel in Padua, and above all in the great Saloon in the same city, the allegorical and the symbolical is replete with poetic character. Indeed that mighty hall with its innumerable pictures, unhappily repainted more than once, and its wide barrel roof, through which an opening is made to allow the sun to draw a line on the floor marking the daily meridian, is to me one of the most interesting buildings in the world.

The profoundest thinker in this partially mystical line of invention was the greatest of modern artists, Michael Angelo, and the most surprising example of it is in the picture of "God the Father creating Adam" on the ceiling of the Sistine. I confess to having lain on my back, the better to examine that ceiling, for hours, and yet to have missed the nature of the figure within the left arm of the Creator—a female figure with smooth parted hair, rising from behind, looking intently on the now living *man*, whose finger is *raised to touch* the finger of God. But when I saw the large photographs by Braun I was at once arrested by the beautiful steady gaze of this figure, unmistakably female, by her bust and smooth hair, not one of the lusty cherub boys that bear up the drapery that envelops the Deity; and I afterwards found that a large, though rude, contemporary woodcut existed. This woodcut was sent by some one to the Burlington Club for examination after my letter was published in the *Athenæum*. The woodcut is inscribed *Gaspar Ruena fecit*, without a date, but from its style may be safely considered contemporary, and if so, probably done from an original sketch of the great artist, as so many large woodcuts at that time were produced from very slight sketches. In this print the sex of the figure within the left arm of the Almighty Father is conspicuously expressed, and I have no doubt Michael Angelo intended to express the coming wife of Adam; the figure is therefore the ante-type or eidolon of Eve!

With respect to strictly allegorical treatment, which was always more affected by sculptors than by painters (indeed Giotto in the Arena Chapel at Padua depicts the emblematic personages introduced between his pictures in monochrome relief, as if sculptures), I found on careful study that it had been always carefully avoided by Michael Angelo. The recumbent statues on the Medici tombs, usually called Night and Day, Morning and Evening, have no such weak and scarcely definable significance. They have always, for these four centuries nearly, passed under the foolish names they bear simply because works of art have never received adequate criticism except for their external qualities. These statues really represent *conditions of life*—sleeping and watching, rest and unrest. How much more significant they are placed on the tombs of the Medici when reviewed under the higher interpretation! Sleep is for the night, therefore the sculptor placed an owl beside the sleeper, and that owl is all the authority for all the figures having received the absurd appellations of Night and Day, Morning and Evening. In the epigram sent to Michael Angelo by Giovanni Strozzi that poet speaks of the sleeper with the owl beside her as *La Notte*, but in the answering epigram the sculptor corrects him by speaking of it as if it *represented* sleep, which of course it does. Michael Angelo's last line is this:

<blockquote>Però non mi destar deh parla basso.</blockquote>

The difference between a piece of sculpture representing a mental or bodily condition and an allegorical human creature flourishing a suggestive implement, or accompanied by a previously understood adjunct, is the difference between the natural and the artificial, between poetry and riddles: recognisable, one would say, by the meanest understanding. Yet at this time Heath Wilson, whom I knew in our earliest active life in Edinburgh, and also in London when I joined the executive of the miserable "Schools of Design," repudiated the distinction I drew in his book on Michael Angelo, and laughed at my elucidation of the female appearing in the group round God the Father in the Creation of Adam. He went farther, showing his want of sense by pronouncing the discovery of no consequence! Mr. Fagan too accepts the old meaningless nomenclature of Night and Day, Morning and Evening, applied to the statues on the Medici tombs, in his smaller work, just out. He was, however, much struck by my suggestion, especially on my definition to him of the last line of Michael Angelo's poetical reply to Strozzi's epigram. But so it will go on; such is the wholly exoteric nature of art-writing, treating the artist only from the point of view of taste and workmanship.

Let me give another instance bearing on the same subject. I had been long interested in the old controversy as to the author of the illustrations to the pedantic romance published in Venice in 1499, the *Hypnerotomachia Poliphili*. This book, thought unique in its way, dealing with the love of Poliphilus, a sort of impersonation of art, for Polia, a representative of classic taste perhaps, is valued mainly for its illustrations, which show minute acquaintance with antique architecture and ornament, and also charming purism of drawing in the figure subjects. The origin of those designs, which are on wood or on the soft metal much used by engravers for surface-printing after the book-making from metal types had arrived at perfection, as we see by the truly wonderful cuts in the Books of Hours by Simon Vostre and others in Paris, was a favourite subject of inquiry. All the greatest painters of the greatest period of painting were accredited with them, from Raphael, who would appear to critics to have had as many hands as Briareus, with eyes in proportion to direct them, down to the least of all those exclusively known by their extant pictures. I knew practically that no painter in great repute and practice would be found to have had any hand in the work. Ottley and others attributed the engraving of Albert

Dürer's best prints on wood to his own hand, as if he who never, as far as we know, cut a single line on wood, could at once surpass the most expert *holzschneider* in Nürnberg. Had they selected the worst as probably done by the painter, they would have been nearer the rational understanding of the matter. How is it at the present day so few of our best masters of the palette are great designers? As for the designer or inventor of the illustrations in the *Hypnerotomachia* being also the engraver, that did not follow; even in Venice, where engraving either in wood or copper had scarcely penetrated as yet, it is very unlikely that he was. The earliest volume printed in Venice bears a German name as printer, and the immediate rise of a number of noble editors, issuing works with admirable woodcut title-pages, suggests that German *formschneiders* resorted thither at once.

Ottley had indeed suggested that the designer and engraver of prints in an Ovid printed in Venice shortly after the *Hypnerotomachia* was the same person. Dr. Lippmann too suggested that not only that engraver, but also Jacob Wälsch or Walch[1] had been connected with that work, because he had returned to Venice to undertake as draftsman, no

[1] This artist was formerly considered to belong to the German school, if indeed he was not a German by birth; now he is given up to the Italians. He was living in Nürnberg at the end of the fifteenth century when Dürer returned thither from his Wanderjahre, and finding Jacob there as an engraver, must have learned much from him. Jacob's style of engraving is so much more closely allied to the German manner that it is probable his stay in Nürnberg was to educate himself in engraving, and even after his return to Venice he had no effect on Italian engraving.

doubt, a large view of Venice to be cut on wood, a copy of which is to be seen in the British Museum. But a book came into my hand, just then published, which enabled me to identify the style of drawing of the much-disputed illustrations with that of other illustrative works publishing about the same year, 1499, in Venice, and to find the initials of the name to be those of an artist who has been accredited with many *nielli* or *quasi-nielli*. This book was *Die Bücherornamentik der Renaissance*, Leipzig, 1878, a collection of a hundred reproductions of the title-borders of Venetian and other works at the end of the fifteenth century. Several of these had an absolutely unmistakable resemblance to the style of those in the *Hypnerotomachia*, and on one were the initials S. C. P., with I. below them, no doubt representing the word *Inventor*. Five minutes' examination by an artist, especially one expert in drawing on wood, is worth a year's deliberation of men who do not possess special knowledge, and internal evidence, the evidence of style, is worth all other. Here were the initials of the name of the artist of these illustrations; they were done by a quite obscure draftsman Vasari had never heard of. I showed the title-border Herr Butsch had faithfully given by means of some new scientific process to several artists, painters, illustrators, and engravers; they were all agreed as to the identity of the style of drawing, and I wrote a letter to the *Athenæum*, which was published 27th March 1880, with considerable satisfaction.

And who was this S. C. P.? I called him a *quasi-niellist*, because the works attributed to him in the British Museum, signed by these initials or various combinations of them, had the lettering in the ordinary way—not reversed, as the true *niello* inscriptions always were. The name in full, as given on one of these doubtful *nielli*, and as repeated without question by Passavant, an unquestionable authority, is Stephanus Cæsenas Peregrini. Unhappily these little engravings have been all, or nearly all, invalidated as ancient works, and are now believed to be modern forgeries; at least they have lately come to light in extraordinary numbers. This, however, is nothing to me. The forgers may have taken the name from this title-border, which is beyond dispute, or they may have invented the name from the initials; I know nothing of that matter.

Looking up this letter to the *Athenæum* I find some notes on the very earliest rudimentary beginnings of imitative art, with sketches to illustrate them, which may be interesting enough to preserve here. They were made in the exhibition of Dr. Schliemann's Collection of Antiquities from Hissarlic, 1877-78. Among these the most important things, in fact, were an immense number of red clay vessels for water, called by him "Owl-headed Vases." He found these in great numbers, and in his very interesting work lays considerable stress on them, conceiving that they are capable of bearing evidence to a favourite doctrine that the Trojans were originally Hellenes, the owl here supposed to be represented being " the great-great-great-grandmother of the bird of Pallas Athena " !

The indefatigable excavator, in descending below

the very cradle of Greek civilisation, has persuaded himself to believe anything ; these vessels are not in the shape of the owl, but in that of the human figure. Some of them have ears, the later ones mouths, and the eyes quite differently represented. It is this difference, showing the progressive steps of imitative art, that drew my attention to them. If we observe a child's earliest attempts at drawing or modelling, the eyes are represented not as a feature but as an organ, the iris and pupil are expressed as a circle. The child and the savage feel alike in this, and art in this follows nature herself, the earliest true eye being bare as in the fish. The second stage of delineation is to express the eye as a feature; the appearance becomes the important thing, the lids are mainly represented, and a long slit is the aspect of the organ. Some of the heads on these vessels have the eyes so modelled. These are the product of a later period, a period of years or centuries. The handles are more developed also to represent arms. The ears and the mouth are much more expressed, and as the body of the vase really represents the upper part of the human body—to follow it any farther, keeping the purpose of the vessel in view, being impossible—the breasts and the navel are carefully recorded.

These particulars, as indicating, to use Dr. Schliemann's phrase, the great-great-great-grandmother of the art of the Parthenon, appear to me amusing as well as interesting, and render the vases worthy of a place in our Museum. The presence of the mammæ as elevations or knobs, and the navel as a third lower down, the smallness of the mouth, seem to prove the head to be that of a female, more probably that of Aphrodite than of Pallas Athena.

# CHAPTER XIX

PENKILL—Æ. (MISS BOYD), 1880

It has been well said, the nation is happy that has no history. It is so with individuals as well as nations, and as years creep on with less struggle and more ease there is less to record, life becomes more orderly, and time fleeter on the wing, one year resembles another. As spring advances into summer and my work at South Kensington draws to a close, we prepare to emigrate to Scotland. Æ., who has wintered with us in London, has gone in May, and our almost daily exchange of letters or journals goes on till July, when we follow, thirsting for the quiet of the *Old Scotch House*, its gray walls chequered by the shade of the great trees, and the jackdaws sitting for ever on its vane or towers.

The absolute silence of the country after noisy Chelsea, and after trying to sleep with one's ear on a railway pillow, if we travel by a sleeping carriage, is like a suggestion of preternatural life. Sounds inaudible in London to the human sense begin to grow on the ear; the silence becomes animest in with charming, soothing characteristics, the already filled with the hum of insects, the fine winnowing of small birds' wings, the rustle of a dress on the grass. In my usual restlessness in the early morning, I got up to-day to find a book wherewith to return to bed. From the window the landscape was as still as the house within. The sky was white, the sun unspeakably white, making the shadows of the trees faintly chequer the smooth green terrace. On the point of one of the leaves of a great aloe below, perched a thrush, silent and motionless; two wild rabbits were sitting on the green terrace still as if they were carved in stone. In the clear air every leaf on every tree had an individuality, and every pebble on the walk, as if shade and even colour were defects of nature, yet there was a luminosity at that hour that gave a peculiar unity to the whole scene, removing it from mid-day impressions. It was as if I had looked from the palace of the Sleeping Beauty, in its enchanted and limitless repose. But it suggested a higher tone of feeling than this; it was as if I had awoke into another world beyond the pulsation of the senses, a state of things that would last for ever. Repeatedly in earlier times I had felt this almost awe-inspiring impression from absolute silence and stillness, and I have tried to express it in a sonnet.

Certainly such an emotional moment as this is not possible in town. Town is the theatre for activity in relation to the actual world, solitude in see-country creates reflection, the luxury or the pain probab I say solitude, because a perfect understanding and sympathy with a single friend of twenty years' standing is something more not less than solitude. Anxiety about the house in Chelsea with all its belongings carries my wife back thither earlier than I care to return. She had no jealousy; the perfect friendship, the ambition of my life, had come within my grasp, and year after year had made its possession secure. To Æ. I had been of use in the affairs of life; on her

> The vanward clouds of evil days
> Had spent their malice and the sullen rear

had exhausted itself in vain; her mind had retained all its elasticity. She had an inexhaustible power of perceiving what was in the mind of any one she loved, and of meeting them midway, as if she, too, had thought as they did; she would rather please them than herself. It was so truly; she enjoyed others' happiness and others' ideas exactly as if they were her own. There is a couplet, said to be by Prior, a very imperfect poet, that I have seen quoted, and have a hundred times repeated to myself, inwardly connecting it with Æ.

> Abra was ready ere I named her name,
> And when I named another Abra came.

She had, moreover, a quickness in attaining to any handicraft or artistic accomplishment that made her critically the most perceptive arbiter I have ever known.

Our way of life was this. She was our guest in winter, and we were hers in summer. I have already spoken of Chelsea as a country town, though a portion of the mighty metropolis. We had or could have had many friends there, but we become more self-centred as we get old, and our environment, the scenery of life, becomes more important. This division of the year between the two localities, with local improvements or other businesses employing spare hours in both, became our habit. November found us settled into a life of fires and books, and the eve of the New Year found us waiting with unabated pleasure for the midnight bells of Battersea rising and falling over the running river. The first winter I spent in London I heard the bells ring out the old year while walking through St. James's Park to my Pimlico lodgings. Last year we were sitting in my library playing bézique, with a hurricane carrying the sounds fitfully over the Thames to us. This contrast suggested these two sonnets :

### NEW YEAR'S EVE. 1879-80

I

Long years ago when love was lord of me,
   And all life's gifts were in the impending year,
   At this same hour I heard afar and near
These New Year's bells flood heaven with melody
Over the snow-clad Park, as over sea
     Voices of welcome to the mariner
     Returning fortunate, till in the rear
St. Paul's great voice made lesser voices flee.

And now again I hear them! far-off Bells,
   Across the rushing river, in the wind,

Fainting or rising as the tempest swells ;
The river rushing like dark years behind
Chasing dark years gone by, and those sweet knells
High overhead like memories intertwined.

II

Ring out again, ye Bells of Battersea,
  Over the seaward Thames, as I sit here
  Lamplit with moistened eyes and hungering ear,
Recalling thoughts of things once hoped to be,
Past now, forgotten ; for to me
  Those wild harmonics in the waves of air
  Changing, yet still repeating, here and there,
Yet truly ordered, ring life's history.

Life's history and life's prophecy withal :—
  Shouted the sons of God when a new ray
  Showed them this infant world, and each new day
They shout, and each new year renews the call
  To higher hopes, continuous and alway,
  Rhythmical, storm-borne, past life's echoing hall.

As spring advances, we begin to look forward to the change. ÆB. must see all the Exhibitions of the season opening in May. But before that time, on the morning of the 18th of March, a note from Sir Frederick Burton informed me at breakfast that a good copy of the picture painted by Dürer in Venice, the " Rosenkrautzfest," was to be sold that day at Christie's. It was the anniversary of my first meeting with ÆB., and we both determined to go, and if possible to buy it in commemoration of the day, to me the day of days. The copy of the " Rosenkrautzfest" was the size of the original and brought too much money, but we persevered in our determination so far, we bought a little Florentine picture, an Annunciation imitative of the manner of Fra Angelico, which is now here at Penkill, to be hung in the great Hall, now in course of erection from my design.

Towards the end of May then Miss Boyd leaves us in town and towards the end of July my wife and I follow, and all through the late summer and

autumn I remain at Penkill. The garden attains its perfection and slowly diminishes again, the harvest becomes yellow and disappears, the equinoctial winds begin to blow and the white horses appear on the distant sea. But now and again our friends appear on the scene, like birds of passage; and here while I write arrives a doggerel note from my dear Reverend but humorous Dr. Littledale, who promised to be one of this year's visitors. He has been suddenly seized with one of his visitations of illness, still his indomitable spirits survive. " I have been mending," he says, "but am still too utterly weak and tired to do any work, even to write a chant-royal or a villanelle. Still I begin to think I shall try, and here it goes :

> " I sit in town the weary weeks,
> I cannot reach the Northern land
> Where hurdies do without the breeks,
>
> Where sporran still the Gael bespeaks,
> Where Farintosh is aye at hand,
> And salmon kippered in the reeks—
>
> You'll say 'Don't try poetic freaks,
> The lyre responds not to your hand,
> By rights tears should be on your cheeks!'
>
> But no, I love not snivelling sneaks,
> I can no waterworks command,
> Like infant thieves before the Beaks,
>
> Though I must pass those aimless weeks
> In Holborn, Fleet Street, or the Strand,
> Where hansom rolls and waggon creaks,
>
> While you are supping cock-with-leeks
> And haggis too, I understand,
> 'Neath Penkill's pepper-boxy peaks—
> Stop, stop, I hear protesting shrieks—
> From the thistly Northern land!—F. R. L."

Here on rainy days, with no painting or writing in progress, I have got acquainted with the oddest collection of books. Books on *Horse-shoeing*, on the *Grape*, the *Kitchen Garden*, and so forth; the once fashionable novels, neatly-bound little volumes such as *The Female Quixote*, and *The Adventures of a Guinea*, and some of the works " no gentleman's library should be without;" but the old Magazines are the most interesting. Here are the *Universal Magazines* of the end of last century with the accounts of the French Revolution and the doings of the guillotine, succeeded by a page or two of poetry, called *The British Muse*, amusing by its now incredible badness. In the advertisements of new publications we see in the same number with the account of King Louis's death, Godwin's *Political Justice*, 2 volumes, 4to, £2 : 2s.; an answer to Paine's *Rights of Man* by Mr. Adam, 1s. 6d.; Priestley's *Appeal on the Riot of Birmingham*, part 2, 3s. 6d., all indicating the topics agitating England in its sympathy with France. We see from the specimens of the British Muse how unpoetic the age was just before the uprising of the Lake poets. Even Horace Walpole found it hard to beat out a few rhymes on the three Vernons, the beauties of his circle. In the volume for 1789 we find also ample evidence of the brutality both of the people and of the law, lawyers having always been the last to move towards reform. In the December session that year there were at the Old Bailey 26 condemned to death; 5 to be publicly whipped in different streets named, then imprisoned; 2 more to be discharged after whipping; and 36 to be transported; while Robert Kelly stood in the pillory twice and was so savagely treated by the populace that the sheriff took him away after an hour and twenty minutes, his full time being two hours. This brutality we find also indicated by the boxing matches at which the royal Dukes were spectators. The principal sawdust pit was in Tottenham Court Road, established by subscription, where these fights were sometimes fatal; a man called Tyne kills his antagonist in 1788, and reappears in the next volume as having died of bruises "received last Tuesday in a battle at Wimbledon."

On the same page with this intimation we find the Judge, Lord Kenyon, "with his usual humanity," as the editor has it, and Mr. Erskine, counsel for the Crown, protecting these royal Dukes by trying "Mr. Walter for publishing (1st February 1789) in a newspaper called *The Times* two libellous paragraphs reflecting on the character of the Dukes of York, Gloucester, and Cumberland," as "having been insincere in their expressions of joy in his Majesty's happy recovery"! Not till five months afterwards do we find the sentence recorded. Mr. Walter is to pay a fine of £50, to be imprisoned for a year, to stand in the pillory one hour at Charing Cross, and to find ample security for good behaviour for seven years! The same judge and counsel a few days later try and convict the Rev. Dr. Withers to the same penalties less the pillory, for a libel on Mrs. Fitzherbert. Here the leading counsel, Mr. Erskine, who was of course shortly after raised to the Bench, said "he had the honour to be acquainted with the lady, who was a person of the most amiable character and gentle manners," and the judge, among other observations, lamented that "the most exalted virtue was no shield against calumny." A third case of libel is that of Mr. Stockdale, the bookseller, accused of reflecting on the House of Commons for their course of procedure against Mr. Hastings. This of course was nobody's interest, and the jury acquitted him.

On 19th November the King (George III.), now remarkably cheerful and well, goes in state to the theatre with the Queen and three Princesses, to see the pleasant comedy of the *Dramatist*. The house was kept in a roar of laughter in which their majesties and the Princesses most heartily joined. The King was dressed in blue velvet embroidered with gold lace. The Queen's dress was a deep rose-coloured satin trimmed with diamonds; a white cap ornamented with a black velvet bandage studded with diamonds, and diamonds in different parts of her hair. The Princesses were in buff satin striped with silver and adorned with point lace, white caps, with blue and white feathers and diamonds in the hair.

Old magazines are some protection against a wet day in the country, but a shortlived one; another was rummaging in a great iron box containing the family documents. No one except myself had ever thought of this as an amusement, and I did not find it remunerative. I found, however, a great seal of Mary Queen of Scots appended to a very small charter, and dated to my surprise only a year or two after the death of her father James V., when she must have been still a child.

Neither this nor any other paper or parchment

was of the least interest, and the only curiosities I found were the singular monograms appended to their signatures by the Scotch lawyers of the sixteenth century. Some of them I copied, as here reproduced.

To close this chapter, perhaps the last in these notes, I will transcribe a sonnet recording the twenty-first Anniversary of my first meeting Æ.

To Æ., 18th March 1880.   21st Anniversary

Spring comes with all the firstlings of the year,
  Leaping around her careless of the cold ;
  Soon summer's tale so charming will be told,
The rose-leaves fall, the sun shrinks back in fear.
Alas, the hours fly faster, and more near

Yule draws to Easter when the hair turns gray,
Sooner it seems the swallows fly away,
And wintry floes brim full the quivering wear.

What matters it? These are but things we know,
    Things that pass by as Chronos gives command ;
Your smile is still as bright as long ago,
We still are gathering shells on life's seashore,
    We still can walk like children hand in hand,
Friendship and love beside us evermore.

# CHAPTER XX AND LAST

*Begun August 1882*

MY POET'S HARVEST HOME—DEATH OF ROSSETTI

WHEN I left off the previous chapter with an anniversary sonnet to Æ., I laid this MS., such as it is, aside with the feeling that it was closed; but already since then two incidents have unexpectedly transpired of vital importance, such as cause me to add another chapter to my story. The unexpected incidents are — my writing without premeditation and with a quite novel feeling of spontaneity a hundred or more little poems, expressing the mental state of the day in the simplest manner, with the comparatively successful publication of the same under the name of *A Poet's Harvest Home*; and the death of my dear friend for so many years, whose intercourse has occupied a very considerable space in this manuscript.

With regard to the poems, the novelty of their unplanned production, while it deprived them of recognised form, gave them simplicity of expression, not one elocutionary or unnecessary word being admitted. This has indeed been always more or less characteristic of the advent of my poems, good, indifferent, or bad as they may be judged; but in the present case this centum of poems or rhymes—many of them abrupt as epigrams should be, others, ballads or short narratives or sonnets—came to me fully dressed, as it were, every morning between waking and rising, in the autumn months of 1881. The motive, with every line to be employed in its development, came to me as if from memory; they were written down in pencil on pieces of paper I had placed under my pillow the night before. Every day I thought, now the good fairy has exhausted himself, I shall have no more! but still it went on till I had a good many over a hundred, some mornings bringing me two or three. The house was full of company, but I found time to make fair copies, and to read them over to *B.* in the garden bower, where in 1870 I used to read the wonderful war news in the daily paper. Then we threw out or tore up a number, as she objected violently to such as were either satirical or metaphysical.

While this incubation was going on, I was surprised by a letter from Rossetti, whom we had left in a very low state of general health, even suffering from a total loss of the hope of recovery, the greatest loss a sick man can suffer. The letter was dated from an out-of-the-way farmhouse in Cumberland, whither he had passively allowed himself to be carried by a young man to whom he had suddenly become exclusively attached, Mr. T. Hall Caine.

When our time came for returning to town I was shocked to find the dear old Gabriel prostrate on the old sofa we had so often in the earlier times seen filled with the most genial friends. He was, it now appeared to me, going down fast; but I tried to keep up the usual deception we apply to invalids. I had gone alone, thinking it best to make this first visit so; but he was by himself, no one attending or trying to cheer the man whose spirits were down to zero.

When he and I were alone, he wept and complained, and made unkind speeches, or showed me things he thought would wound me, as when he made his servant lay before me a large chalk sketch he called "Questioning the Sphinx." This wounded me, because it happened that I had made an illustration in my first issue of *The Year of the World*, that juvenile "poem with a purpose," of the hero-traveller leaning on an augural staff with his ear to the mouth of a Sphinx, which I called by that name, and which the beloved D. G. R. of that early time used to make game of, as if I had mistaken the ancient fable in which the Sphinx was the questioner, not the questioned. I had besides written a poem called "To the Sphinx considered as the symbol of religious mystery." Lying on the sofa dying, as he was, I saw that singular expression of ferocity that used to take possession of his face if he surmised a quarrel was coming. I laid the sketch aside, but he kept staring at me; I refused to take up the gauntlet, and I could not venture to speak of the sketch itself, the style of drawing being so bad as to show his illness was destroying his work.

As the year drew to a close I was variously harassed and occupied, among other things, with reading my new poems to literary friends, and in trying to find a publisher, as, since the death of Mr. W. Longman, I had no interest in that world. Had it not been for the favourable verdict pronounced on the majority of my poems I would not have published at all; in Rossetti in particular, when very short readings sufficed to tire him, the old enthusiasm in my verse burst out, and the tears that came to his eyes were answered by mine, alas! from a different cause. One or two such effusions of feeling were the last flashes of ancient friendship I have to record.

Professor Marshall's object in sending young Mr. Maudsley and a nurse was to cure, by sub-cutaneous injections of morphia gradually decreased, his consumption of chloral—of late enormously enlarged by his increasing insomnia. The result was a complete success. Maudsley decreased the dose, and gradually diluted it without the knowledge and without the consciousness of the patient, till at last he injected only water, Rossetti actually going to sleep immediately after the operation! Altogether before this treatment, with its surprising result, a new idea had taken possession of his mind which caused us painful agitation. He wanted a priest to give him absolution for his sins! I mention this hallucination as I have related previous ones; for example, that of the chaffinch on the highway, so long ago as 1869, not loving him the less but the more, sympathising with him almost mesmerically. Italian as he was, he had no living tie to the country, had never visited it, although Italy is conventionally the country of painting. His mother was affectionately attached to the Church of England, and his father's book of poems called *Arpa Evangelica* was evangelical enough. But the æsthetic side of anything was his exclusive interest; in poetry and in painting the mediæval period of history was necessary to him. Everything he ever did in either art was mediæval in date and in spirit, except his picture called "Found" and his poem called "Jenny," which had both one origin and inspiration. I am nearly certain he never entered a Romish church in his life, except to look at some picture that might be there, and that he knew simply nothing of its ritual or its sacraments.

At first no one took any notice of this demand for a confessor. We thought his mind wandering, or that he was dreaming. But on its earnest repetition, with his eyes open, I for one put him in mind of his not being a papist, and of his extreme agnosticism. "I don't care about that," was his puzzling reply; "I can make nothing of Christianity, but I only want a confessor to give me absolution for my sins!" This was so truly like a man living or rather dying in A.D. 1300, that it was impossible to do anything but smile. Yet he was serious, and went on: "I believe in a future life. Have I not had evidence of that often enough? Have I not heard and seen those that died long years ago? What I want now is absolution for my sins, that's all!" "And very little too," some outsider in the room whispered, as a gloomy joke; none of us, the deeply-interested few who heard him, could answer a word.

Shortly after this he had a slight attack of paralysis, or fancied he had. He was carried upstairs to bed, and never came down again. The difficulty in believing in his sensations made his illness a problem to every one, and I remember William Morris, when he came one evening to hear some of my new poems read, asking me if I really thought Rossetti so ill, or was he only acting to keep those about him in suspense? I declared I knew him to be very ill, but Morris still hesitated to accept my assurance. He was in fact preparing to die. He became weaker, more natural, without the chloral, perhaps, but less vital; and one morning I was surprised by J. P. Sedden, the architect, who had been building houses of the bungalow type at Birchington-on-the-Sea, calling with the information that he had placed one of them at the service of the invalid, who was, at the moment of our conversation, leaving for that place with the young doctor, and others attending. I felt it was too late to see him again, before going; but he never returned, so I saw him no more.

The picture I have drawn had been a painful one to witness in the original, and has been only less so to indicate in narrative, even carefully omitting the most repulsive elements of the scene.

At Birchington he lived four months or more, till the 9th of April, but the presence of his mother and sister, Christina, cleared the air of the sickroom, and made the period sacred. I saw him no more.

My *Poet's Harvest Home* had been issued just the day before. Let me finish my task by my usual method, quoting, or giving entire letters of friends about it. Here is one from Morris himself:

KELMSCOTT HOUSE, UPPER MALL,<br>
HAMMERSMITH, 27<i>th April</i> 1882.

MY DEAR SCOTT—I have never written to thank you for sending me your book, because I have been trying to get round to see you to do so in person, but I must put that off till next week; so I write now.

I have just the same impression on me now I have seen the poems in print, as I had when I heard you read them: that they are original and full of thought, and that their general atmosphere is most delightfully poetical and real; that there is real beauty about them, and I congratulate you heartily on the book, which for the rest is a very pretty little book. . . .—With best wishes, yours ever, WILLIAM MORRIS.

Some other letters within the bundle I have untied I cannot resist the impulse to copy here, they are so pleasant to me as expressions of friendly feeling. Here is one from "our Director," as some of us call him, F. W. Burton:

43 ARGYLL ROAD, KENSINGTON, W.,<br>
21<i>st April</i> 1882.

MY DEAR SCOTT—Having had to return to the National Gallery late yesterday afternoon, I found there on my table a little book, packed up, which I, being hurried at the moment, put into my pocket as it was, and brought home with me.

Great was my pleasure when on uncovering and opening the tiny volume, I found my name inscribed in it by the hand of one whose innate worth, whose high and varied talents, and whose close friendship I value the more deeply the longer I know him, and as to whom my earnest prayer is that he may long be spared to us all as an affectionate and dear friend, and an example of thorough integrity of heart and mind, and of spotless honour.

Before going to bed last night I read a few of the verses in the *Poet's Harvest Home*, but will not attempt to say with what delight. Later on we may talk over the whole matter. At present I will only return my thanks for the book.

One thing I must say here, which could not be so well said face to face—that among the many associations which make dear to me the memory of our great and lost Gabriel Rossetti, not the least dear is that it was through him I first learned to know William Bell Scott.—Believe me ever your affectionate friend,    F. W. BURTON.

From my friend, Sir Frederick, this note gave me a great deal of pleasure, knowing the usual moderation of his language. But if I went on in my selection of letters still extant, I might bring into one bouquet all the valued friends left me whose names appear in the previous reminiscences. This would be pleasant, and artistically proper withal; but was there ever an autobiography or even a memoir by a closely-attached friend produced which was not overdone? and I hold brevity more and more imperative nowadays; it is not the "soul of wit" certainly, but rather the body. I found the stringency with which I held in my little steed in these "Hundred Short Poems" confirmed my views on this matter, and I can less and less understand why Swinburne, publishing a poem ten books long, of two hundred to eight hundred lines each, in which he has glorified passion by presenting it in an atmosphere of poetic splendour almost unparalleled—should load the volume with two hundred pages more of inferior matter!

So I must allow myself to give one or two more letters, nearly entirely relating to my book, coming from men I have mentioned before in these pages. The first is from Holman Hunt, somewhat autobiographic in its nature, and showing, moreover, that he had in his mind a renewal of the ancient amity and intercourse with D. G. R., which had died out with bitterness many years before. It is dated 17th April 1882.

MY DEAR SCOTT—My first thought on getting your little volume is to envy you. I wish so much that I could write poetry! I tried a little in early youth, but then, as with music at a still earlier time, and for somewhat similar reasons, *i.e.* that I had almost more than I could do to avoid being driven from painting, I was discouraged, and lost the chance, if ever I had one, of training my ear in the melody of sweet sounds. It seems to me that I have been assailed more than most men in attempts to work by obstructing demons, so that it has been impossible to listen duly to angels' lessons. In poetry, I may say, that I try to console myself by fancying out poems without words; but I long for the further power, that I might tell my dreams to others.

Although I have by no means had time to go through your little volume thoroughly, I have read enough to feel that the poems are very dainty and thoughtful, with that tender pitifulness that can only be expressed by an Ancient justified by confidence in the authority he holds, but who would not imitate the defiant neck of men of earlier days; an elder doubtful whether the objects of a holy war have not often been missed by the hectoring spirit of the young who have adopted the confidence in their mission of the enlisting sergeant. Your poems have the ripeness of Age without the loss of faith in effort which is so often a mark of length of days, and I treasure the book in the hope that some day I may talk to my children about its author as one they have desired to know more of.

Rossetti's death is ever in my mind, for all my old thoughts turn up in order to be fresh marked with the painful fact. I had long ago forgiven him, and forgotten the offence, which, in fact, taken altogether, worked me good rather than harm; indeed, I had intended in recent times to call upon him, but the difficulties arising from this Jerusalem canvas had already humiliated my spirit so much, that when the visit was in question I felt the need of conquering the task before I went, and awakened memories of early days, when, partly by the noisy blundering of followers, we were driven to stand as though we were reckless in our challenge of the whole world of self-seeking fools. Illness of Rossetti hindered our meeting still more, and thus our talk over the past is deferred until our meeting in the Elysian fields, when, if, as you suggest in your little book, he may defer so long to drink the waters of Lethe, and I retain my memory so long, we may talk over back history as having nothing in it not atoned for and wiped out long ago, and as having value only as experience which has done its work in making us both wiser and better.—Yours ever affectionately,

W. HOLMAN HUNT.

What this ancient but now forgiven offence was we shall not now inquire, but this admirable letter deserved preservation.

I shall now give a few extracts from verses furnished by the same occasion.

Dr. Littledale, my comic versifier, quoted before in similar strains, sent me now a sheet of verses in the newest measures—a Triolet, a Kyrielle, a Rondeau, and a Villanelle. The Rondeau he published in the *Academy*.

> His "Harvest-home" the poet brings,
> Harvest of rich and lovely things,
>  Piled high upon the loaded wain
>  That bears the fruitage of the brain,
> Begirt with flowery garlandings.
>
> With generous hand its gift he flings
> To all with gracious welcomings;
>  And so to scatter wide is fain
>   His Harvest-home.
>
> Not like the niggard's grasp that clings
> To hoarded gold is his who sings,
>  Sings for pure love and not for gain:
>  Then sing we too, with glad refrain,
>   His Harvest-home.

"I began," he says, "by amusing myself with parodying a public favourite, and then thought it a shame not to put down my real sentiments also. I send them to you exactly as they were scribbled off in the original draft. But an hour and a half is not enough time to write four poems in, even for a great poet like myself." This was the *Villanelle*:

> The harvest-home of seventy years—
>  Not scant and thin but lush and fair,
> And rich with heavy golden ears.
>
> In sooth a pleasant sight that cheers,
>  And half unloads the heart of care,
> This harvest-home of seventy years;

> For should not youth discard its fears
>   If eld can home such harvest bear,
>   All rich with heavy golden ears?
>
> The honoured eld which still endears
>   The singer-artist's boon we share—
>   The harvest-home of seventy years.

Swinburne's sonnet I need not transcribe, as it is printed in his Tristram volume; but here, in answer to a complimentary copy, is a trifle by Christina Rossetti, which has an exceedingly interesting reference to the first visit I paid to her household about thirty-five years ago, when I first saw her standing writing at a small high desk, as already recorded in these notes: "before I was twenty" indicating her age pretty nearly at the epoch I mean:

> My old admiration before I was twenty,—
> Is predilect still now promoted to se'enty!
> My own demi-century plus an odd one
>     Some weight to my judgment may fairly impart.
> Accept this faint flash of a smouldering fun,
>     The fun of a heavy old heart.        C. G. R.

This was sent me a month or more after Gabriel's funeral. I will end by "A Rhyme to W. B. S." from Professor Dowden, who says in the accompanying letter: "I was happy in reading your *Harvest Home*, because I had not to look into the clear serene through hangings and trappings of rhetoric. The worst of this rhetoric is the injury it does to the vital variety of true feeling by its uniform high-pressure glare and blare."

A burden of tired thoughts to ease
    I called your "little dears"[1] to me,
And set a pair upon my knees,
    For I had heard their voices free
And seen the sunlight on their hair ;
    And but to touch their cheeks, I thought,
To make my circling arms their lair,
    To lay in mine each tiny palm,
To feel the clinging of small feet,
    To live within their breathing sweet,—
        It will be balm
        For fretted heart and brain o'erwrought.

I had no fear, no touch of awe :—
Ah, "little dears," what gifts you brought
Beyond my careless reckoning !
For they had questions far more wise
Than our accustomed old replies ;
And in their baby eyes I saw
The deeps of life, and in their breath
        Heard the strong song of death.

Some few last words on the actual death of Rossetti may be given here, derived from letters from his brother, written immediately after, from Birchington-on-Sea ; and also an account of his funeral, which indisposition prevented me from attending, in a letter kindly written me by Judge Lushington, who had been intimate with Rossetti in his earlier and better days. He had seen nothing of D. G. R. through all the later period of his career, but still retained so much interest in the singular

---

[1] [In the Prologue to *A Poet's Harvest Home* the writer had spoken of his poems as " Little Dears," and asked—
    Ah me ! then, reader, can you say
    " Little dears " to these to-day ?—Ed.]

endowments of the poet as to assist at the honours of the funeral.

W. M. R. writes to me in answer to my telegram. He says: "It is too true that we have lost Gabriel. He died about 9½ P.M. yesterday. The immediate cause of death said to be uræmic poisoning, or, as we might say, functional derangement of the kidneys leading to a bad state of the blood." William had been at Birchington on Saturday and Sunday, and had formed a bad opinion of his brother's condition, so on receipt of a telegram from Christina he returned again at once on Good Friday, and found the invalid fatally sinking. Up to 9¼ in the evening the anxious watchers did not see that he was getting worse, but then the blood-poisoning, "as the doctor says," went to the brain; Gabriel cried out twice, immediately fell into a sort of convulsive lethargy, and to all appearance expired unconscious and unsuffering.

For more reasons than one the family had concluded to have the funeral there, not at Highgate, where old Rossetti lies, and Gabriel's wife. Would it be consistent with my feelings, he asks, and otherwise manageable for me to attend on Friday, the day appointed for the funeral? If so, they would like to see me. They mean to write to a few other intimates to the same effect.

William writes me again three days later. "We continue here," he says, "in that state of hushed sorrowfulness which can be imagined, waiting for the funeral to-morrow." In all their minds there was the feeling that it really was an alternative between loss of life and gradually increasing, and finally, perhaps, total loss of his powers, even of all force of mind, and that the loss of life was ten thousand times the less painful and miserable branch of the alternative. D. G. R. looked in death serene and restful, and so natural as to suggest sleep rather than death. This is usually the case, but they could see no alteration up to the morning of the funeral. On Monday, a mould had been taken from the face and hand, one of the smallest of full-grown male hands.

His Honour, Judge Lushington, on reaching home wrote me as follows :

> 36 KENSINGTON SQUARE, 14*th April* 1882.
>
> DEAR MR. SCOTT—I think you will like to hear how your dear friend Gabriel Rossetti was buried, so I will tell you—for, thanks to your kind telegram, I was there ; I had hoped to see *you* there, and was grieved to hear that you were prevented by illness.
>
> The church at Birchington stands back about three-quarters of a mile from the sea, on slightly rising ground, which looks over the open land and the sea. It is of gray country flint, built in the twelfth or thirteenth century, and restored a few years ago, I thought simply ; it is nicely kept, and to-day was full of Easter flowers. It has an old gray tower, and gray shingle spire, which went up, as I noticed during the ceremony, into a pure blue sky. The churchyard is nicely kept, too ; it was bright with irises and wallflowers in bloom, and close to Gabriel's grave there was a laurestinus and a lilac. The grave is on the south side close to the porch ; it was cut so clearly it seemed carved out of the chalk. Altogether it was a sweet open spot, I thought.

At the graveside, wonderful to say, was the old mother, supported by William on one side and Christina on the other—a most pathetic sight. She was very calm, extraordinarily calm, but whether from self-command or the passivity of age, I do not know—probably from both; but she followed all the proceedings with close interest. Then around was a company of about fifteen or twenty, many of them friends of yours, and several whom I did not know. The service was well read by the vicar. Then we all looked into the resting-place of our friend, and thought and felt our last farewells—many flowers, azaleas and primroses, were thrown in. I saw William throw in his lily of the valley.

This is all I have to tell you. Sad it was, very sad, but simple and full of feeling, and the fresh beauty of the day made itself felt with all the rest.

I shook hands with William, and came home with Mr. Graham. Dear Gabriel, I shall not forget him.

I hope you are getting better. Pray remember me to Mrs. Scott.—Always very truly yours,

VERNON LUSHINGTON.

And so my Notes bring themselves to an end, at least as far as we can be sure of anything we say or do ending as long as we live. My work has not been *Art for Art's sake*, but truth for truth's sake. There is no other writing quite honourable for a man to do; and I shall miss the little task I have always fallen back upon as an occupation in the absence of any other more urgent in this pleasant retirement I enjoy, invalid as I am, waiting till the fatal bell shall call me home. The day is a fine, warm day in late September; Miss Boyd and the gardener are among the flowers preparing for the next spring beforehand, by cutting and layering such as are preservable; so the seasons bring their everlasting repetition of interest. I shall go to join them as soon as I have wound up by transcribing the following poem, written last year :

### On my Birthday, Æ. 70

So many years I've gone this way!
So many years! I must confess
Waste energies, much disarray,
Yet can I own no weariness,
Nor see I evening shadows fall
Down my much-inscriptioned wall;
The warm air still is like mid-day,
And many mournful ghosts have past,
    Laid still at last.
The Fabulist's fardel lighter grew
As near the bourne the bearer drew;
Life can, alas, no more surprise
By its continuous compromise;
New faces fill the chairs, and so
Our interest in the game runs low;
Quiet pleasures longest stay;
Experience packs so much away.

I wait and wonder: long ago
This wonder was my constant guest,
Wonder at our environing,
And at myself within the ring;
Still that abides, and still some quest
Before my footsteps seems to lie,
But quest of what I scarcely know,
And life itself makes no reply:
A quest for naught that earth supplies,—
This is our latest compromise.

So many years I've gone this way,
It seems I may walk on for aye;

"Long life, God's gift," my brother prayed,
Nearing the confines of the dead,
Going reluctant, not afraid ;
With thankful breath I bow the head
Thinking of those grave words to-day.

The ancient tempter well divined
This longing of the sunlit blind :
"Ye shall be wise as gods," he said :
"If ye obey me undismayed."
Ah, never may this be ! though still
In hope we climb the topless hill.
'Tis but the ending of the strife,
Calms while it crowns the weary head,
Weary yet anxious still with eyes
Bent forward to some hoped-for prize.
But not until beyond our life,
Can the life's oracle be read,
When the unanswered brain and heart
Have ceased to ask and ceased to smart,
And all the centuries to come
Like centuries past to us are dumb.

# CONCLUDING CHAPTER
## BY THE EDITOR

NINE more years remained to Mr. Scott after he wrote the grave and touching verses with which his Autobiography ends. When he died on the 22nd of November 1890, he had nearly completed the full sum of fourscore years. During the last six of them his strength was greatly impaired by recurring attacks of *angina pectoris*. That his long extension of life beyond the ordinary span was not labour and sorrow, was due entirely to that other "God's gift" besides "long life" for which he has recorded his gratitude, the gift of a noble woman's devoted friendship. When it became apparent that he could no longer stand the strain of active work, Miss Boyd put her house at his service, devoted her whole time to him, and nursed him with a care and skill to which it would be hard to find a parallel. The poet's dreams of an ideal friendship were realised as such dreams can seldom have been. Often and often has Dr. Valentine, the kindly and efficient doctor who attended him in those last years at Penkill, a sympathetic philosopher as well as a physician, spoken to me of Miss Boyd's self-sacrificing devotion, of the tender care and cheerful tact with which she guarded her patient from excitement and worry, from everything that might remotely bring on one of the dreaded paroxysms, and the ready and resourceful presence of mind with which she administered the necessary remedies when attacks came in spite of all her care.

I have asked Miss Boyd to furnish me with some notes of the beginnings of this intermittent illness and the invalid's habits in its intervals. I give them here in her own words.

The weakness of his heart first showed itself on the 23rd April 1885.

He had been working at South Kensington, at the examination of students' drawings, from the 13th of April, and did not feel well, but had no idea of anything serious being the matter till the 23rd of the month at three o'clock in the morning, when he was seized with frightful heart-spasm, and from that time till his death he was liable to dreadful attacks of the same, and never recovered his bodily strength, always requiring to be most careful of cold or exertion of any kind.

This beginning of his illness took place at his Chelsea home (Bellevue), where he remained till his doctors thought him well enough to bear the journey to Scotland. They considered this change might be useful to him. Dr. R. Thompson and Professor John Marshall were his medical advisers.

So we made an arrangement for a through invalid carriage from Euston to take us to Girvan without change.

' Unfortunately, owing to the stupid carelessness of the officials, clerks at the ticket-office, and porters, he had so much exertion at the station before starting that he was greatly exhausted, and almost fainted. We (he and

I) went by the 8.45 P.M. train, and journeyed all night, on the 25th-26th of June. As the night advanced he became very cold, and at about three o'clock in the morning, when the train was going at great speed, he was attacked by a frightful heart-spasm, and I thought he was dying. I could hardly get the necessary medicines given, from the swinging of the carriage; a dreadful night of suffering it was. At last the paroxysm passed away, and though much exhausted and very weak, he appeared to have recovered by the time we got to our journey's end.

Alas! this was not the case, for on the night of the 28th there was a dreadful return of illness, with congestion of the lungs. When we got to Penkill on the 26th it would have been right for him to have gone to bed and kept quiet, but the pleasure of finding himself at last back at the old place made us imprudent, and we walked and drove about, thinking our troubles were over.

A very long illness followed, and the first time he got out again into the sunshine was the 20th of July. After this he regained strength to some extent, and we were always hoping that in time he might be able to resume a more active life, but on the 28th September another attack, followed by congestion of the lungs, showed that this was not to be, although sometimes months would pass without a relapse. Once, indeed, he was free for eight months, and even *I* was rather hopeful.

Looking back one sees how each year there was a change; something had to be given up, until at last he had no power of walking or taking the least exertion.

It was wonderful how the mental powers were unchanged, and how alive he was to everything that before had interested him; but all this you know better than I can tell you.

I give you this painful, short sketch of the progress of his illness as you ask me to do so; but from your own observation you can understand better than I can tell you how patiently and nobly he endured five long years of sickness, how unselfish and thoughtful he was for those about him, and kindly and loving to all his friends; always ready, if in his power, to help those in trouble, even thinking of what he could do for them when suffering greatly himself.

He read a good deal, as you know, and friends were most kind (you among the number) in sending him books that they thought would interest him.

Now and then he painted a little when well enough, and his hand and eye never lost their power—the one as firm and the other as clear as ever to the last, as his handwriting can show.

The picture which he painted from a sketch done years ago of the landing-place of St. Columba, on Iona, shows how he retained his sense of colour and feeling for the beauties of wild, rugged landscape scenery, and the painting of the sea is as good as at any time of his life, and that is not saying a little. He began this picture on the 10th September 1887, and from time to time worked upon it to within about a year of his death. It is not quite finished, but is a beautiful work, full of poetic feeling. He always had a great love of the sea, seen from the land, for he was no sailor, and one of the drives he loved best was along the coast, south of Girvan, where you and I went the last time you were here. Sometimes when the sea was very calm he would stop the carriage to listen to the wash of the waves till his eyes filled with tears.

Fortunately his love of Penkill was so great that he never tired of it; and the enjoyment he had in the change of the seasons—the flowers as they came, and the farming operations, ploughing in the autumn, with flocks of white sea-birds following in the new-turned furrows, the sower going out to sow, scattering the seed as he goes—was always a delight. Then the harvesting—the strong man on the reaping machine, his powerful arms regulating the swathes of corn with his large rake, and the "gatherers" ready, each in his place, quickly and deftly securing and binding his or her sheaf. When possible, we used to drive

our brougham into the field, and watch row by row of the golden corn fall as the large horses slowly wended their way.

The fact was that work, big or little, *really done well*, gave very great delight to his true artist's eye. When our new hall[1] was building he would (this was before his illness) sit watching the masons placing their stones and proving their lines by the "plumb," and anything done not as it should be was very disturbing to him; and often have I been made to do things over again when I thought them pretty good!

This desire to do the best possible ran through all his actions in life, and a most severe critic he was of himself, and so tender-hearted that I have known him deprived of sleep by the thought that perhaps a spoken or written word of his might hurt the feelings of a friend.

I should like it to be recorded how very ready he was to give wise advice to young men entering upon life; and however busy he might be when called upon, he seldom, if ever, sent them away without a hearing, and to many he became a loving, helpful friend.

To read a list of the many good, kind friends who came from far to see him here, as he could not go to them, shows the loving interest they had in him. I give you a list of those I remember. Others there were who would have come, but his illnesses prevented him from seeing them.

Vernon Lushington (*many times*).    Eyre Crowe.
F. Hueffer.    J. W. Gibb.
H. Bowler.    William Morris.

---

[1] [The foundation of this extension of Penkill (the exterior of which is shown in the annexed photograph) was laid in March 1883; the building was finished by the end of the season, and it was ready for habitation in the summer of 1884. It was designed entirely, outside and inside, stonework and woodwork, down to the smallest detail of decoration, by Mr. Scott. He had no professional assistance except from the local master-workmen, and he was naturally proud of it as his solitary achievement in architecture. The annexed view of the interior is from a painting by Mr. Arthur Hughes.—ED.]

Arthur Hughes (*many times*).
Hubert Horne.
Mr. Hipkins.
J. W. Mackail (*many times*).
William Minto (*many times*).
Sydney Morse.
W. J. Linton (*twice*).
F. G. Ellis (*from Torquay*).
T. Bayne.
Professor Nichol.
Rev. W. Anderson.
Walter C. Smith.
J. M. Gray.

From what Miss Boyd says it will be seen that the dear old Hermit, as we used to call him, though invalided from active work, had lost none of his interest in life, and kept up many of his old occupations. For more than a year after his enforced seclusion at Penkill, he cherished the hope of being able to return to London, but as his strength was gradually weakened by attack after attack of the painful malady, he resigned himself to the inevitable. Thus I find him writing as follows in a letter dated 11th June 1886:

As to myself. I have been very much the same all through this long winter and longer and worse spring. In general health well, but unable to bear the very least fatigue of body or exposure to the air. I am not allowed to go up a stair even; and the other day (three weeks ago indeed) I tried to walk the very short way to the garden, and that night suffered one of the breathless attacks so painful and which throw me back. The result is my medico gives it as his opinion that I can't be allowed to travel, so here I remain, an idle man trying to fill up my time by writing a little, drawing or painting a little, reading a little, and being read to a great deal. Sometimes a friend comes for a few days; the last was Vernon Lushington, so long ago as in the beginning of the year. If I could induce you to come, I should be so glad. Miss Boyd tells me to say how glad she should be also.

Later on in the same year, in a letter dated 30th November, he says:

I daresay you are surprised to find me still here. The truth is I remain exactly the same, very weak and unable almost to go about, now and then having those dreadful night attacks of heart disturbance that make my doctor prohibit travelling, and my best of friends, Miss Boyd, is not tired of me. Mrs. Scott comes and stays a month or so, and in the intervals of my attacks I am quite well, that is to say, I apply myself to writing, painting, or any other work that does not require athletic exercise.

In the autumn of the following year, *à propos* of a visit that I proposed to make, after saying that it was "the most delightful proposal he had had since Christmas, when F. S. Ellis came from Torquay, 'once errand,' as we say in Scotland, all that way, for a good long talk about old friends," he wrote:

About my health. You will do me a great deal of good. Living here so much alone—with Miss Boyd, the best of company, indeed, but without the concussion of the robuster nature, after spending all my life in the society of sets or coteries, if you like, men closely associated and seeing each other daily—I sometimes get into a lowish key which prevents me applying myself to anything whatever, and does not assist to get me out of the invalid groove. At present I am amazingly well, having had none of the night attacks of congestion for some months, but I am so weak and so unable to walk that I am never out except in a brougham. When planted in an easy chair I may say I am as well as ever I was, and expect you will treat me as an impostor, as many of my friends have done, thinking to meet a ghost of a creature with a voice scarcely articulate.

Another extract or two from his letters to me, which gradually became less frequent, will show

how fit after fit of the terrible *angina* pulled him down, and how buoyantly he continued to rally after each successive attack. In January 1888 he writes :

I am again clothed and I hope in my right mind, being trusted with a pen in my hand, although under a severe admonition not to write much, nor about anything very trying to the nerves. Do you know this last month of 1887 has been the severest trial in life I have yet had, and yet I have got over it remarkably well, and can look forward to your promised visit in the spring with great pleasure.

More than a year later, in April 1889, he writes :

You see I have just been allowed to write by the medico, but I feel no difference after so long a cessation, and suppose you don't see any difference in my scrawl. Yet this latest heart-spasm has pulled me down more than any of my late attacks have done. . . . Having just been allowed pen in hand I am expected to write only a few words, so I shall stop, having little more to say. This morning I have got by post a copy of W. J. Linton's volume of poems just published by Nimmo. It is full of spirit, and beautiful lyrics, and is dedicated to me, as the friend of fifty years. He is my age, yet all his later poems are on LOVE, a fack that baffles me to understand.

His wide knowledge of men and books and art, and the scope and freshness of his interests, made him one of the most delightful of partners in a talk, and my visits to Penkill must always remain among my most pleasant memories. In the morning and early afternoon we had no fear of the effects of over-excitement on the night's rest, and he was equal to

the toughest of conversation, always eager to hear and keen to discuss any kind of inquiry, literary or philosophic, that I happened to be engaged in, or to bring on the tapis any book or article that had attracted his attention. In the evening we had to be more careful. I then did my best to second Miss Boyd's skilful efforts to turn the tide of talk on pleasant reminiscences. A very picturesque figure he looked propped up in the curiously-carved bed in the tapestried chamber, of which a photograph is printed in this volume. His scarlet biretta and cowl made one think of an invalid Cardinal Inquisitor, but very far from inquisitorial was the laugh with which he capped our little jokes and anecdotes. These evening hours were the happiest hours of his invalid day, when the lamps were lit, a little square red box ranged on the bed before him, and placed thereon the glass of hot grog which was one of the milder features of his severe regimen.

A certain hankering after serious work, a desire to be still producing " were it but the infinitesimallest fraction of a product," never quite left him. He had been so indefatigable a worker all his life long that he could not be idle without uneasiness, and never could quite get rid of an uncomfortable feeling that he ought to be doing something. This restlessness was Miss Boyd's greatest difficulty as an ever-vigilant nurse. She quickly discovered how much he could do without risk, and kept him within safe limits with the most delicate and delightful tact. Only a brute would have been refractory under such tender authority, enforced as it was with the liveliest wit, and he was as docile as a good-natured child. The smile of placid content with which after some demur and protest he resigned himself to a judicious restriction on his freedom of will was one of the most perfect expressions of happiness it has ever been my lot to see.

One of his occupations was to prepare a series of etchings from his paintings on the Penkill staircase, with a preface on *The King's Quair* from which the subjects were taken. This he had privately printed, and issued to his friends in 1887. He wrote very little verse. All his life it had been a principle with him never to write verse except under a strong inspiration, and this excitement being dangerous was not encouraged. Now and again, however, the impulse seized him and would not be denied, and one of his last labours was to prepare for the printer in his punctiliously neat manner a small collection of pieces to follow a second edition of his *Harvest Home* as an *Aftermath*. This he asked me, in the spring of 1890, to see through the press, the condition being that he was to see nothing of it till the book appeared; but the negotiations with a publisher were hardly begun when Miss Boyd saw that the prospect made him anxious, and it was given up. Perhaps his chief occupation during his years of illness was reading and revising the Autobiographic Notes now printed. In the last chapter he speaks as if his intention had been in 1882 to lay them aside for ever. But this he could not do. Miss

Boyd tells me that she often left him apparently tranquil, quietly reading or disposed to sleep, and returned to find him with the MS. before him, busily revising, re-writing, and interpolating. Till I discovered that this had been his practice, I was often puzzled by allusions that seemed to be of later date than the ostensible time of writing, and any confusion arising from this I have tried to put straight. With characteristic love of order he neatly pasted in every correction, so as not to break the continuity of the MS.

If he wrote little during those last years, he read and was read to a great deal, keeping himself well abreast of everything going on outside his quiet hermitage. Like his other friends I went to Penkill only when his kind hostess had the doctor's consent to the invitation. But to the last I could never see any falling-off in the old breadth and variety of his interests. His mind continued to be a mirror of the English world of art and letters. Any new movement at once caught his attention and was eagerly followed. To take the first examples that occur to me, I heard of Robert Bridges from him before Mr. Lang's praise had made that name as familiar as it is now. Of his interest in Mr. Lang's own brilliant career he has spoken in his Notes; it continued to the last. I sent him Mr. Henley's *Book of Verses* when it came out: my copy was returned by and by with a message that he had ordered one for his own use. Before his illness he had designed a frontispiece for *Love in Idleness*. One of the three then youthful authors, Mr. Mackail, is in Miss Boyd's list of frequent visitors to Penkill. Another name also there is Mr. Hubert Horne's. The ideas and aims of the Century Guild were likely to commend themselves to one who was in himself an embodiment of the unity of the Arts. He contributed a poem to the *Hobby Horse* as in years gone by he had contributed to the *Germ*. And while young men found his appreciation of their work as fresh as it was in the Pre-Raphaelite days, he continued to maintain pleasant relations with many old friends, and to receive public acknowledgments of respect and affection. I have quoted from a letter in which he speaks of Mr. W. J. Linton's dedication of a new volume of Poems and Translations to " the friend of nearly fifty years." A poet of a younger generation, Mr. Cosmo Monkhouse, inscribed *Corn and Poppies* to his veteran friend. But the tribute in this kind which naturally gratified the old man most was the splendid poem in which Mr. Swinburne dedicated to him his third series of *Poems and Ballads*.

That Mr. Scott should have kept the love and respect of so many friends was but just, for he was essentially a man of a genial and friendly disposition, as these autobiographical notes abundantly testify. With some, as I have been surprised to hear since his death, he had the repute of saying severe things, of taking characters to pieces in a grudging spirit, of reducing personal pretensions to the lowest possible denomination something after the manner of Carlyle. This I simply cannot understand, except as a misunderstanding. Those who knew him best do not say this of him. It is very far from being my own impression. I had many a long talk with him in the sixteen years during which I had the privilege of knowing him, and I can aver that I have never heard him say an unjust or uncharitable word, and that I have heard him say many a generous one. It is true that though he lived all his life, as he says in one of the letters I have quoted, in sets or coteries, he had not the coterie weakness—an amiable enough one in its way—of seeing only the merits of his fellow-members. He had too scrupulous a literary and artistic conscience for this. He simply could not praise what he did not honestly admire. Perhaps he was sometimes too outspoken about shortcomings. The less a member of a coterie says about the work of his fellow-members, except in the way of upholding it against the envious and calumniating tooth of the world, the better for his peace of mind, for a bird of the air, in the shape of a candid friend, is generally ready to carry the voice. Mr. Scott had the knack of putting things happily, in graphic phrases that exactly expressed his meaning, and when they came to his lips, he could not always judiciously keep them back. Thus I have heard him, after a very just and liberal allowance of merit, sum up by saying that So-and-so "had no devil in him," or that So-and-so "was no doubt a very respectable codger"—the remark, of course, applying to the artist, not to the man. He would not, of course, say such things to So-and-so himself. The friendliness of his nature would lead him rather to keep any sense of demerit or defect in the background. But a candid friend might carry the voice.

I do not, however, conceive that it is any part of my duty to comment on the character of my much-beloved old friend. It is very fully and frankly revealed in these Autobiographic Notes. A wise and charitable soul makes itself felt in every chapter of them. I have no doubt that those who knew him will have the same feeling that I had myself on first perusing them. So direct and sincere is their utterance, they are written so exactly as the man was in the habit of speaking, that one seems to hear his voice behind every sentence—the grave-pitched kindly voice with its slow measured articulation which was so true an index of the grave, thoughtful, kindly nature.

He died on the 22nd of November 1890. A few weeks after his death there appeared in the *Athenæum* a noble tribute to his memory which I have Mr. Swinburne's permission to reprint here.

## MEMORIAL VERSES
### ON THE DEATH OF WILLIAM BELL SCOTT

A life more bright than the sun's face, bowed
Through stress of season and coil of cloud,
    Sets: and the sorrow that casts out fear
Scarce deems him dead in his chill still shroud,

Dead on the breast of the dying year,
Poet and painter and friend, thrice dear
    For love of the suns long set, for love
Of song that sets not with sunset here,

For love of the fervent heart, above
Their sense who saw not the swift light move
    That filled with sense of the loud sun's lyre
The thoughts that passion was fain to prove

In fervent labour of high desire
And faith that leapt from its own quenched pyre
    Alive and strong as the sun, and caught
From darkness light, and from twilight fire.

Passion, deep as the depths unsought
Whence faith's own hope may redeem us nought,
    Filled full with ardour of pain sublime
His mourning song and his mounting thought.

Elate with sense of a sterner time,
His hand's flight clomb as a bird's might climb
    Calvary: dark in the darkling air
That shrank for fear of the crowning crime,

Three crosses rose on the hillside bare,
Shewn scarce by grace of the lightning's glare
    That clove the veil of the temple through
And smote the priests on the threshold there.[1]

The soul that saw it, the hand that drew,
Whence light as thought's or as faith's glance flew,
    And stung to life the sepulchral past,
And bade the stars of it burn anew,

Held no less than the dead world fast
The light live shadows about them cast,
    The likeness living of dawn and night,
The days that pass and the dreams that last.

---

[1] [The reference here is to Mr. Scott's picture of the theme:—
"And, behold! the vail of the Temple was rent in twain from the top to the bottom, and the earth did quake, and the rocks rent."—ED.]

Thought, clothed round with sorrow as light,
Dark as a cloud that the moon turns bright,
    Moved, as a wind on the striving sea,
That yearns and quickens and flags in flight,

Through forms of colour and song that he
Who fain would have set its wide wings free
    Cast round it, clothing or chaining hope
With lights that last not and shades that flee.

Scarce in song could his soul find scope,
Scarce the strength of his hand might ope
    Art's inmost gate of her sovereign shrine,
To cope with heaven as a man may cope.

But high as the hope of a man may shine
The faith, the fervour, the life divine
    That thrills our life and transfigures, rose
And shone resurgent, a sunbright sign,

Through shapes whereunder the strong soul glows
And fills them full as a sunlit rose
    With sense and fervour of life, whose light
The fool's eye knows not, the man's eye knows.

None that can read or divine aright
The scriptures writ of the soul may slight
    The strife of a strenuous soul to show
More than the craft of the hand may write.

None may slight it, and none may know
How high the flames that aspire and glow
    From heart and spirit and soul may climb
And triumph; higher than the souls lie low

Whose hearing hears not the livelong rhyme,
Whose eyesight sees not the light sublime,
    That shines, that sounds, that ascends and lives
Unquenched of change, unobscured of time.

A long life's length, as a man's life gives
Space for the spirit that soars and strives
    To strive and soar, has the soul shone through
That heeds not whither the world's wind drives

Now that the days and the ways it knew
Are strange, are dead as the dawn's grey dew
    At high midnoon of the mounting day
That mocks the might of the dawn it slew.

Yet haply may not—and haply may—
No sense abide of the dead sun's ray
    Wherein the soul that outsoars us now
Rejoiced with ours in its radiant sway.

Hope may hover, and doubt may bow,
Dreaming. Haply—they dream not how—
    Not life but death may indeed be dead
When silence darkens the dead man's brow.

Hope, whose name is remembrance, fed
With love that lightens from seasons fled,
    Dreams, and craves not indeed to know,
That death and life are as souls that wed.

But change that falls on the heart like snow
Can chill not memory nor hope, that show
    The soul, the spirit, the heart and head,
Alive above us who strive below.

                ALGERNON CHARLES SWINBURNE.

# INDEX

## A

ACADEMY, Royal, i. 107, 109, 110
Allan, Sir W., i. 80
Allingham, W., ii. 31, 32
*Antiquarian Gleanings*, i. 220
Arloshes of Woodside, i. 221
Armitage, painter, i. 169
Art and Artists in 1837, i. 105-13
Art, Italian, heresies on, i. 231; Bavarian, 318
*Atlas, The*, Editor of, i. 123
Autobiography of 1854 destroyed, i. 3, 276

## B

BALDER, i. 80, 100
Ballads, Jacobite, i. 79
"Ballad Singer, Old English," picture, i. 108, 110, 114
Ballantine, James, fellow-pupil in Edinburgh, i. 81; ii. 2, 206
Barker, Fiott, i. 342, 343
Barnby, Goodwin, the Proto-Shiloh, i. 174, 175
*Battersea Bells*, sonnets, ii. 294, 295
Bavarian Art, i. 318
"Bede, Death of," picture, ii. 7
*Bee, The*, i. 21
Beetham, Father, i. 349
Beham's "Fountain of Rejuvenescence," ii. 278
Bell, Henry Glassford, i. 78
Bell's English Poets, i. 14
Bentham, Leigh Hunt's opinion of his atheism, i. 129
Bewick, compared with Rösch, i. 194
Bewick, Robert, i. 194-96

Blair's *Grave*, i. 21, 68, 74
Blake's designs for *The Grave*, i. 21, 23; Sonnet on, 23; *Songs of Innocence*, 22
"Boccaccio and Dante's Daughter," picture by W. B. S., i. 305
Bowler, H. A., sketch by, ii. 296; 325
Boyd, Miss, ii. 54, 56, 57, 59; removes from Newcastle to London with the Scotts, 73; tries to defeat a prophecy, 79; 163, 169, 181, 182, 291-302, 318, 321
Boyd, Spencer, ii. 75, 77; death of, 78; name "thought-read" by a medium, 81
Boydell's Shakespeare, i. 16
Brown, F. Madox, D. G. R. a pupil of, i. 287; might have gone to Australia, ii. 48; his family circle, 183; the high character of his painting, 189; a funny mistake, 190
Brown, John, letter from, ii. 26, 27
Brown, Samuel, as medical student in Edinburgh, i. 92; in London, 157, 158; rhabdomancy, 219; his laboratory in Portobello, ii. 1; death of, 25-27
Brown, Tom, engraver and man of science, i. 45, 82
Browning, performance of *Strafford*, i. 124; W. M. R. on Sordello, ii. 57; D. G. R. on *Balaustion's Adventure*, 138; *Fifine at the Fair*, 180
Browning, Mrs., *Aurora Leigh*, ii. 34; in Paris, 30; in Florence, 35
Burchett, R., ii. 272-75
Burnet, John, engraver and printer,

apprentice with R. Scott, a "genius," i. 19; his career, 46, 47
Burns, sonnets on, ii. 164; Rossetti's criticisms of, 152, 155; W. B. S.'s edition of, 166; unpublished letter of his, 177
Burton, Sir F. W., letter about Wallington, ii. 259-60; letter about *Fons Juventutis*, 279-81; letter in acknowledgment of *Harvest Home*, 309, 310

## C

CAINE, T. HALL, ii. 304
Campbell's *Pleasures of Hope*, i. 70
Carlyle, his *Hero-worship*, i. 158; satire of his *Cromwell*, 159; *Hades* sent to him, 159; first meeting with, 269; droll passage-at-arms with, ii. 20-24; on Millais' staircase, 223; and Thomas Dixon, 270
Carlyle, Mrs., i. 270
Carmichael, Newcastle painter, i. 185, 209, 210
Cartoon Competition for Houses of Parliament, i. 166-73; second competition, 214
*Chevy Chase*, subject of picture at Wallington, ii. 11, 118
Cholera at Newcastle, i. 341
Clennell, Luke, painter, i. 163; son of, 198-201
*Cloud Confines*, poem by D. G. R., ii. 146, 154, 155
Cole, Sir H., head of Science and Art Department, i. 181, 329
Collins, Charles, P.R.B., i. 285, 286
Collinson, James, P.R.B., i. 281; ii. 273
Constable, in 1837, i. 106
Cope, painter, i. 169
Cowen, Joseph, M.P., i. 122, 338
Crowe, Eyre, ii. 325
Crowe, Mrs., i. 218, 219; ii. 2
Curate, muscular, in cholera epidemic, i. 340, 347, 348
"Cuthbert, St.," picture, ii. 7; D. G. R.'s criticism, 35, 36

## D

DADD, RICHARD, chairman of mal-

contents, i. 111; in Houses of Parliament Cartoon Competition, 172
"Danes at Tynemouth," picture, ii. 7
Design, Schools of, History of, i. 180, 327-31
De Quincey, i. 98; ii. 3
Deverell, Walter, P.R.B., i. 285; his "Twelfth Night" picture, 286, 315, 321; his ill-health, 305, 320; D. G. R.'s letter on his death, 320
Dixon, Thomas, of Sunderland, ii. 33, 264-72
Dobson, Austin, ii. 198
Doubleday, Thomas, Newcastle poet, i. 198
Dowden, Prof., a "Rhyme to W. B. S.," ii. 314
Dürer, Albert, analogue of his workshop, i. 45; his copper-plates, 50; visit to Nürnberg, 317; picture of his house, 319; W. B. S.'s Life of, ii. 193
Dyce, William, painter, on prospects of historical art, i. 208; and wall-painting, 215

## E

EASTLAKE, Sir C., i. 168-70
Ebsworth, J. W., i. 264
Education, W. B. S.'s early, i. 12-24
Eldin, John Clerk, Lord, i. 18
Emerson, R. W., letter from, i. 240; intercourse with, 241, 242; portrait by D. Scott, 241
Engraver's business at beginning of century, i. 18-20
Enthusiast, an, ii. 237-41
Epps, Dr. John, i. 255; his poetic butler, 256

## F

FAIRBAIRN, J. C., early friend of W. B. S., i. 92; letter from, 93, 94
Fine Arts, chair of, in Edinburgh, i. 124
*Fons Juventutis*, inquiry into myth, ii. 281-83
*Foxglove, The*, a poem, ii. 122

# INDEX

Franco-German War of 1870, ii. 119-26
Franklin, book illustrator, i. 162
Fresco painting, remarks on, i. 214, 215
Frith, painter, in 1837, i. 110, 112
Fuseli's designs, i. 17 ; influence on Blake, 23 ; influence on Von Holst, 162 ; price of a picture by, 263

## G

"GRACE DARLING," picture, ii. 7, 55, 58
*Graffito* paintings in S. K. Keramic Gallery, ii. 107
"George Eliot," ii. 71, 247, 248 ; Carlyle on, 249
*Germ, The,* i. 282-84, 323
Gilfillan, G., on David Scott, i. 267
"Gilpin, Bernard," picture, ii. 7, 56
Gosse, E. W., ii. 193

## H

HALL, S. C.'s *Book of Ballads*, i. 108
Hake, Dr., ii. 172, 176, 178, 180
Hamerton, P. G., ii. 124-26
Hancocks, the, of Newcastle, i. 184
Hannay, ii. 34, 35
Hart, Solomon, ii. 275
Harvey, Sir G., ii. 206
Haydon, B. R., personal traits, i. 166-68 ; at the Westminster Hall Cartoon Competition, 171
Henley, W. E., ii. 331
Henning, sculptor, i. 115
"Hexham Market-Place," picture, i. 224, 322
Hogarth Club, ii. 47
Hogarth's designs, i. 17
Hogg, "Ettrick Shepherd," his *Justified Sinner*, i. 69
Holst, T. von, painter, i. 162-64
Horne, Hubert, ii. 326, 332
Horne, R. H., the farthing *Orion*, i. 253
Horoscope, i. 119
Howitt, W., i. 297, 315
Howitt, Anna Mary, letter from, i. 322, 323 ; her spiritualism, ii. 242, 243

Hueffer, F., ii. 163, 168, 183 ; letters from, 185-87 ; nonsense verses, 187, 188
Hughes, Arthur, ii. 31, 35, 67, 325
Hunt, Holman, his painting in 1848, "Light of the World," i. 280 ; Ayrshire sermon on this picture, 309 ; letter giving its history, 311 14 ; fled to the desert, 320 ; in the East, ii. 31 ; painting at home, "Christ and the Doctors," 35, 49, letter on technical matters, 49 ; proposed return to East, 50 ; sketching at Falmouth, 56 ; sale and exhibition of pictures, 58 ; letters from Jerusalem, 1870, 1871, 88-106 ; his "Triumph of the Innocents," 221, 225-27 ; letter concerning, 228-32 ; the model of "The Prophet," 241 ; letter on *Harvest Home* and death of D. G. R., 311, 312
Hunt, Leigh, i. 125
*Hypnerotomachia Poliphili*, ii. 285-88

## I

ILLUSTRATIONS, character of, in 1830, i. 15
Introspective tendency, i. 3, 329
"Iron and Coal," picture, ii. 7
Italian art, heresies on, i. 231

## J

JONES, BURNE, his first designs, ii. 37 ; his indifference to opinion, 216
Jones, Ebenezer, i. 252

## K

KEATS, early study of, i. 88 ; Leigh Hunt and, 128
Kelly, Father, i. 348
Kelmscott, ii. 130
Kennedy, fellow-pupil in Edinburgh, i. 80
*King's Quair*, subject of wall-paintings at Penkill, ii. 83 ; suggestion of D. G. R.'s *King's Tragedy*, 116

## L

Lang, Andrew, ii. 201, 331
Lawyers' marks from Penkill chest, ii. 301
Leathart, James, picture collector, ii. 48, 207
"Legion, Prince," a series of designs, i. 131, 132
Lewes, G. H., note from, i. 129, 130; his turn for language, 131; reference to early friendship in *Leader*, 132; his youthful ambitions, 133; letter about *Year of the World*, 238; resumes acquaintance, ii. 71, 72; death of, 244; his powers, 245
Lilly, the astrologer, i. 119
Linton, W. J., friend of Mazzini, i. 121; verses by, 121; at Brantwood, 122; and Emerson, 241; and politics, 252; D. G. R.'s opinion of, ii. 36; and Polish refugees, 274; poems, 328
*Little Boy*, poem, i. 41
Littledale, Dr., humorous verses by, ii. 296, 313, 314
Losh, Miss, of Woodside, a Cumberland "Worthy," i. 221
Lushington, Vernon, ii. 37, 47; letter on D. G. R.'s funeral, 317, 325, 326

## M

Mackail, J. W., ii. 326, 332
Maclise, in 1837, i. 107, 112; and wall-painting, 215; price of a picture by, 263; ii. 83-86
Marshall, Calder, sculptor, i. 161
Marshall, Mrs., spirit medium, ii. 80-82
Marston, Philip Bourke, ii. 198
Martin, John, brother of, i. 196
Marzials, Theo., ii. 194
Mazzini, i. 121, 255
Meadows, Kenny, recollections of, i. 113-15; his views of town and country, 175; letter from Jersey, ii. 71
Michael Angelo, "Creation of Adam," ii. 282, 283; figures on the Medici tombs, 283, 284
Millais, as P.R.B., i. 278; "The Carpenter's Shop," 279; his fun,

306-8; resents bad hanging, ii. 29; anecdotes of, 222, 223
Milton, Thomas, engraver, i. 17
Monk, a model, ii. 241
Monkhouse, Cosmo, ii. 336
Mormonism in Newcastle, i. 334, 335
Morris, William, fresh from Oxford, ii. 37; his first picture, 39; his tales in *Oxford and Cambridge Magazine*, 40; his *Defence of Guenevere*, 42; his Red House at Upton, 60, 61; in Iceland, 153; at Kelmscott, 157, 161; letter to W. B. S. on publication of *Poems*, 212, 213; on *Harvest Home*, 309
Morse, S., ii. 326
Motherwell, W., i. 79
Müller, Max, on Thomas Dixon, ii. 271
Munro, Alex., sculptor, makes medallion of W. B. S., i. 307; letters from, 320; ii. 30; busts of Sir Walter and Lady Trevelyan, 68

## N

Nettleship, artist, ii. 196, 197
Newcastle in 1844, i. 182, 183; amusements of society there, 185, 186; art manufactory, 189
Nichol, Professor, astronomer, i. 218, 219, 334; ii. 1

## O

Oliphant, Francis, i. 188
Ord, Walker, i. 78
Orsini, i. 255
O'Shaughnessy, ii. 189, 196

## P

Park, Patric, sculptor, i. 161, 162; his busts of Haydon and Napoleon III., 164; his unlucky generosity, 165
Parliament Square, Edinburgh, engraver's shop there, i. 13, 43-50; its "little masters," 45 *et seq.*; burnt in 1824, 49
Patmore, Coventry, i. 252, 297, 306; ii. 31

Paton, Sir Noel, ii. 206
Pattison, Mrs. Mark (Lady Dilke), ii. 67
Paul, Emperor, relic of his murder at St. Petersburg, i. 212
Payne, John, ii. 197
Penkill Castle, ii. 57; description of, 73; paintings on staircase of, 83, 108, 116; way of life at, 291-302
Perseverance and genius, ii. 217-20
Poems, on Blake's designs, i. 23; *Little Boy*, 41; *Pillars of Seth*, 57-60; *Rosabell*, 135; on W. A. C. Shand, 204; on his brother's death, 261; sonnet to his brother, 266; "My Mother," sonnets, 274, 275; *The Foxglove*, ii. 122; *On Going to Live in Bellevue House*, 123; *Dedicatio Postica*, 209; *New Year's Eve*, 294, 295; to Miss Boyd, anniversary, 301; *Ætat.* 70, 319, 320
Poetry, causes of its popularity obscure, i. 254
*Poet's Harvest Home*, ii. 303
Poets, the rising generation in 1875, ii. 192-201
Poole, painter, i. 111
Pre-Raphaelites, i. 248 *et seq.*; first knowledge of the name, 277; the P.R.B.'s and their principles, 277-87; the *Germ*, 282 *et seq.*; short history of the brotherhood, 323-26; ill-used by the Academy, ii. 52

R

*REQUIESCAT IN PACE*, origin of, ii. 276
Richardson, Anna, Quaker, i. 351-56
Richardson, T. M., Newcastle painter, i. 207
Roberts, David, scene-painter, i. 81
"Roman Wall, Building of," picture, ii. 7, 38
Ronge, Johannes, and Holy Coat of Treves, i. 336-40; letter from, 339
Rosabell Bonally, acquaintance with, i. 101; poem on subject of, 135; Rossetti and this poem, 289, 305, 322

Rösch, compared with Bewick, i. 194
Rossetti, Christina, i. 247; a drawing pupil, 279; verses in acknowledgment of *Harvest Home*, 317
Rossetti, Dante Gabriel, autobiographer's third "friend," i. 88; first letter from, in 1847, 243; sends "Songs of the Art-Catholic," 245; in Holman Hunt's studio, 248; early pictures, 278, 281; visits Newcastle, 287; fascination of, 289; walks back through Shakespeare country, letters, 291-93; his opinion of "Self-Culture," 293; news-letters, 301-3; epitaph on Scotus, 305; development, 314, 315; and Miss Siddal, 316; proposes sketching club, 325; and Ruskin, ii. 8-10; news-letter in 1855, 31, 32; criticism of "St. Cuthbert" picture, 35, 36; designs woodcuts for Tennyson's poems, 35, 36; first impressions of W. Morris and Burne-Jones, 37; paintings in the Oxford Union, 40-42; his habits of painting, 43-45; succeeds in life-size painting, 51, 52; letters after his marriage, 62, 63; his picture "Found," 63; his wife's death, 65; spiritualism, 66; at Penkill in 1868 and 1869, 108-18; is persuaded to resume poetry, 109; in Bennan's Cave, 115; determines to recover the buried MS., 117; letters to W. B. S. from Kelmscott, 127-63; his sleeplessness, 139; the attack on "The Fleshly School," 161; how affected by, 168, 171; his illness, 172; at Stobhall, 173; letters from, 175, 176; at Kelmscott, recovered, 178; mysterious letter from, 179; nonsense verses, 187-89; urges publication of poems, 202, 203; letter on publication, 209-11; letter from Bognor, 213-16; broken health, 304-308; death, 315
Rossetti, W. M., visits Newcastle in 1848, i. 277; sonnet in *Germ*, 324; news-letter in June 1855, ii. 30, 31; in 1856, 32-35; edits Walt Whitman, 33, 267; news-

letter in 1858, 47; letter on Sordello, etc., 58; takes part in a *séance*, 80; anxiety about his brother, 174; one of a party in Italian tour, 182; letters on his brother's death, 315-17
Ruskin, J., ii. 5, 7-12

S

SCHLIEMANN's "Owl-headed Vases," ii. 288-90
Schœlcher, Senator, *Le Vrai St. Paul*, ii. 252
*Scotland's Skaith*, i. 21
*Scots Magazine*, i. 13, 18, 70
Scott, David, early influences on his art, i. 15, 17; *Memoir* of, 26, 267, 268; in Rome, 83; contributes to *Souvenir*, 92; in Cartoon Competition for Houses of Parliament, 168, 169, 171; his egoism, 171; his specimen of fresco, 216; his studio, habits, and character, 216-19; last illness and death, 259, 260; *Requiem*, 261; his character, 262-69; " Maxims from Italy," 265; Rossetti concerning, 283
Scott, George, uncle of W. B. S., i. 29-31; his nursery rhymes, 30; his game eggs, 71; his last days, 219
Scott, Mrs. (L. M. N.), i. 118; takes part in religious inquiries, 332; letter from, ii. 59, 60; 327
Scott, Robert, engraver, his shop, i. 13, 43-50; personal appearance, 28; his Sunday books, 28; his religious services, i. 27, 32; his teaching, 38, 39; his financial troubles, 61-63
Scott, Robert, brother of W. B. S., i. 27; boyish adventure, 65; early death, 67; return from West Indies, 99
Scott, Sir Walter, his strong language, i. 70; interview with, 72-75
Scott, William Bell, birthplace, i. 7-12, 31; home education, 12-24; his father's household, 25-32; his mother, 25; his uncle George, 29-31; reminiscences of childhood, 33-42; early religious influences,

53; first attempts at poetry, 56-60; his first picture, 77; art studies, 80-81; his engraving of "The Martyrs' Tombs," 83; his early friends, 87; poetic and philosophic studies, 88, 89; essays in ballad and octosyllabic, 89; contributes to *Edinburgh University Souvenir*, 91, 92; leaves Edinburgh in 1837, 99, 100; his equipment and hopes, 102, 103; "painter's etchings," 105; first picture in London, historical, 108; his horoscope, 119; makes acquaintance of Leigh Hunt and G. H. Lewes, 123-34; his "Prince Legion," 131; his poem of *Rosabell*, 135; takes part in Cartoon Competition for Houses of Parliament, 168; appointed to mastership in School of Design at Newcastle, 1844, 173; his motives in accepting, 173, 251; his work as art master, 177 *et seq.*; publishes *Antiquarian Gleanings*, 220; anatomical studies at Durham, 220; landscape haunts in the North, 220-28; unaffected by Continental tours, 231; heresies on Italian art, 231-33; writes *The Year of the World*, 234; first letter from D. G. R., 243; makes acquaintance of the Rossetti family, 247; of Holman Hunt, 248; his brother's death, 259; his mother's death, 273; early autobiography (destroyed), 276; visits Paris, 299; gives "Half - hour Lectures on the Arts," 330; inquires into influence of religion on character, 331-56; invited to Wallington Hall, ii. 3-6; pictures commissioned illustrative of Border history, 7; makes acquaintance of Miss Boyd, 56, 57; first visit to Penkill Castle, 59; returns to London, 1864, 70; reflections on town and country life, 70; paints Keramic Gallery windows in *graffito*, 107; completes *Chevy Chase* series, 118; buys Bellevue House, Chelsea, 119; settles there in 1870, 123; writes *Life of Albert Dürer*, 193; edits Burns, 166;

designs door for Lecture Theatre, South Kensington, 170; visits Italy, 182; publishes poems in 1875, 202; artistic investigations, 278-90; way of life at Penkill, 291-302; publishes *Poet's Harvest Home*, 303; last years, 321-34; designs new hall for Penkill, 325; prepares *Aftermath*, 330
Seddon, Thomas, painter, ii. 34
Selous, painter, i. 169
Shand, W. A. C., first friend, i. 87; friendship at first sight, 88; holiday song by, 95; youthful plans, 97; offer to De Quincey, 98; parting festivities, 100; his linguistic ability, 131; reappears at Newcastle, 202; last sight of, 204; poem on, 204
Sharp, William, ii. 180
Shelley, early admiration of, i. 88; how qualified, 89; poem on, in *Tait's Magazine*, 91; Leigh Hunt and, 128; at Lynmouth, ii. 139-40
Sibson, Thomas, early friend, i. 87; career, 153-56; at Newcastle, 205; his genius in art, 206; specimen of his design, 207
Siddal, E. E. (Mrs. Rossetti), i. 315, 316; with D. G. R. in Paris, ii. 30; marriage to D. G. R., 58, 60, 62, 63; death of, 64, 65
Siddons, Mrs., Henning's anecdote of, i. 116
Skipsey, the pitman poet, ii. 269
Spiritualism, ii. 235
"Spur in the Dish, The," picture, ii. 7
Steell, Sir John, sculptor, ii. 2
Stobhall, ii. 173
Stoddart's *Death Wake*, i. 80, 100
Swinburne, A. C., first met at Wallington, ii. 14-18; portrait painted by W. B. S., 18; his physical courage, 19; his dislike of Louis Napoleon, 46; a holiday at Tynemouth, 68; first in W. B. S.'s triple dedication, 212; dedicates poems to W. B. S., 336; memorial verses, 339
Swinburne, Sir John, anecdote of, ii. 19; death of, 55
Symbolism in Art, ii. 283-89

T

TADEMA, ALMA, visits Penkill, ii. 203; contributes etchings to W. B. S.'s poems, 203, 204; his mastery of his art, 205, 216; letter from, 207
Tennyson, Alfred, Lord, i. 297; a political forecast, 300; Woolner's bust of, ii. 29, 35; D. G. R.'s woodcuts for poems, 35, 36
Thomson of Duddingston, clerical amateur painter, i. 83
Trevelyan, Lady Pauline, reviews *Memoir*, ii. 3; first visit to, 3-6; W. M. R. and, 34; letters from, 51-56; her character, 256; selections from her writings, 257
Trevelyan, Sir Walter, ii. 3, 5; W. M. R. and, 34; death of, 253; his bequest to National Gallery, 259-61; bequest of his cellar to Dr. Richardson, 261-63
Turner, J. M. W., anecdote of, i. 84; ii. 9; in 1837, i. 106; on ruin of Royal Academy, i. 109; private sketches, 251

V

VALENTINE, Dr., ii. 321
Varley, the astrologer, i. 118

W

WADE, THOMAS, poet, i. 253
Wailes, W., Newcastle art manufacturer, i. 189-91.
Wallington Hall, first visit to, ii. 3-6; pictures there, 7; exhibited in London, 38, 66; decoration of, 67
"Wallace," picture of, i. 231; ii. 249
Ward, E. M., i. 111, 168
Watts, Theodore, ii. 180, 213
Weatherley, Captain, Chairman of School of Design at Newcastle, i. 179, 197; a Peninsular story, 211
Weingartshofer, Dr., citizen of the world, i. 343-47; his exegesis, 345
Weir, W., i. 79
Whitman, Walt, *Leaves of Grass*,

sent by W. B. S. to W. M. R., ii. 32, 33; 267-69
Wilkinson, Garth, i. 22; his poetry, 298
Wilson, C. H., Director of Schools of Design, i. 179, 181
Wilson, John, "Christopher North," advises W. B. S., i. 71, 72; Carlyle concerning, 75; his after-dinner speaking, 77; at breakfast, 78; receives a dedication, 83; gives opinion of a poem, 89; opinion of Shelley, 91; advice, 100
Woodchuck, the, ii. 159; epitaph on, 163
Woolner, T., introduces W. B. S. to Carlyle, i. 269; his medallion of Carlyle, 270, another, ii. 28; his renunciation of poetry, i. 271; *My Beautiful Lady*, 282; goes to Australia, 295; letter after his return, 305; news-letter from, ii. 29; his Wentworth statue commission, 30, 31; central sculpture for Wallington Hall, 33, 34, 67; bust of Tennyson, 35; on W. Morris's poems, 42
Wordsworth, not so congenial to his youth as Shelley, i. 88; a humble imitator, i. 256
Wornum, R. N., i. 112; his wife, Miss Selden, 156; a Swedenborgian, 160; in Cartoon Competition, 168; lecturer to School of Design, 328; death of, ii. 244, 249, 250; his "Saul of Tarsus," 251

Y

*YEAR OF THE WORLD, THE*, projected, i. 100; written, 234; account of, 235-38; reception of, 238, 239; letter from G. H. Lewes concerning, 238; from Emerson, 240
Young's *Night Thoughts*, i. 21, 68


THE END


*Printed by* R. & R. CLARK, *Edinburgh*

www.ingramcontent.com/pod-product-compliance
Lightning Source LLC
Chambersburg PA
CBHW030743250426
43672CB00028B/383